WHAT'S PUBLIC ABOUT PUBLIC HIGHER ED?

What's Public about Public Higher Ed

*Halting Higher Education's Decline
in the Court of Public Opinion*

Stephen M. Gavazzi
&
E. Gordon Gee

JOHNS HOPKINS UNIVERSITY PRESS | *Baltimore*

© 2021 Johns Hopkins University Press
All rights reserved. Published 2021
Printed in the United States of America on acid-free paper
9 8 7 6 5 4 3 2 1

Johns Hopkins University Press
2715 North Charles Street
Baltimore, Maryland 21218-4363
www.press.jhu.edu

Library of Congress Cataloging-in-Publication Data

Names: Gavazzi, Stephen M., author. | Gee, E. Gordon (Elwood Gordon),
    1944– author.
Title: What's public about public higher ed? : halting higher education's
    decline in the court of public opinion / Stephen M. Gavazzi and
    E. Gordon Gee.
Description: Baltimore, Maryland : Johns Hopkins University Press, 2021. |
    Includes bibliographical references and index.
Identifiers: LCCN 2021002623 | ISBN 9781421442525 (hardcover) |
    ISBN 9781421442532 (ebook)
Subjects: LCSH: Public universities and colleges—United States. | Public
    opinion—United States. | Public universities and colleges—United
    States—Administration. | Public universities and colleges—Ratings and
    rankings—United States.
Classification: LCC LB2341 .G38 2021 | DDC 378/.050973—dc23
LC record available at https://lccn.loc.gov/2021002623

A catalog record for this book is available from the British Library.

Special discounts are available for bulk purchases of this book. For more information, please
contact Special Sales at specialsales@jh.edu.

CONTENTS

ACKNOWLEDGMENTS

This book was made possible by the assistance of many people. First and foremost, we wish to thank Dr. Elizabeth Cooksey and her staff at The Ohio State University's Center for Human Resources Research. Without their support and attention to detail, there would have been no survey, and thus no book.

As we were formulating ideas for our survey, the guidance of two individuals stands out. First, Dr. Michael Neblo, the Ohio State professor of political science who provided invaluable assistance in the development of our politically oriented variables. Second, Dr. Trevor Brown, dean of the John Glenn College of Public Affairs at Ohio State, who helped us to think through the political nature of the questions we were asking and situate them in the larger context of higher education policy.

Once our data were gathered, we very much appreciated the thorough assistance afforded to us by several individuals. First, we wish to acknowledge Dr. Deanna Wilkinson, associate professor of Human Sciences at Ohio State, who led the way on the qualitative data analyses that appear in our eighth chapter. Additionally, the more quantitative analyses contained in chapters 3 through 7 were reviewed by Dr. Sandra Reed and other staff members associated with the Data Access and Analysis Core within the Office of Research, Innovation, and Collaboration in Ohio State's College of Education and Human Ecology.

The survey itself was funded by a generous grant from the Koch Foundation. We wish to thank Michael Tolhurst and Michael Wilt for their assistance in shaping the grant and moving our proposal to funded status. As well, we wish to thank our current program officer, Ewan Watt, for his continued support as we look to expand our initial surveying efforts.

In conclusion, we wish to recognize those individuals who provided critical behind-the-scenes support throughout the writing process. First and foremost, we would never have been able to put together a second book without the continued enthusiasm for this work by our editor at Johns Hopkins University Press, Gregory M. Britton. Greg and the JHUP staff members have been a delight to work with throughout these past four years.

Finally, we remain grateful for the devoted support we have received from our loved ones—Courtney Gavazzi and Laurie Erickson—who continue to keep us anchored in reality and connected to those things that matter most while we completed this work.

WHAT'S PUBLIC ABOUT PUBLIC HIGHER ED?

Introduction

We are not enemies, but friends. We must not be enemies. Though passion may have strained, it must not break our bonds of affection. The mystic chords of memory, stretching from every battle-field, and patriot grave, to every living heart and hearth-stone, all over this broad land, will yet swell the chorus of the Union, when again touched, as surely they will be, by the better angels of our nature.

We begin our book with the ending paragraph of Abraham Lincoln's first inaugural address, given on March 4, 1861, at the US Capitol Building in Washington, DC. While several Southern states already had declared succession from the Union at the time of Lincoln's inauguration, the American Civil War had not yet officially commenced. That would happen the following month, when Confederate forces attacked Fort Sumter on April 12, 1861. This was a momentous time in our nation's history, a threat to the very existence of the United States of America.

Lincoln would go on to provide the leadership that was necessary to win the war on the battlefield, and then, just as importantly, would move quickly to bind and heal the nation's wounds. We find ourselves inspired by Lincoln's words and actions, and for so many reasons. We elected to begin our book with Lincoln's inauguration speech because we found ourselves drawn to the idea of "the better angels of our nature." Although we write this book over one hundred and fifty years after the end of hostilities between the Northern and Southern states, we are painfully aware of the increasingly sharpened divisions that have emerged between the political factions of our day.[1] Just as Lincoln would beseech the American people in 1861 to put aside their differences for the good of the country, so, too, do we implore today's citizens to place our national interests above that of partisan gain. Where, oh where, are our better angels to be found right now?

The Culture Wars and Our Public Universities

Fortunately, at present, we are nowhere near the state of armed insurrection and conflict that Lincoln faced, despite the violent storming of the US Capitol on January 6, 2021, and the demagoguery of political opportunists that has periodically surfaced. Rather than a shooting match, we find ourselves in a cultural war.[2] On the left side of the current political equation, we see attempts to focus attention (and governmental action) on social justice issues, among other progressive concerns.[3] On the right side of the aisle, we find individuals not only "standing athwart history, yelling stop" but also working to reinvigorate the social value of those traditional concepts and ideals they are hoping to conserve and protect.[4] Both sides have valid points to make, even as they remain at least partially blind to the positive intentions of one another.

Amid this ideological conflict, we see our nation's universities as having become—unintentionally or otherwise—part of a contemporary battleground for the hearts and souls of the American people. There is a fight taking place within academia itself, as terms such as "truth" and "social justice" are juxtaposed against one another in discussions about the nature and production of scholarship.[5] If universities were hermetically sealed entities, we would have little about which to worry. These sorts of dialectical exercises have been going on for millennia, of course, and are part of the backbone of university life.

Of greater concern to us instead is the corrosive impact that these culture wars have had on the public's perceptions of the value of a college degree itself. The pursuit of higher education has never been more important for the individual well-being of the American citizen and for the public good of these United States. In the briefest of terms, the long-term economic value of a college degree is well worth the cost, at least for the vast majority of people.[6] And yet, we are witnessing a growing number of surveys that indicate our country's men and women are increasingly skeptical about the importance of attending an institution of higher learning.[7] This may seem to be more true of those American citizens who lean Republican in their political orientation, although there has also been erosion in Democratic support for higher education over the years as well.[8]

A Republican himself, Abraham Lincoln might have been flabbergasted by such survey results. The son of illiterate parents from the country's vast frontier, Lincoln proclaimed in his first political speech ever given that education was "the most important subject which we as a people can be engaged in."[9] In America's darkest moments, in the turmoil of civil war, he expanded the promise of public education to higher education, extending opportunity beyond the wealthy and well connected.

With the stroke of his pen on July 2, 1862, President Lincoln signed into law the Morrill Act, setting into motion a series of activities that would lead to the founding of some of America's finest public universities. We cannot overstate the dire straits facing our country at that time. The year of 1862 included the Battle of Shiloh, Second Bull Run, and Antietam. The losses incurred by the armies of North and South were nearly beyond comprehension. Uncertainty was high and hope was scarce. Yet, Lincoln keenly recognized that the story of human progress was inextricably bound to education.

Unforced Errors

What is happening now to our citizens' evaluation of education during this time of relative peace and tranquility? How have we gotten ourselves to the point where our fellow Americans look askance at the great public universities that we have built? As members of the academy, we believe we need look no further than ourselves to fix blame.

We have met the enemy, and he is us, to borrow from Walt Kelly's infamous comic character Pogo.

The saddest part of all is that the mistakes we have been making within our great public universities, at least in the eyes of the public, have largely been due to unforced errors. In tennis terms, this means that a player misses a shot or loses a point because of the individual's own mistake and not because of anything that their opponent has done. As applied to our public institutions of higher learning, then, we mean to say that we have been creating problems for ourselves, especially in how citizens assess the activities we undertake.

We assert here that critical problems have arisen from higher education leaders often assuming that what was good for universities was good for the public at large. For example, most public institutions have placed more and more emphasis on research pursuits, often at the expense of teaching and learning efforts and of making investments in outreach and engagement activities. Worse yet, many universities have shown a tendency to brag about the amount of research dollars that is awarded to and expended in their institutions. We cannot help but believe that such boastfulness serves to further confuse the public's understanding of not only what we are supposed to be doing but also the extent to which we need public funds to carry out our mission.[10]

Our bottom-line statement is this: the university-centric viewpoint that has evolved on campuses across America has contributed significantly to the growing rift between our nation's public universities and the representatives of those citizens they were supposed to be serving. Which brings us to the original working title of this book—*Fallen Angels*—which came from your second author's own professional experience as a university president over the past four decades. When he took his first university president position in 1981, Gee believed that higher education could do no wrong in the eyes of the public, including those lawmakers elected to represent the viewpoints and interests of their constituents. Universities were on a pedestal, highly revered angels of enlightenment. Fast forward four decades later, and we bear witness to a very different landscape. The angels have fallen quite far from their revered perches of yesteryear.

Is there a way back from this present sense of estrangement between campuses and communities? Yes, there is, we believe, which is why this book is subtitled *Halting Higher Education's Decline in the Court of Public Opinion*. The return to roost can only happen if university leaders, faculty members, students, and governing boards take the time to really listen to what the citizens of their states are asking of them. This is precisely what our book is meant to offer to its readers. The primary objective of this work is to unflinchingly present a no-holds-barred exploration of what citizens really think about their public universities. Along the way, we hope to create opportunities for university personnel to revive and rediscover their better angels, both internally and in the eyes of the public.

Higher Education at the Time of the COVID-19 Pandemic and Social Unrest

This book was conceived conceptually in January 2019 when our editor at Johns Hopkins University Press, Greg Britton, asked what we were going to do as a follow-up to our *Land-Grant Universities for the Future* book. A lengthy series of in-depth discussions produced a book proposal that was handed off to Mr. Britton in March 2019. Shortly afterward, we submitted a grant proposal to the Koch Foundation to support our research efforts, and we were pleased to receive word in May 2019 that our proposal was to be funded. That grant award set into motion our data collection planning efforts, which subsequently were launched in November 2019 and terminated in early January 2020. Soon afterward, we received official notification from Johns Hopkins University Press regarding the formal acceptance of our book proposal. Almost no one in the United States had any familiarity with the term *coronavirus* at that time.

Fast forward half a year later, and the entire world has been turned upside down as we put the finishing touches on this book. The COVID-19 pandemic closed large sections of society, wrecked the economy, and placed great strain and uncertainty upon the entire world, including, of course, the realm of higher education. As we go to press with this book, many questions remain unanswered, including what will happen to colleges and universities both in the near-term and further out into the future. Some have opened their campuses again to residential students, while others remain online for the time being. As if that were not enough change to account for at the latter stage of this book's composition, our nation next witnessed the death of George Floyd at the hands of the Minneapolis police on May 25, 2020. The riots and social unrest that followed were unlike anything seen in America since 1968.

It was clear we could not ignore current events, especially as the global pandemic and the antiracism protests had such an immediate and profound effect on several important topics contained in this book. While the gathering of survey responses from participants were concluded prior to the emergence of the coronavirus in the United States, our discussion of findings with national experts was ongoing throughout the beginning months of these twin crises. We also had front row seats to the daily impact that COVID-19 and the protests were having at our respective institutions of higher learning, and so we could resonate with the experiences of faculty members and university presidents alike. Simply put, these were times that were not comparable to anything seen in over one hundred years.

And so, our writing efforts in this book reflect the bifocal nature of our higher education experiences through 2019 and 2020. Much of what we had formulated in terms of our original purpose—to take the themes that were generated through our interviews of university leaders and check on their applicability in terms of how well they lined up with the public's viewpoints regarding higher education—remained intact. As previewed in the next section, the findings related to these primary objectives will be laid out in detail throughout chapters 1 through 8. While the COVID-19 pandemic does receive brief mention in chapter 5 due to its logical connection with global activities, it is in chapter 9 that we included a more intensified focus on both the coronavirus issue and antiracism activities as part of our discussion of the results generated from our quantitative and qualitative data analyses. In essence, we portray the events of 2020 as a major inflection point for understanding the implications of our entire study amid the broader repercussions for higher education's future as an enterprise.

What Lies Ahead in This Book

In our first chapter, we explore various opportunities and threats that institutions of higher learning are facing at this moment in history. This chapter includes a description of the seven themes that were generated from the interviews we conducted for our 2018 book on land-grant universities, as well as our rationale for paying closer attention to public sentiment on higher education issues. We review laudable efforts over the past twenty years undertaken by higher education leaders to better understand the difficulties they have faced in the eyes of the public, yet we also provide pointed criticism that these same leaders have not bothered to ask community stakeholders what they want and need from their public universities. We also review some seminal literature—including the historical writing of Nathan Sorber and the more contemporary viewpoints of Holden Thorp and Buck Goldstein—as part of a conceptual exercise designed to underscore the idea that those who cannot remember the past are doomed to repeat it.

In chapter 2, we lay out the framework for ground truthing our main assertion that university leaders must take steps to better understand what American citizens think about the public universities of their state. This includes a description of our efforts to create survey items for our study that were based on the "formula for success" we had established as part of the earlier work reported in our 2018 book on land-grant universities. We then briefly discuss our selection of additional items pertaining to political affiliations and voting behavior under the direction and guidance of Ohio State political science professor Michael Neblo. We also describe our use of the American Population Panel and the work we undertook in partnership with personnel from the Center for Human Resources Research, including its director, Dr. Elizabeth Cooksey. We end this chapter by providing a description of the overall sample gleaned from our recruitment efforts, which we deemed to be a great success. That is, we state our belief that the individuals selected for participation from the American Population Panel were representative of their state populations in terms of educational attainment (our proxy for socioeconomic status), gender, age, race/ethnicity, and political affiliation, thus allowing us to be confident in the generalizability of our findings.

Chapter 3 provides an in-depth discussion of how the study participants would distribute public funding across university activities. More specifically, our first survey question asked survey respondents to consider how—in an ideal world—every $100 of taxpayer money provided to public universities should be spent in terms of teaching, research, and community outreach programs and services. We report on findings from the overall sample first, whereby study participants expressed the desire to provide almost half of all public monies toward teaching efforts. In turn, the respondents divided up the remaining 50% of funds almost equally to research and community outreach programs and services. Next, we discuss the important lack of differences surrounding the politically oriented variables, as well as the significant differences we uncovered in terms of three demographic characteristics: gender, age, and level of educational attainment. The remainder of this chapter provides some contextualization of these findings in terms of teaching responsibilities and the growth in employment of nontenure-track faculty members, the true costs associated with conducting research, and the evolving nature of community outreach and engagement activities, with special focus on Cooperative Extension Services.

In chapter 4, our attention turns to a focus on our second higher education survey question, one that asked participants to consider who should be prioritized by public universities in their state: rural communities, urban communities, or if both rural and urban communities should be treated equally. In fact, more than 70% of respondents did believe that public universities should place equivalent emphasis on rural and urban communities. At the same time, however, our analyses revealed significant differences on this question as a function of several demographic variables—gender, age, educational attainment, and geographic location—as well as significant differences on political variables involving party, orientation, and predicted voting behavior in 2020. We report on all these significant differences and discuss their implications regarding university prioritization of rural and urban communities.

Chapter 5 focuses on findings related to the third survey question, which asked participants to consider whether public universities in their state should place more of their emphasis on global/international issues, more emphasis on those issues closer to home that more directly impact the communities in which they lived, or if the public universities of their state should emphasize international and local issues equally. More than 40% of the overall sample reported that there should be no difference in emphasis between global/international concerns and local issues and, much to our surprise, another third of the sample endorsed the idea that global concerns should be more greatly emphasized. Analyses using the demographic variables revealed significant differences as a function of gender, race/ethnicity, age, and educational attainment, and further significant differences were found for political variables associated with party, orientation, and predicted voting behavior in 2020. We unpack all these significant results and discuss their implications regarding university emphasis on international concerns and local issues. Although only briefly mentioned, the COVID-19 pandemic does receive mention in this chapter due to its logical connection with global activities.

In chapter 6, we report on the fourth higher education survey question that asked participants to consider what should be prioritized for student-directed funding by public universities in their state: needs-based aid (based on family income) or merit-based aid (based on student academic performance). Almost half of the sample endorsed the idea that merit-based aid should be prioritized for funding over needs-based aid. Analyses using the demographic variables revealed significant differences only as a function of age, and further significant differences were found for political variables associated with party, orientation, and predicted voting behavior in 2020. These significant results are discussed in terms of their implications regarding university emphasis on needs-based and merit-based aid.

Chapter 7 focuses on findings from the fifth survey question, which asked participants to agree or disagree with the following statement: When it comes to university rankings like *US News and World Report*, it matters a lot to me where the public universities of (my state) are ranked. While a majority (51%) of the respondents were neutral or disagreed/strongly disagreed with that statement, almost half of the sample (47%) endorsed the idea that national rankings mattered in terms of their state's public universities. Analyses using the demographic variables indicated significant effects for gender and educational attainment, and additional significant differences were found as a function of party and voting behavior in 2016. We conducted an additional analysis that combined answers to the fourth and fifth survey questions, and we found an interesting and somewhat contradictory (at least to us) pattern of responses; namely, those participants who prioritized needs-based student aid by percentage were most likely to report that national rankings mattered, whereas participants prioritizing merit-based aid, or reporting that both merit-based and needs-based aid should be equally prioritized, by percentage were more likely to be neutral or report that national rankings did not matter.

In chapter 8, we report on the sixth and final higher education survey question that asked participants to consider the following statement: If there was one thing that the public universities in your state could do that would make you feel more comfortable about how taxpayer money was being used to support higher education, what would it be? The open-ended responses to this question were deconstructed into themes and emergent patterns that matched the purposes of this study. We report on five themes that, together, create a "central idea" in terms of paths to helping citizens feel more comfortable about how taxpayer money is being used to support higher education. These themes cover issues related to access and affordability, financial stewardship, faculty and the teaching mission, community focus and services, and student-centered experiences. In addition, we report on four additional emergent themes comprised of a lesser number of open-ended responses, yet nevertheless were deemed to contain important information about participant perceptions of how taxpayer money was being spent by public universities. These four emergent themes cover issues related to campus climate issues, communicating with the public, college sports, and research.

Chapter 9 concludes our writing efforts through an exercise in charting the future of our nation's public universities. Here, we provide an overall interpretation of the findings generated from our survey of citizens from the four most populous states in America, plus Ohio and West Virginia, as well as paying close attention to the impact of issues related to COVID-19 and the antiracism social unrest. To do so, we began by examining some of the present challenges that university leaders are facing when it comes to understanding public sentiment. We then interpret some of the main findings of our study in the context of events that had occurred throughout the year 2020. We do so by first describing the results of an additional (albeit brief) survey we conducted amid the twin pandemics of COVID-19 and racial injustice. Next, we return to the results of our initial survey to further discuss findings related to the distribution of university funding, the future of international higher education, and the pursuit of national rankings. We also attend to issues tied directly to the themes generated from the qualitative data reported in chapter 8, including access and affordability, community engagement, and college sports. Finally, we discuss issues that specifically focus on diversity and inclusion concerns on America's public university campuses.

In Closing

All our friends. They are too numerous to be now named individually, while there is no one of them who is not too dear to be forgotten or neglected.

In closing the introductory section of this book, we wish to explicitly acknowledge the people who have generated the scholarship on various topics we have relied upon in the writing of this book, or otherwise helped us to shape the academic contours of this book. Similar to the quote above, which was part of a toast offered by Abraham Lincoln on July 25, 1837, during a dinner celebrating the naming of Springfield as the capital of Illinois,[11] we find ourselves with a gratitude of debt to so many individuals who are too numerous to name here. Nonetheless, we endeavor to mention at least a few of those colleagues and scholars whose work and colleagueship have helped shape our thinking.

Special thanks for assistance in the overall design of the study is given to our two Ohio State colleagues, Elizabeth Cooksey and Michael Neblo. We also owe a debt of gratitude to Ohio State's Deanna Wilkinson for her assistance in analyzing our qualitative data, to Penny Pasque for lending her expertise on topics related to higher education's public good, and to Vladimir Kogan and Stephane Lavertu for the directions they gave on policy-oriented issues. Our thanks as well are offered to West Virginia University friend and colleague Nathan Sorber, whose book, *Land-Grant Universities and Popular Revolt*, continues to influence our understanding of the higher education's extraordinary beginnings in America's history.[12] Likewise, *Our Higher Calling* written by Washington University's Holden Thorp and Buck Goldstein of the University of North Carolina at Chapel Hill has had a profound influence on our conceptualization of what it would mean to host a conversation on higher education among university and community stakeholders.[13] We also received invaluable insights into financial aid issues from Michael Nietzel, president emeritus of Missouri State University, through his prolific writing for *Forbes* magazine and his 2018 book *Coming to Grips with Higher Education*.[14] It is literally impossible for us to imagine coherently pulling together our chapter on global issues and concerns without the immense help of Philip Altbach, research professor at Boston College and author of the book *Global Perspectives on Higher Education*.[15]

Further appreciation is expressed to the Cato Institute's Neal McCluskey, Ohio State's Matthew Mayhew, and Ohio University's Richard Vedder for connecting us to your networks. As a result, we were able to benefit from the expertise of many and varied scholars and thought leaders. Alphabetically, this included Sonja Ardoin (Appalachian State University), Sandy Baum (Urban Institute), Nick Bowman (University of Iowa), Andrew Gillen (Texas Public Policy Foundation's Center for Innovation in Education), Rick Hess (American Enterprise

Institute), Nick Hillman (University of Wisconsin at Madison), Diane Jones (US Department of Education), Andrew Kelly (University of North Carolina system), and Miki Kittlison (Arizona State University).

Last but certainly not least, we also wish to mention the book "in between" books for Johns Hopkins University Press that both of your authors made contributions toward as an additional prelude to the present work. Gavazzi (along with colleague David Staley, who among other things wrote the book *Alternative Universities*[16] that also was influential in our thinking) coedited a book for The Ohio State University Press in celebration of Ohio State's sesquicentennial celebration. Entitled *Fulfilling the 21st Century Land-Grant Mission*,[17] this collection of essays reflects a wide assortment of authors from across the university—representing fields as various as agriculture, dance, English, engineering, family science, geography, medicine, social work, and veterinary science—to showcase how the land-grant mission continues to shape the work being conducted within public universities at present. We highlight this assemblage of writings because both of us wrote essays that foreshadowed certain topics that are covered in the present book.

First, in addition to serving as the lead coeditor, Gavazzi authored or coauthored four separate essays for this collection. In each case, these contributions were designed to speak directly to the question of the public university's current relevance to the well-being of our nation. Using his home institution as a focal point, Gavazzi's writing[18] provided myriad examples of excellence in teaching, research, and community engagement activities at Ohio State, and how those efforts—in combination—were directly meeting the most pressing needs of citizens at the local, state, national, and global levels.

In turn, Gee provided readers with an insider's view of what it means to lead a university, having served as the president of both public (The Ohio State University, the University of Colorado at Boulder, and West Virginia University) and private (Brown University and Vanderbilt University) institutions of higher learning. While Gee expressed appreciation for the time spent at those private universities—especially the relative liberty he experienced from having to deal with legislators, governors, newspapers, and Freedom of Information Acts—at the same time he wrote about his heart and mind being more firmly lodged in the trappings of the public university. The reasons he gave for this are quite simple: "I know my exact responsibility, which is to the people of the state I am serving and to work non-stop to make their lives better."[19]

It is with this clarity of purpose that we end our introductory chapter and thus turn our attention to the main purposes of this book. Our sincere hope is that we will provide readers with sufficient motivation to locate our better angels and enough information to begin (or strengthen) everyone's efforts to have an authentic conversation about our public universities and their contribution to the health and well-being of our great nation. So, without further ado, let us begin!

1

Opportunities and Threats to Higher Education

The dogmas of the quiet past are inadequate to the stormy present. The occasion is piled high with difficulty, and we must rise with the occasion. As our case is new, so we must think anew, and act anew.

A braham Lincoln was only one month away from issuing his Emancipation Proclamation when he forwarded his annual message to Congress on December 1, 1862, which included the quote above.[1] While the sending of such a message was customary for the presidents of his day, the contents of that communication—and the harbinger of what was to follow—could be viewed as anything but routine. In a similar fashion, we believe that the doctrines of the past are insufficient for the demands of what our public universities are facing today. New situations call for new ways of thinking about how institutions of higher learning can best serve the public good.

In forging such an innovative path forward, our straightforward aim here is to pick up where we left off in our 2018 book *Land-Grant Universities for the Future: Higher Education for the Public Good*. This earlier book was based primarily on interviews conducted with 27 presidents and chancellors of America's public land-grant institutions who were asked to comment on the strengths, weaknesses, opportunities, and threats facing contemporary higher education. Our analysis of the interview data resulted in the development of seven themes that told a story about the dynamic tensions being faced by the leaders of our nation's public universities. The seven themes, presented in dialectic fashion due to the continuum of thought expressed by the senior leaders on each of these topics, were as follows:

1. Concerns about funding declines versus the need to create efficiencies
2. Research prowess versus teaching and service excellence
3. Knowledge for knowledge's sake versus a more applied focus
4. The focus on rankings versus an emphasis on access and affordability
5. Meeting the needs of rural communities versus the needs of a more urbanized America
6. Global reach versus closer-to-home impact
7. The benefits of higher education versus the devaluation of a college diploma

Taken together, these seven themes covered various aspects of the three-part mission of the land-grant university: (1) teaching and learning, (2) research, and (3) outreach and engagement with the communities they were designed to serve.

Further interviews were conducted with more than 35 higher education thought leaders who offered reactions to these seven themes that also were reported in our book on land-grant universities. The qualitative data produced from these interviews allowed us to outline a clear roadmap—discussed as a formula for success—that was designed to increase the public's appreciation for the return on investment these higher learning institutions offered toward the public good. Nothing else would matter, we contended, unless these universities reclaimed their mantle as the "people's universities." To do this, these public institutions of higher learning would have to "pick a side" in terms of the dialectical themes discussed above. As a result, universities wishing to reassert the benefits of a college degree would have to become more efficient, cultivate increased teaching excellence, better engage with community stakeholders, conduct research that mattered, clarify how their university's activities impacted the needs of local citizens (even amid internationally based efforts), and refocus attention on being more affordable and accessible instead of worrying about national rankings.

In addition to providing a formula for success that would enhance the reputation of higher education institutions in the eyes of the public, our previous book also provided a critical examination of how university leaders have attempted to deal with the readily identified disconnect between universities and their constituents. To illustrate what had been done to date, we reviewed three major efforts that had been launched over the last two decades, including the "Returning to Our Roots" reports issued by the Kellogg Commission on the Future of State and Land-Grant Universities,[2] the "Classification for Community Engagement" offered by the Carnegie Foundation for the Advancement of Teaching,[3] and the "Innovation and Economic Prosperity (IEP)" designation created by the Association of Public and Land-Grant Universities (APLU).[4] These efforts, coming as they have at regular intervals over the past 20 years, have created noteworthy calls to action for university leaders to better connect with community constituents.

The Kellogg Commission's work on this topic warrants a bit more consideration here as they paid great attention to the concept of the "engaged institution." Among other things, the reports from the Kellogg Commission's efforts provided seven guiding characteristics (dubbed a "seven-part test" by the report's authors) that, together, defined engagement with the community ostensibly being served by public universities: responsiveness, respect for partners, academic neutrality, accessibility, integration, coordination, and resource partnerships.[5] While each of these seven characteristics purportedly held relatively equal value in the engagement process, we were particularly interested in the responsiveness factor from the standpoint of valuing stakeholder feedback. From the executive summaries of the Kellogg Commission (2000) report, responsive engagement was described as follows:

We need to ask ourselves periodically if we are listening to the communities, regions, and states we serve. Are we asking the right questions? Do we offer our services in the right way at the right time? Are our communications clear? Do we provide space and, if need be, resources for preliminary community-university discussions of the public problem to be addressed? Above all, do we really understand that in reaching out, we are also obtaining valuable information for our own purposes? (16)

Despite this sort of rhetoric, however, these reports, classifications, and designations seem to have had a negligible impact on public perceptions of higher education as evidenced by the surveys of public opinion we described above and elsewhere.[6] We believe that this scarcity of influence can be explained in large part by the almost complete lack of input from the public supposedly being served by these institutions of higher learning. In other words, despite the speechmaking, it is our contention that universities typically have not sought to gather this sort of routine feedback from community stakeholders, regardless of their status as an engaged institution.[7]

In all candidness, that sort of activity does not seem to have been the primary intention of the three major efforts introduced above. As we have noted previously in our land-grant universities book, for example, while the Kellogg Commission members (comprised of former and present university presidents and advised by an elite group of stakeholders from business and industry) were overtly committed to rethinking public education for the twenty-first century, their activities were both a subtle and not-so-subtle attempt to sway public opinion and otherwise stabilize perceptions during a time of great criticism and uncertainty about the value of America's colleges and universities. The Carnegie Foundation work, in turn, was largely meant to provide a voluntary badge of honor for those universities whose self-studies were deemed to be worthy of such an endorsement.[8]

Only the IEP designation generated by APLU began to address the need for outside input from members of the community. Designed to recognize those colleges and universities that are more intensively involved in economic development efforts, institutions of higher learning are put through an assessment process that includes both a self-study (similar in form to the Carnegie endorsement) as well as external stakeholder input. This latter component requires universities to specifically identify community partners who essentially are willing and able to vouchsafe for the university's involvement in some aspect of economic development in the community.[9] However, even the APLU effort is quite limited in the sense that it focused mainly on a rather small yet essential segment (business and industry) of the larger community served by America's public institutions of higher learning.

Thus, we draw important attention here to the fact that higher education leaders to date have spent a great deal of time talking inwardly to each other about the difficulties they have faced in the eyes of the public. Although hindsight is always 20-20, we remain puzzled by the lack of attention to public input. Does it not seem a bit bizarre to profess concern about your university's impact on the community, and yet not invite community stakeholders to the table for a discussion about what they might want and need? This is why we set out to conduct the study we report in this book. If you are going to think anew, you need to act anew. So, we thought, let us do just that. Let us start a conversation by asking for the opinions and perspectives of the citizens themselves.

Those Who Cannot Remember the Past Are Doomed to Repeat It

Our efforts to gauge the public's perceptions of American colleges and universities at this moment in time were influenced directly by our having read and digested many books on higher education. Out of these, there are two relatively recent works that we wish to mention and cover in some detail here. The first book to be discussed is Nathan Sorber's *Land-Grant Colleges and Popular Revolt: The Origins of the Morrill Act and the Reform of Higher Education*, which provided us with a keen sense of the historical importance of paying attention to public sentiment (and remembering just how variable those attitudes and opinions can be in real life). The second book, written by Holden Thorp and Buck

Goldstein and entitled *Our Higher Calling: Rebuilding the Partnership between America and its Colleges and Universities*, helped guide and direct us as we developed a framework for a twenty-first-century dialogue between university representatives and the citizens they are supposed to be serving. Together, they are bookended works which have led us to believe, like George Santayana, that those who cannot remember the past are doomed to repeat it.[10] Or, perhaps more accurately, they are ill-equipped for present and future challenges because they don't know how we got here, nor do they understand who did what to create the present situation.

Nathan Sorber's *Land-Grant Colleges and Popular Revolt* tells the deromanticized story of the founding and evolution of America's public land-grant universities.[11] Sorber underscored the need to be pragmatic about the birth and development of our nation's land-grant institutions because there has been a tendency to look back on this historical period with rose-colored glasses. Instead of a time where everyone was holding hands and singing "Kumbaya," this author argues that the passage of the Morrill Land-Grant Act of 1862 and the decades that followed were marked by intensive conflict over exactly what these universities should be and who they should serve. As Sorber put it, "In breaking away from romantic memory, this history reveals that the land-grant movement was forged not through a shared vision of democratic higher education but instead through a pragmatic accommodation of competing class interests" (175).

This friction was especially present in the northeastern United States, where agriculture was in decline as an industry. Farmers in these states were facing enormous financial pressures due to deflated crop prices and land values, caused in large part by bank failures and related negative economic conditions beginning in the early 1870s that lasted until the turn of the century (until the 1930s came along, this previous period of time was known as the Great Depression). Making a difficult situation worse, there was an exodus of labor through outmigration of the former farm workers to better paying jobs in the cities. Sorber described how farmers responded to this agricultural crisis by forming granges that became politically active and, with the aid of populist politicians, initiated a variety of lobbying efforts that would ease their plight.

The organizers of the granges soon set their sights on the newly emerging land-grant colleges. These movement leaders argued that the scientifically oriented curricula of these institutions of higher learning were intensifying the problems faced by the farming community. The politicization of this situation in several states—most notably Connecticut, New Hampshire, Rhode Island, and Vermont—resulted in these granges seeking nothing less than the takeover of the land-grant colleges themselves. Their goal, according to Sorber, was to install a farmer-friendly curriculum that emphasized agricultural methods and placed higher value on rural living.

Over time, this dynamic tension was alleviated as the land-grant colleges transformed themselves in response to this public outcry. Most noteworthy in this regard were the outreach and engagement activities aimed at rural communities that these institutions of higher learning began to develop. Eventually, these efforts culminated in the development of the Cooperative Extension Services system through passage of the Smith-Lever Act of 1914. According to Sorber, "the three-part mission of teaching, research, and service emerged as the solution to the riddle that baffled higher education leaders in the nineteenth century" (17). Hence, we have historical evidence of highly controversial opinions about what higher education should be doing for the public good in the 1800s that were resolved by university administrators both listening to public sentiment and then doing something that directly addressed those concerns.

We spoke at some length with Dr. Sorber about his written scholarship and its place within the context of our book. There is much to be gained from the adoption of a deromanticized viewpoint regarding the early days of land-grant universities, he explained, with special emphasis on rejection of the notion that these institutions of higher learning came into existence because of a shared democratic vision among its citizens. Instead, the reality was that their historical development was much more contentious and fragmented, which, over time, demanded a more pragmatic accommodation among competing interests. Ultimately, citizens got some of what they needed from these land-grant institutions, and, in turn, these universities benefited from innovations—Cooperative Extension Services, curricular reform, and alternative course delivery methods—that were generated as a function of seeking this common ground.

Despite all of this, however, Dr. Sorber felt it was necessary to sound a cautionary note about the place that public universities find themselves in today. "The future of public universities is based on two-way communication, as it always has been. The reason that land-grants have persisted has been a function of the partnership struck between the university and the public, where both sides brought something to the table. I get worried now about populist critiques that undermine the value of scientific knowledge, and I get equally upset about faculty members who want to keep that knowledge within the ivory tower." In the end, Dr. Sorber explains, there must be a welding of these university and societal interests, where faculty are free to follow their scientific pursuits and, at the same time, are expected to apply the resulting knowledge to local and state issues and concerns.

By extension, *Our Higher Calling* by Thorp and Goldstein walked us right up to the doorstep of our desire to develop a twenty-first century conversation between higher education leaders and citizens that would replicate what had evolved over the course of the latter part of the nineteenth century.[12] Starting from a similar place set forth by other higher education scholars,[13] Thorp and Goldstein asserted that the relationship between universities and the public has historically been a partnership that most resembles a compact: institutions of higher learning were supposed to create a vibrant workforce and generate new knowledge that benefited society at large, and in return they were to be adequately funded and allowed to manage themselves in the pursuit of whatever subject matter they deemed to be essential to the betterment of their areas of expertise. The problem at present, these authors maintain, is that this contractual arrangement is breaking down, with both sides seemingly not holding up their end of the bargain.

What we found particularly appealing about this work is their call for both parties—universities and the public—to work cooperatively in *dialogue* with one another to reconstitute the compact. Thorp and Goldstein state that "the effort to rebuild the partnership will necessarily involve a conversation among parties inside and outside the university, each with distinctly different points of view, but it is critical that we bridge those divides" (3–4). These authors go on to provide evidence that the distance between academia and the public is widespread at present. As but one example, Thorp and Goldstein cited a Brookings Institution article that reported on the disparity between the percentage of business leaders (11%) who believe current college graduates are adequately prepared for the workforce in comparison to the percentage of those chief academic officers (96%) who believe the same thing.[14] How in the world can those perspectives be so far off from each other, we might ask?

We did some further digging, and it turns out that this finding was part of a survey conducted by the Lumina Foundation and Gallup in 2013. This larger report contains additional results that provided further evidence of a profound disconnect between university efforts and public needs and desires.[15] For instance, this report noted that a fairly large percentage of Americans (89%) believed that colleges and university need to change in order to better serve the needs of contemporary students, yet not quite half of these same citizens (49%) thought that universities were actually making those changes. Perhaps even more telling is the finding that, while the majority (84%) of business leaders believed that the amount of knowledge brought to the table by a candidate was very important in terms of a decision to hire that individual, roughly a quarter (28%) of those polled thought the *type* of degree was important, and only 9% valued the place *where* the candidate received their degree. So much for the idea that selected majors are important, this report seems to indicate, to say nothing about the idea that the institution from which you received your degree matters.

Another survey conducted by *Inside Higher Ed* and Gallup—this one focused on the perspectives of college and university presidents—provides further evidence of the disconnect between universities and the citizens they are meant to serve.[16] Among the findings was the fact that only 12% of these senior leaders either agreed or strongly agreed that "most Americans have an accurate view of the purpose of higher education." Additionally, 84% of these presidents believe that citizens have been misled into thinking college is less affordable by the attention that has been paid to student debt. Further, almost this same number (80%) of leaders report that fanfare related to the growth of university endowments has skewed public perceptions about the actual financial well-being of institutions of higher learning.

Returning to the Thorp and Goldstein book, we find that plenty of the blame for the breakdown in the university-public compact can be placed on the inability of university leaders to create strategies and implement necessary changes, even in the face of overwhelming evidence that would support such tactical adjustments. The biggest culprit? The authors state that "the reason is clear: strategy is about being different and about making hard choices. But a university community—which is typically governed by consensus—resists direction from the top and has great difficulty choosing among competing priorities that create winners and losers" (34).

Therefore, the main challenge here, as stated most simply by Thorp and Goldstein, is that the consensus sought by denizens of the university quickly becomes the enemy of strategy. Higher education is not the only business sector facing such dilemmas, of course.[17] That said, this sort of problem does not, at least on the surface, bode well for the further introduction of those additional competing demands that would be voiced by community stakeholders who, external to the university, would be invited into the conversation. This may provide at least a partial explanation about why university leaders are not engaging community stakeholders in dialogue at present. After all, why ask for feedback from citizens when it seems unlikely you can be responsive to that input?

And yet, there is no other way around this sort of predicament. Thorp and Goldstein state emphatically that "the disconnect is one that can no longer be ignored" (137). In fact, the failure of higher education to take part in such a conversation with the public will only generate further evidence in support of Santayana's maxim. Quite frankly, we do not believe it would be in the best interests of any public university to wait for the emergence of the next "grange" movement as the motivation for action. To underscore our point with another adage, universities can either be at the table or they can be on the menu.

We spoke at length with Buck Goldstein about some of the issues that have arisen out of the present situation faced by public universities and the communities they are supposed to be serving. Our wide-ranging discussion focused on a variety of topics, some of which can be viewed as logical extensions of the contents of that book. For example, in discussing how difficult it is to promote strategic change inside of universities, Professor Goldstein noted that "in academia, no wants to do something different for the first time. More often, the impulse is to try to match or exceed a perceived competitor." This self-inflicted shortcoming seems to hold up even when there are clear and relatively undemanding adjustments to be made that would prove beneficial to all parties concerned.

In a fashion parallel to our discussion with Dr. Sorber, however, our conversation with Professor Goldstein also contained some advisory notes about how we might proceed in terms of promoting the kind of campus-community dialogue we were seeking. One of those primary cautions surrounded the role of faculty members in such an enterprise. We understand a great deal more about what the public's expectations of universities are, Goldstein remarked, than we are certain about what faculty members expect of themselves regarding this compact with communities. "Typically, we don't sit down and explain 'the deal' to a young faculty member in terms of their obligations to the betterment of communities," Goldstein said. "And so, part of the problem is the disconnect between what the public expects and what we end up offering as rewards to faculty members, which don't always comport with the bargain we have struck."

Essentially, Professor Goldstein was urging us to consider how our efforts to survey citizens might be followed up with an attempt to give voice to what faculty members think about their role in working directly on behalf of communities. This suggestion was grounded in his belief that university leaders tell two very different stories depending on their audience. When in front of the state legislature, Goldstein stated, presidents and other top administrators provide a narrative that emphasizes all the public good that is being done on behalf of citizens. Upon their return to campus, however, leaders tell a very different tale. It is a storyline that places much greater emphasis on support for faculty members' more individualized pursuits, especially in the realm of research. What happens when you try to bring those narratives together? "You get a pretty serious problem," Goldstein remarked. This is a problem of our own making, which is why we now turn our attention to a series of other mistakes we have been making in academia that have seriously hampered our ability to create meaningful dialogue about university engagement to date.

Emancipation from the Tyrannies of Our Own Making

In our *Land-Grant Universities for the Future* book, we identified several "tyrannies" or stumbling blocks that, we believed, serve to obstruct and delay a university's ability to adapt successfully to the challenges and needs of twenty-first-century America. We highlighted three such stumbling blocks: the tyranny of the university department, the tyranny of the university gerontocracy, and the tyranny of university complacency. Recognition of the tyranny related to the university's departmental structure was meant to highlight the foot-dragging that can occur in the face of change by faculty members who simply do not want to get out of their comfort zone. In turn, the tyranny of the university's gerontocracy marked the fact that an aging faculty workforce[18] often translates into situations where older faculty members—who typically have greater power through their higher rank and seniority—more typically support the status quo.

Over time, these two related forms of inflexibility are thought to contribute to the tyranny of complacency, one where self-satisfaction with the accomplishments of the past have prompted university personnel to rest on their laurels. The result is what Robert Sternberg called "mediocracy," a situation where mediocrity becomes rewarded by universities who fail to keep up with external standards of performance excellence.[19] In naming these tyrannies, we meant to lay out a path for academics to set themselves free from various subjugations of their own making, to become agents of transformation instead of change-adverse obstructionists.

To our list of warnings, we now wish to add one more self-inflicted form of oppression that universities suffer from at present: the tyranny of the echo chamber. The thought that campuses are political echo chambers—especially regarding left-leaning ideologies—is not new.[20] What we are describing here goes beyond politics, however, and gets at the very core of our mission to give voice to the public at large. We wish to witness personnel from our public universities stepping out of their oftentimes hermeneutically sealed worlds of teaching and research and beginning to listen and to act upon—in fact, to serve—the wants and needs of the very citizens for whom they are supposed to be working. This translates into a stepping into something else; in this case, into a "servant university" mentality.

Borrowing extensively from Robert Greenleaf's discourse on servant leadership,[21] we used the concept of the "servant university" to introduce this sort of position in our land-grant universities book. What we were advocating for was the idea that a public institution of higher learning would place primary emphasis on the stewardship responsibilities they have been given by society to provide for the development and well-being of its communities. Said in a slightly different way, we believed that the original agreement struck between the public and its colleges and universities meant that critical decisions made at all levels of leadership should be filtered first through the lens of what provides maximum benefit for the citizens of each state and for American society at large.

We are encouraged to see that this sort of mentality may be beginning to creep into the thinking of some quarters of academia. One particularly promising endeavor surrounds the work being undertaken on certain "Grand Challenges" (also described as "Moon Shots") related to pressing problems in such diverse areas as precision medicine, space exploration, environmental sustainability, and mental health.[22] This work purports to "violate Weber's injunctions against engagement with the nonacademic world and working across specialties," meaning that faculty members work collaboratively with each other instead of in isolation from one another, and with the public good in mind.[23] We remain cautiously hopeful that such efforts are being done in direct collaboration with stakeholders in those communities, states, provinces, and countries that are targeted as the recipients of these efforts, rather than on the belief that these universities know what is best for the public at large.

That brings us to our evolving thoughts about the servant university and our earlier writing on this subject matter. We know now that we did not go far enough in making our argument about the need for institutions of higher learning to adopt such a stance. What we should have included was a set of direct statements that underscored the importance of hearing directly from citizens about what they want and need public universities to be doing on their behalf. Saying "we are the experts of our academic areas, so we know what to do" rings as hollow as "we're from the government, and we're here to help" to the ears of far too many citizens these days. The ideal servant university, therefore, is asking what is needed and desired by stakeholders in the community—in this case, the very public that ostensibly is being served by the institution of higher learning—before acting.

Summary

When the Varsity Blues admissions scandal broke in early 2019, we were appalled. Rich and famous parents were caught cheating the system in order to allow their sons and daughters to gain admittance to some of the nation's premier universities.[24] Even now, at the time of this book's writing, the fallout continues unabated.[25] One of us (Gee) felt so incensed that he decided to pen a letter[26] to the editor of USA Today. In this op-ed article, it was stated that significant portions of our society had rather radically distorted its value system, including how institutions of higher learning were evaluated. To move us back to a more balanced appreciation of what our universities offer to us, Gee said that we must "learn how to be elite without being elitist, which means not impressing and intimidating each other with our academic credentials but helping each other to grow better educated, better prepared and better attuned to each other's needs." This was a statement about valuing purpose over prestige, plain and simple.

We raise the issue of purpose to set the stage for all that follows. The extensive use of material from our 2018 *Land-Grant Universities for the Future* book in this first chapter not only provided a rationale for university leaders to pay closer attention to public sentiment on higher education issues, but also served to underscore the prior work we had done to lay out an argument for institutions of higher learning to become more visible and consistent contributors to the common good. In turn, this chapter's review of efforts undertaken by higher education leaders to better position themselves in the eyes of a wary public was sprinkled with the criticism that these leaders—as yet—have not engaged in any sort of meaningful dialogue with community stakeholders about what they want and need from their public universities. Finally, our consideration of both the historical writing of Nathan Sorber and the more contemporary viewpoints of Holden Thorp and Buck Goldstein were presented as evidence that public universities that forget their main purpose are likely to be devalued by the very citizens whom they are supposed to be serving.

2

What Citizens Think about Their State's Public Universities

Steps toward Ground Truthing

In this and like communities, public sentiment is everything. With public sentiment, nothing can fail; without it nothing can succeed. Consequently, he who molds public sentiment, goes deeper than he who enacts statutes or pronounces decisions. He makes statutes and decisions possible or impossible to be executed.

This chapter begins with words uttered by Abraham Lincoln during his first debate with Stephen Douglas. The place was Ottawa, Illinois, and the date was August 21, 1858, when he made those remarks.[1] This underscores just how early Lincoln had emphasized the importance of finding out (and acting upon) what citizens thought about the issues of the day. We find ourselves in complete agreement with Lincoln's position at the outset of his candidacy to become president of the United States of America. Power resides in the will of the people and especially within those durable opinions that are "the product of history and culture."[2]

Stated slightly differently in the context of higher education, universities ignore public opinion at their own peril. To date it would seem to be the case that leaders of our public institutions of higher learning largely have been indifferent, if not fully oblivious and unresponsive, to the wants and needs of the very citizens they are supposed to be serving. We wish to change this situation and so, without further ado, we move to introduce the study that was designed to provide just that sort of information about public sentiment regarding higher education. Those with ears to hear, let them hear!

The Study

We designed this study as a direct follow-up to and extension of our previous empirical work as reported in our book, *Land-Grant Universities for the Future: Higher Education for the Public Good.* In brief, we wished to test the degree to which the seven themes generated through a thematic analysis of interview data—based as they were on the viewpoints of university presidents and higher education thought leaders— would display any sense of alignment with the views of the public at large. As such, we created survey items for the present study—described next—that were based on the "formula for success" we had established as part of our earlier work. Following the discussion of how these items were developed, we then briefly describe our selection of additional items pertaining to political affiliations and demographic characteristics. The solicitation script and all items asked of participants are contained in appendix 1. Next, we go on to describe our use of the American Population Panel as the mechanism for accessing study participants, and we end this chapter by providing a description of the overall sample gleaned from our recruitment efforts. In subsequent chapters we present an initial overview of the main findings from these items, we disaggregate the results according to the available demographic and political affiliation data, and then we provide a discussion of the implications of our findings.

The Higher Education Items

The first higher education-based survey question asked respondents to consider how—in an ideal world—every $100 of taxpayer money provided to public universities should be spent in terms of teaching, research, and community outreach programs and services. This question was based on two of the themes described in our land-grant universities book: "research prowess versus teaching and service excellence" and "knowledge for knowledge's sake versus a more applied focus." Participants were told that their answers must add up to $100, and they were told to assume that all basic operating costs (electricity, heating/cooling, etc.) and other expenses (student housing, dining services, recreation, etc.) were already covered by non-taxpayer monies. Based on our previous work regarding the formula for success, we anticipated that participants would direct the greatest amount of money toward teaching. We further hypothesized that participants would spend more of the remaining money on community outreach programs and services in comparison to funding put toward research.

The second higher education-based survey question asked participants to consider who should be prioritized by public universities in their state: rural or urban communities. This question was predicated on the theme reported in our land-grant universities book regarding "meeting the needs of rural communities versus the needs of a more urbanized America." Possible responses included (a) rural communities should be prioritized; (b) urban communities should be prioritized; or (c) there should be no difference between how rural and urban communities are prioritized. Based on our previous work regarding the formula for success, we believed that the preponderance of study participants would endorse the idea that there should be no difference between rural and urban counties when it comes to prioritizing public university activities.

The third higher education-based survey question asked participants to consider whether public universities in their state should place more of their emphasis on global/international issues or on those issues closer to home that more directly impacted the communities in which they lived. This item was based on the theme reported in our previous book regarding the dynamic tension between "global reach versus closer to home impact." Responses included (a) global/international concerns should be emphasized more than issues impacting my community; (b) issues impacting my community should be emphasized more than global/international concerns; or (c) there should be no difference in emphasis between global/international concerns and issues impacting my community. Based on our previous work regarding the formula for success, we hypothesized that participants were most likely to report that local issues should eclipse more global-based activities.

The fourth higher education-based survey question asked participants to consider what should be prioritized for student-directed funding by public universities in their state: needs-based aid (based on family income) or merit-based aid (based on student academic performance). This survey question was predicated on the theme presented in our previous book regarding "the focus on rankings versus an emphasis on access and affordability." Possible responses included: (a) needs-based aid should be prioritized for funding over merit-based aid; (b) merit-based aid should be prioritized for funding over needs-based aid; (c) there should be no difference in funding provided for needs-based aid and merit-based aid; or (d) none of the above (I do not believe public universities should provide either needs-based or merit-based aid). Based on our previous work regarding the formula for success, we believed that study participants would endorse the idea that there should be no difference between needs-based aid and merit-based aid, or perhaps even that needs-based aid should be prioritized for funding over merit-based aid when it comes to prioritizing public university activities.

The fifth survey question asked participants to agree or disagree with the following statement: When it comes to university rankings like *US News and World Report*, it matters a lot to me where the public universities of (my state) are ranked. Possible responses on a five-point Likert-like scale ranged from "strongly agree" to "strongly disagree," with an anchor point in the middle labeled "neither agree nor disagree." Comparable to the previous survey item, the fifth question was also based on the theme presented in our land-grant universities book regarding "the focus on rankings versus an emphasis on access and affordability." Here, we predicted that study participants would endorse the idea that national rankings were inconsequential, meaning that more respondents would be neutral or would not care (disagree or strongly disagree) about university rankings.

At a more complex level, we hypothesized additionally that *if* respondents endorsed the idea that needs-based aid should be prioritized for funding over merit-based aid in item four, *then* those same participants would be more likely to disagree or strongly disagree about the importance of national rankings. We thought that the opposite case would be equally likely. That is, *if* respondents endorsed the idea that merit-based aid should be prioritized for funding over needs-based aid in item four, *then* those same participants would be more likely to agree or strongly agree about the importance of national rankings. Finally, *if* respondents endorsed the idea that there should be no difference in funding provided for needs-based aid and merit-based aid, *then* those same participants would be more likely to remain neutral about the importance of national rankings.

The sixth and final survey question asked participants to respond to the following open-ended question: If there was one thing that the public universities in your state could do that would make you feel more comfortable about how taxpayer money was being used to support higher education, what would it be? Based on our previous work on the formula for success, we predicted that participants would provide text-based responses that would fall into several categories related to the seven themes presented in *Land-Grant Universities for the Future*. More specifically, we anticipated that the greatest amount of attention would be paid to how universities were spending the money that was provided by public tax dollars, followed by the related issue regarding how much time faculty members were spending in the classroom as compared to other activities. That said, the fact that we interviewed only those individuals connected to higher education in our previous study also sensitized us to the possibility of other as-yet-to-be identified themes developing out of this open-ended question.

Items Targeting Political Affiliation and Voting Behaviors

Because the data collection efforts for our land-grant universities book took place between August 2016 and January 2017, we were compelled by the comments of the interviewees to pay attention to certain ramifications related to the 2016 US presidential election. That is, we listened intently to how those senior administrators we interviewed prior to Election Day were typically making remarks about the potential consequences of the election as small talk either before or following the semi-structured interview questions. As well, we also took note of how, following Election Day, the presidents and chancellors we interviewed were embedding commentary about the electoral results directly into their responses to our questions about the strengths, weaknesses, opportunities, and threats faced by their universities.

Almost without exception, the higher education leaders we interviewed had voiced great concern about the divisiveness of the election. Many also wondered out loud about the role that our public universities might play in sorting out the aftermath, especially in creating what we ended up describing in our book as the "neutral ground" that would be required for all sides to be heard and understood. This, of course, triggered consideration of other issues and concerns, not the least of which surrounded the need to take into account the public's perception that America's universities displayed a distinctly leftward skew on the political spectrum, something that has been widely reported in the media.[3]

This led us to an examination of polling results[4] in and around institutions of higher learning during the 2016 US presidential election, an analysis that generated evidence of exactly this sort of political slant. That is, communities in and around universities (and apparently, especially land-grant universities) were skewed toward more democratic voting patterns. With these findings in mind, we took great pains to describe how university leaders must heed the public's sensitivity to such political biases. In tandem, we strongly suggested that these same leaders double their commitment to actions that clearly and unequivocally would provide messaging to the public at large that their campuses would remain "neutral ground." That is, a fair and balanced approach would be adopted by their campuses regarding any number of issues that might be seen (and voted on) differently by campus representatives in comparison to their host community brethren. Precisely because academics are supposed to pursue truth—veritas—this stance promotes the airing of all opinions into healthy and ongoing dialogues that sort the wheat from the chaff.

All this prior work created a heightened awareness of the "multiverse of communities" that were being served by our nation's public universities. Therefore, we believed that any solicitation of public sentiment about these institutions of higher learning ideally would be interpreted through an examination of the political inclinations of those participants whose viewpoints we were seeking. After all, we hoped to stand an even chance of getting folks from both sides of the aisle to tell us what they thought about higher education. That brought us to the point where we realized we needed a set of questions that would allow us to gather some important political background information about our respondents.

We were fortunate enough to have the opportunity to work with Michael Neblo on this aspect of the study. Dr. Neblo is a professor of political science at The Ohio State University, where he conducts research that focuses on deliberative democracy and political psychology.[5] In brief, deliberative democracy involves consensus-building within diverse groups of constituents, activities that focus on the development of commonly shared viewpoints.[6] With the guidance and direction of Dr. Neblo, we were able to fashion a small set of items that, we believed, generated a coherent sense of participants' political affiliation and the voting behaviors of citizens. Our goal was to find a Goldilocks moment regarding these variables; that is, not too much but also not too little information on this important topic.

First, to generate some basic information about political affiliation, we began with a very general first question about how respondents thought of themselves in terms of political parties. That is, we asked participants to tell us if they considered themselves to be a Republican, a Democrat, an Independent, or something else ("Other" or "no preference" were the additional choices provided to respondents). Next, if they selected Republican or Democrat, we asked a follow-up question about whether they considered themselves to be a "strong Republican" or "strong Democrat" respectively. If instead they had selected Independent, other, or no preference, they were given a follow-up question that asked if they thought of themselves as closer to the Republican party, closer to the Democratic party, or neither.

Next, we wished to locate our participants on a continuum that ranged from "extremely liberal" to "extremely conservative" in their political orientation. The midpoint was anchored by the response of "moderate or middle of the road." Finally, in terms of voting behavior, we asked one question about the 2016 presidential election (did you vote: yes or no) and one question about the likelihood of their voting in the 2020 presidential election. Possible responses here ranged from "I definitely will vote" to "I definitely will not vote" with the midpoint response anchored by the statement "there is a 50/50 chance I will vote."

The American Population Panel

The American Population Panel (APP)[7] is a growing collection of citizens from across the United States who have registered voluntarily to participate in research surveys of their own choosing. The APP is housed in the Center for Human Resources Research (CHRR) at The Ohio State University. The CHRR has been in existence for more than 50 years and is best known for their design and management of the national longitudinal surveys sponsored by the Bureau of Labor Statistics inside of the US Department of Labor.

At the time that this study was conducted, the APP included approximately 35,000 panelists, the majority of whom had been recruited via the internet. Other methods of recruitment have included mailings, emailing, calling both landline and cell phone numbers, recruitment from other studies conducted by CHRR researchers, and face-to-face recruiting at state and local events where a broad cross-section of the population is more likely to be present. The APP panelists are paid for the time it takes them to complete surveys. Experience has taught the CHRR personnel that people are more likely to answer questions thoughtfully and thoroughly when they are compensated fairly for their time. Because the present study was relatively brief (taking approximately five minutes on average to complete), panelists earned five dollars that were dispensed as gift cards.

The CHRR is directed by Elizabeth Cooksey. Dr Cooksey, who is also a professor of sociology at The Ohio State University, provided important consultation to us throughout the data collection portion of this project. In discussing our aims, Dr. Cooksey underscored the fact that it has become more and more difficult to recruit people for research studies the old-fashioned way. Even with a sampling frame explicitly drawn to create a carefully crafted, nationally representative sample, she went on to say, efforts to recruit by mail and by telephone increasingly are less and less successful. Potential participants often ignore their mail and many people no longer have landline telephones—even if they do, they tend to let their answering machines take the calls. These societal developments have made it much more difficult to create truly representative samples.

We further learned from Dr. Cooksey that lists of emails and cell phone numbers could be purchased for our project. Emailing potential respondents would be inexpensive, of course, but those messages are often ignored or end up in spam or trash folders. Calling people on their cell phones is a time-consuming activity and, with sharp increases in robocalling, tends not to yield healthy response rates either. Additionally, not everyone has a cell phone and the area code for cell phone numbers doesn't necessarily match up with their current area of residence making it difficult to get full geographic representation from cell phone numbers alone. Of course, texting is a good way to get people's attention, but it is illegal to text a cell phone number without first getting permission from the owner.

Given this situation, we selected our sample from APP members. Dr. Cooksey explained that this sort of strategy is becoming more common as less and less people have the resources to create their own survey samples. She also noted that an increasing number of panels available for researchers are drawn from internet users responding to requests on social media platforms. That said, we were concerned about the representativeness of the APP sample. As with email samples, panelists recruited through the internet must be internet users, and these panels are going to be biased accordingly. The APP continues to recruit panelists via more expensive and time-consuming mechanisms to minimize this kind of bias as much as possible. By using a well-defined and specifically chosen sample of respondents from a large panel such as the APP, which uses a wide range of recruitment methods, we feel confident that our results represent a diverse set of people and views. We describe our strategic sampling methods next.

The Sampling Strategy

When recruiting for our study, we wanted to end up with a sample of approximately 600 respondents (100 participants coming from each of the six states we had targeted). Ideally then, we would achieve relatively equal numbers of participants coming from California, Florida, New York, and Texas (the four most populous states in the nation) plus Ohio and West Virginia (our home states). We selected the four most populous states precisely because we were so laser-focused on public sentiment. In other words, we wished to begin our exploration of what citizens thought about higher education in those places where the most people lived. Our addition of Ohio and West Virginia were purely for parochial purposes. We were curious about the opinions of those citizens who resided in the states that supported our universities. In the end, this was never intended to be a nationally representative sample, but rather an effort to launch a research project that might indicate the value of asking people what they thought about their state's public institutions of higher learning.

That said, the individuals selected for participation would need to be as representative of their state populations as possible in terms of socioeconomic status (using highest level of education attained as a proxy for SES), gender, rural/urban residence and age (18–44 and 45+). Hence, US census data were employed for each of these six states to calculate the distribution of the population by two educational attainment groups, two age groups, rural/urban residence, and gender. This produced 16 categories or "buckets" that represented all the unique permutations potentially possible for each state. Across the six states, there ended up being a total of 96 unique buckets.

Our CHRR/APP colleagues sent invitations out in batches or "replicates." Knowing that not everyone would respond positively to the survey invitation, more respondents were sent invitations than were needed to fill each bucket. So, for example, if we wanted to end up with 11 older females who had a high school diploma and lived in California, in our first replicate we might send an invitation to 15 such women. Invitations were also sent out to individuals who had missing data on, for example, their state of residence, and those panelists were asked for their zip code in the survey. In this manner, CHRR/APP staff members were able to update information on panelists and place them in the correct "bucket."

Sometimes, of course, people had moved to a new state, and, therefore, they would have to be reclassified. Other times, people had completed more education since the time they had last participated, and so they, too, were reclassified. As soon as a bucket was filled with the required number of survey takers, that bucket was closed it off and included no more people with those specific characteristics in the next round of survey invites.

Sample

We report here on the first 844 respondents that were successfully recruited into the sample. We were able to exceed our original target of 600 participants due to some additional fiscal resources being freed up in tandem with a more robust than expected response from panelists in several of the states. Data collection is ongoing at the time of this book's writing, and our hope is to incorporate responses from panelists hailing from several additional large population states (including Georgia, Illinois, and Pennsylvania). With an eventual cohort of at least 1,200 participants residing in the eight most populous states (plus West Virginia), our plan is to replicate the initial results described in this book with this larger and more geographically diverse sample. Pending the availability of additional funds connected to ongoing grantwriting efforts, eventually we wish to create a fully national sample that would include panelists from all fifty states. Then and only then, of course, will our results be generalizable to the country as a whole.

Demographics

There were 344 (41%) males and 500 females (59%) in the sample gathered for this study. In our analysis plan, we sought to compare male and female scores to examine potential gender differences. The average age of participants was 45.7 years, with a range of 18 to 95 years of age. Our analyses also aimed to examine potential age-related differences through use of the two main age groups employed in our solicitation strategy described above. That is, we wished to compare the viewpoints of participants who were aged 18 to 44 years (n = 403, or 48% of the sample) to those citizens who were 45 years and older (n = 441, or 52% of the sample).

A total of 663 (79%) participants were White/Caucasian. Additionally, there were 57 (7%) Hispanic participants, 52 (6%) African American participants, 20 (2%) Indian participants, 13 (1%) Asian American participants, 6 (0.5%) participants of Hawaiian descent, and 33 (4%) participants who considered their race/ethnicity as "other." In our analysis plan, we set out to examine potential race/ethnicity-related differences by comparing the viewpoints of White/Caucasian respondents with the combined group of participants reporting other race/ethnicity backgrounds.

A total of 232 (28%) participants reported having a high school diploma or some lower amount of educational attainment. An additional 246 (29%) participants reported having completed some college course and/or an associate degree. The remaining 366 (43%) participants completed a four-year college degree or greater. In our analysis plan, we set out to examine the potential impact of educational attainment using these three categories.

We also wanted to ensure that we had some geographic variability within the sample. As noted above in the sampling strategy section, buckets were created for solicitation of participants from rural and urban residences. As a result of our sampling efforts, a total of 663 (79%) of the respondents resided in an urban area, with the remaining 181 (21%) of participants residing in a rural location. In our analysis plan, we sought to examine potential geography-related differences through use of this rural and urban distinction.

In order to get some sense of participants' political affiliations, we asked the question "generally speaking, do you usually think of yourself as a . . ." with the possible responses being Republican, Democrat, Independent, other, and no preference. In the overall sample, 178 (21%) participants in the sample reported themselves to be Republican and 372 (44%) considered themselves to be Democrats. The percentage of Republicans who considered themselves to be "strong Republicans" (74%) was slightly higher than the number of Democrats who considered themselves to be "strong Democrats" (67%).

Additionally, a total of 203 (24%) thought of themselves as Independent, and the remaining 91 (11%) participants in the sample selected "other" or "no preference." Relatively small numbers of these participants think of themselves as closer to the Republican party (11%) or closer to the Democratic party (13%). In our analysis plan, we set out to examine potential political affiliation differences by combining the other and no preference participants into one group for comparison purposes with the Republican, Democrat, and Independent groups.

As shown in table 1, the political affiliations of respondents in each of the six states represented in the sample generally follows the overall percentages, with some important variations. The subsample from New York contained the most Democrats (54%), for example, while the Texas subsample displayed the most Republican (31%) and Independent (16%) participants.

Table 1. Political Affiliation of the Sample (in percentages)

	CA	FL	NY	OH	TX	WV	Total
Republican	15	20	12	24	31	25	21
Democrat	58	47	54	44	29	30	44
Independent	19	25	19	23	24	36	24
Other / No Preference	9	8	15	9	16	9	11

As a secondary check on political affiliation, we asked the question "when it comes to politics do you usually think of yourself as . . ." with the possible responses including extremely liberal, liberal, slightly liberal, moderate or middle of the road, slightly conservative, extremely conservative, or none of the above. A total of 386 (46%) of the respondents chose one of the liberal responses, 176 (21%) of the respondents chose "moderate or middle of the road," 230 (27%) of the respondents chose one of the conservative responses, and the remaining 52 (6%) of the sample chose "none of the above." In our analysis plan, we set out to examine potential political spectrum differences by comparing the liberal, middle of the road, and conservative group perspectives along with the "none of the above" group.

Those respondents who reported themselves to be Republican described themselves as conservative 73% of the time (versus 17% middle of the road and 10% liberal), while those respondents who reported themselves to be Democrats described themselves as liberal 75% of the time (versus 20% middle of the road and 5% conservative). A total of 45% of Independents and all others reported themselves as middle of the road as compared to being liberal (32%) or conservative (23%). Although there seemingly is considerable overlap between the Democrat and liberal groupings on the one hand and between the Republican and conservative groupings on the other hand, there are roughly 25% of participants in each political party who do not conform to that polarized stereotype. In addition, the fact that a preponderance of the Independent labeled group sits in the middle of the political spectrum must be tempered by the knowledge that an additional one-third of these Independents are liberal and another one-quarter that claim conservative bona fides.

We also asked about voting behavior in the 2016 US presidential election. In answer to the question "did you vote in the 2016 presidential election" a total of 707 (84%) of the sample reported having voted. Almost identical numbers of Democrats (90%) and Republicans (90%) reported having voted, whereas those who identified as Independent or other had a 75% voting record in the last presidential election.

Finally, we asked the question "how likely are you to vote in the 2020 presidential election" with possible responses including: I definitely will vote, I probably will vote, there is a 50/50 chance I will vote, I probably will not vote, and I definitely will not vote. A total of 652 (77%) of the sample reported that they were going to definitively vote in the upcoming presidential election. Democrats reported being most likely (89%) to vote, followed by Republicans (79%) and then those who identified as Independent or other (71%).

When the two voting behavior questions are combined, we see that a total of 595 (84%) participants who voted in the 2016 presidential election reported that they were definitely going to vote in the 2020 presidential election versus the remaining 57 (16%) participants who had voted in 2016. Less overlap was seen in the participant group that did not vote in the 2016 election, however. A total of 57 (42%) of those participants who did not vote in 2016 stated that they were definite voters in the 2020 election. In our analysis plan, therefore, we sought to examine potential political voting behavior-related differences by comparing 2016 voters and nonvoters as well as 2020 definite voters versus those less certain of their future voting behavior.

Limitations

Before moving ahead with a discussion of our findings, we thought it would be wise to enumerate all the inherent limitations of this research undertaking. First and foremost, there are concerns about the national representativeness of our sample, as noted above. There is no immediate reason to assume that our recruitment of survey participants from the four most populous states—California, Florida, New York, and Texas—plus Ohio and West Virginia provides us with any special insights into the viewpoints of citizens from Wyoming, Vermont, Alaska, or North Dakota, for example. Those are the four least populated states in our nation and as such are likely faced with at least some different issues that might be related to the number of their state's inhabitants.

At the same time, there is no reason to assume that there would not be at least some similarity in the public's sentiment about institutions of higher learning within their state's borders, regardless of the size of their population. The point is, we don't know, because no one has ever bothered to ask citizens across the nation to provide their opinions about the sorts of issues we are examining in this research study. Our contention is that one of the main contributions of this book is beginning to ask such questions as an initial step toward fostering a dialogue among university personnel and their civilian stakeholders.

As we are hoping this project is only the very beginning of a more nationwide effort to gather this sort of information from our citizens, we hope that readers will be tolerant of the fact that we had to start somewhere. The same can be said for the relatively small numbers of citizens that were polled within each of the six states we did select. But for a relatively modest research budget, we certainly would have wanted to have surveyed larger numbers of citizens within each of those states. At the same time, we trust that the methods we employed to ensure relatively equal numbers of males and females, rural and urban residents, Democrats and Republican and Independents, and so on gave us at least some license to provoke a meaningful initial conversation regarding public sentiment of higher education.

Speaking of which, another limitation that must be mentioned here is the lack of specific knowledge about which of the public universities our participants were thinking of when they responded to our survey items. Were they only thinking about their state's flagship institution, for example, or solely about the university that had the winningest football team? Or were they only thinking about the public university that was geographically closest to them? Or the one they attended as an undergraduate? Or did they fail to understand that some of the schools they were thinking about were not public universities but rather private institutions of higher learning?

Again, we have no way of knowing what our participants were thinking about when they responded to the items within the survey. While that certainly is a limitation worth mentioning, we also believe that, at least in some ways, it may not have mattered which specific universities our respondents had in mind. What we mean to say here is that there likely is some "idealized university" that we all conjure in our minds when it comes to discussions about the role that higher education plays in the lives of our citizens. It is precisely that venerated image of the university held in the minds of the American public—God's "almost chosen people" as described by Lincoln[8]—that we wished to interrogate within this study.

There are also other limitations related to the likely large range of understanding about practically every one of the higher education issues we examined in this study. For example, some participants were probably well-versed in differences between merit-based and needs-based aid, while at least some respondents may never have been exposed to those terms before taking this survey. Some participants might have been thinking about medical research conducted by universities while others might have been thinking more about empirical work funded by the Department of Defense. Again, we cannot estimate the breadth and depth of participant understanding of these issues. That, in a nutshell, is why we remain so interested in expanding our work in this area. At the end of the day, we do not see these limitations as fatal but rather as further food for thought as we dissect these initial findings.

Summary

In this chapter we began by describing our interest in better understanding public sentiment about higher education. Next, we described the items we created for this study that would allow us to better understand citizen viewpoints. We then set out to explain how we worked to ensure that the sample we pulled from the four most populous states of our nation and the two additional home states of your authors was as representative as possible and thus generalizable. We believe that the individuals selected for participation from the American Population Panel were quite representative of their state populations in terms of educational attainment (our proxy for SES), gender, age, race/ethnicity, political affiliation, and voting behavior. At the same time, we also recognized many of the limitations inherent to this sort of study. As such, we now move on to an analysis of our findings.

3

Public Funding for Teaching, Research, and Community Engagement

A capacity, and taste, for reading, gives access to whatever has already been discovered by others. It is the key, or one of the keys, to the already solved problems. And not only so. It gives a relish, and facility, for successfully pursuing the unsolved ones.

The quote that begins this third chapter came from a September 1859 speech that Abraham Lincoln gave to the Wisconsin State Agricultural Society. We are convinced that our sixteenth president deeply valued education in all its forms, which is why he was so keen to sign the Morrill Land-Grant Act of 1862, among other actions he had taken in that tumultuous year. What would Lincoln say about the way that our modern universities choose to spend their financial resources in the twenty-first century? We do not pretend to know the answer to that question, but what we are certain about is this: Lincoln would have cared deeply about what the *public* thought their universities should be doing with their tax dollars.

This chapter examines the data collected on our first higher education-based survey question, which asked survey respondents to consider how—in an ideal world—every $100 of taxpayer money provided to public universities should be spent in terms of teaching, research, and community outreach programs and services. As a reminder to readers, participants were told that their answers must add up to $100, and they were told to assume that all basic operating costs (electricity, heating/cooling, etc.) and other expenses (student housing, dining services, recreation, etc.) were already covered by non-taxpayer monies.

We noted in chapter 2 that this question was based on two of the themes described in our book, *Land-Grant Universities for the Future*: "research prowess versus teaching and service excellence" and "knowledge for knowledge's sake versus a more applied focus." Also noted in chapter 2 was our belief that participants would direct the greatest amount of money toward teaching. We further hypothesized that participants would spend more of the remaining money on community outreach programs and services in comparison to funding put toward research.

This chapter begins with the simple and direct reporting of the aggregated responses of the participants in our study, as well as some of our initial reactions to the findings. We then contextualize the results by raising three sets of issues we believe are of great importance in any discussion of teaching, research, and public service efforts undertaken by our nation's public universities. This includes teaching responsibilities and the growth in employment of nontenure-track faculty members, the true costs associated with conducting research, and the evolving nature of community outreach and engagement activities, with a special focus on Cooperative Extension Services.

Findings from the Overall Sample

On average, participants in the entire sample reported that they would spend the greatest amount of money on teaching ($46.10), with the remainder of the funds to be split relatively equally between research ($28.20) and community outreach programs and services ($25.70). This finding is aligned rather nicely with the "formula for success" we alluded to in earlier chapters and in our 2018 land-grant universities book, where excellence in both teaching and community engagement were valued at or above that of research prowess.

In order to test for potential differences in how respondents appropriated money to teaching, research, and service to communities, we ran a multiple analysis of variance (MANOVA) procedure using all of the demographic variables (gender, age, race/ethnicity, geographic location, and educational attainment) and the politically oriented variables (party affiliation, liberal/conservative orientation, actual voting behavior in 2016, and predicted voting behavior in 2020). The full multivariate results, which are reported in full detail in appendix 2, indicated that three variables had a significant impact on respondents' allocations of funding to teaching, research, and service to communities: gender, age, and educational attainment.

The specific manner by which these three demographic variables had an impact will be discussed in more detail below, guided by tests of between-subjects effects (found in appendix 3) and post-hoc comparison tests (found in appendix 4). We then consider the ramifications of the lack of differences found as a result of the remaining demographic, political, and voting behavior variables.

Gender, Age, and Educational Attainment

Comparing the viewpoints of male and female participants, we see that there are significant differences in terms of money put toward teaching and money put toward services to the community (but no significant differences regarding money put toward research). The male participants on average put $50 toward teaching, $29 toward research, and $21 toward services to the community, whereas female respondents on average put $46 toward teaching, $27 toward research, and $27 toward services to the community. Hence, although gender was not a factor in allocations made to research, males wanted to put more public money toward teaching, whereas females wished to see more money put toward services rendered to the community.

When the viewpoints of participants who were aged 18 to 44 years are compared against the viewpoints of those citizens who were 45 years and older, we see that there were significant differences in terms of money put toward teaching and services to the community (but again, no significant differences with regard to money put toward research). The younger participants put $44 toward teaching, $29 toward research, and $27 toward services to the community, whereas older respondents put $50 toward teaching, $28 toward research, and $22 toward services to the community. Although age was not a factor in allocations made to research, younger citizens wanted to put more public money toward services to the community, whereas older citizens wished to see more money put toward teaching.

Examining potential variation related to level of educational attainment yielded significant differences between the three groups regarding money put toward teaching and services to the community (but once again, not research). Those participants with a high school education or less on average put $42 toward teaching, $29 toward research, and $29 toward services to the community. Respondents with some college or an associate's degree on average put $45 toward teaching, $29 toward research, and $26 toward services to the community. Those participants with a four-year college degree or greater level of educational attainment on average put $51 toward teaching, $28 toward research, and $21 toward services to the community. Although educational attainment was not a factor in allocations made to research, participants with a high school degree or lower wanted to put more public money toward services to the community, whereas those respondents with a four-year degree or greater wished to see more money put toward teaching.

Initial Reactions to the Findings

The general findings related to the entire sample—where participants allocated approximately $50 to teaching and roughly $25 to research and $25 to community-based services—was supported by the "formula for success" we discussed in earlier chapters and in our previous 2018 book. At the very least, we had believed, teaching and community engagement were both going to be valued at or above that of research prowess. As it turned out, teaching was much more highly valued, and community-based work was placed on a relatively equal plane.

That said, the findings largely replicated an earlier study that engaged participants in a very similar exercise.[1] As part of a larger effort to understand how citizen perceptions of Cooperative Extension Services had changed over time, Warner and colleagues asked respondents to allocate $100 of taxpayer money to teaching, research, and Extension activities (such as nutrition and health, leadership development, 4-H programming, etc.). A random sample of just over 1,100 respondents indicated that, on average, they would allocate $45 to teaching, $30 to Extension, and $25 to research. According to the researchers, these allocations did not differ by age, educational attainment, income, race/ethnicity, or geographic location.[2]

Comparing Public Sentiment Against What We Know

How does the public's desire to spend money stack up against the current reality of the situation? Data on 2016–2017 expenditures from the National Center for Education Statistics (NCES) indicated that public four-year institutions spent 28% of their budgets on instructional activities.[3] In turn, the NCES data indicated that these same public universities were spending 11.5% of their budgets on research and 4.5% on public service. Where does the large remainder of money get spent by four-year public universities? As it turns out, the funding is spent mainly on noninstructional activities, including expenses such as academic support (22%), hospitals (15%), auxiliaries (10%), outside services (5%), and grant aid to students (3%).[4]

Of course, in the scenario we presented to survey participants, they were supposed to assume that all other expenses beyond teaching, research, and community-based services were already taken care of by other sources. Therefore, a fair comparison would be to examine the ratio of expenditures excluding noninstructional activities (the 44% of the total expenditures dedicated to teaching, research, and public service). This would translate into 64 percent of those expenditures going toward teaching, 26 percent toward teaching, and 10 percent toward services to the community.

By this calculation, America's public universities are spending almost two-thirds of their nonadministrative funding on instructional activities, exceeding the public's allocation by a significant (and one would assume welcome) factor. At the same time, the remainder is lopsided in favor of research activities, although the shortfall in funds expended on community-based services is due mainly to the overage given to teaching. Research expenditures as a portion of the total expenditures, excluding noninstructional activities, is very close to the allocation provided in the ideal world scenario allocations provided by our survey participants.

Demographic Differences as Related to the Findings

The significant differences that were found regarding the demographic variables of gender, age, and level of educational attainment are interesting, if somewhat unsurprising. First, the fact that males put more money toward teaching while females put more money toward community services would seem to fall in line with theories in social psychology surrounding agency and communion.[5] Here, we would expect males to be more focused on agency-related phenomena, or those activities that are oriented around the individual. In contrast, we would anticipate that females would be focused more on communion-related experiences, or those activities that surrounded relationships and community-oriented phenomena.

Second, the fact that younger citizens put more public money toward community services and older citizens allocated more funds to teaching also provided little shock value to us. What came to mind here was the well-worn adage that if you are not a socialist when you are young you have no heart, and if you are not a conservative when you are older you have no head. In this case, older citizens want universities to do what they are in the primary business of doing (that is, teaching), whereas younger citizens have a greater stake in the community and its welfare. Alternatively, however, we did find some social psychology literature that might also have provided some support for the opposite case. That is, there are studies which have reported the finding that older individuals, with a shortened life horizon, downplay agency-related phenomena and express a more communion-focused orientation within their life perspectives.[6]

Third, and finally in terms of demographic variable contrasts, the significant differences found as a function of educational attainment levels was also unsurprising. Those respondents with a four-year degree or greater displayed a tendency to put more money toward teaching precisely because they had actual experience in a university setting and would, therefore, be in the best position to place greater value on instructional efforts. In turn, those participants with a high school degree or lower—a strong indicator of lower socioeconomic status—would have the greatest need for investment in community-oriented services as opposed to teaching or research activities.[7]

The Lack of Political Differences in Funding Allocations

In terms of the lack of significant differences found regarding the relationship between resource allocations and this study's politically oriented variables, we believe there was some very good news generated within this finding. Unlike the results we will report in later chapters, there appeared to be a complete lack of partisanship with respect to how citizens allocated taxpayer money for teaching, research, and community-based service activities. Republicans, Democrats, and Independents, liberals and conservatives, and voters and nonvoters alike, all seem to have wanted to put the most money toward teaching, while still seeing appreciable amounts of funding directed toward research and engagement with the community.

In fact, this lack of disagreement among citizens about funding allocations, regardless of their political stripes, may be the most noteworthy finding of our entire study. We say this simply because it is so very difficult to find *any* topic or concern that individuals on the right, left, and middle of the political spectrum agree upon these days. Not to put too fine a point on this, but one recent survey conducted by the Pew Research Center indicated that Americans of different political stripes agree only that things are going to get worse in terms of the polarization between our two major parties, even as they profoundly disagree about the means to solving the problems we are facing.[8] Indeed, it appears as if "The Big Sort" continues unabated in so many different ways right now across our nation, making these nonpartisan findings all the more extraordinary.[9]

Contextualizing Teaching, Research, and Community Engagement Activities

If we were going to gain any traction in promoting the kind of campus-community dialogue we were seeking, we believed that we needed to make a concerted effort to contextualize the results we were going to report from our survey efforts. While we identified numerous issues that impacted the ability of our public universities to carry out their teaching, research, and community engagement efforts, we settled on one particularly significant example within each of those activity spheres. In terms of teaching, we focused on the steady increase in the use of nontenure-track faculty to carry out the teaching mission of the public university. For research, we concentrated on the costs of conducting scientific studies. In the realm of community engagement, we centered our attention on the precarious nature of Cooperative Extension Services, born from the original mandate for public universities to directly serve the needs of the public.

Teaching and the Employment of Nontenure-Track Faculty Members

First, let us examine issues surrounding the employment of nontenured faculty. In our previous book, we described the faculty tenure-track position as the gold standard for university employment. In general, the granting of tenure is thought to be a guarantee of lifelong employment at a university (that is, barring fiscal emergency within the university or grossly inappropriate behaviors on the part of the professor). Universities grant tenure for two main reasons: (1) the protection of academic freedom, allowing professors to teach and conduct research on whatever subject matter they wish to pursue as scholars; and (2) the offering of enough economic security to make the position financially appealing to individuals with high ability.[10] While the tenure process results in permanent employment, we believe that the lengthy probationary period which precedes the granting of tenure is typically used to maintain the highest standards of academic value within the university.

However, most of the individuals who are responsible for instructional activities within our public universities are not on the tenure track. Across all institutions of higher learning in our country, it has been estimated that three out of every four faculty members fall into the nontenure-track category.[11] There are various titles that are used to describe these nontenure-track faculty members, including but not limited to titles such as lecturer, adjunct faculty, auxiliary faculty, casual faculty, and contingent faculty. So, while the tenure-track position may be most exalted within the university, the nontenure-track faculty members are the instructional worker bees, as they are responsible for teaching most of the courses being taken by students in our nation's universities.[12]

In our reading of current public sentiment as expressed through various articles that have been published in mainstream media over the past decade, there appears to be rather strong and vocal opinions surrounding the need for university faculty members to do more teaching.[13] Members of the academy themselves have certainly noted this drawdown in teaching responsibilities for tenure-track faculty members. One scholar has labeled this the "Great Disappearing Teaching Load," complemented by a description of an "arms race" scenario among universities seeking to attract the best and brightest faculty members with promises of lower and lower teaching responsibilities.[14]

This reduction in instructional activities has not gone unnoticed by those who are elected to serve the public good. Lawmakers in various states seemed to have lost patience with university officials on this issue, and, as a result, they have attempted to legislate increased teaching loads.[15] More recently, the idea of pushing faculty members to do more teaching has surfaced as a means toward staving off budget cuts as well.[16]

So, if these tenure-track faculty members are not teaching in the classroom, what then are they doing with their time? In large part, increased research activities are one of the primary reasons that faculty are not teaching in their classrooms more often.[17] As we have discussed extensively in our previous book, high research productivity is currently the coin of the realm within most universities, and so exceptional empirical work is more highly rewarded in comparison to excellence in teaching and community engagement. Relatedly, faculty with advanced research skills tend to be expensive and demanding, whereas faculty who only are given teaching responsibilities are typically hired at a much cheaper rate. This shift in teaching responsibilities is one of the main reasons why universities have been hiring so many nontenure-track faculty members. To wit, they carry on with the instructional activities that tenure-track faculty have been released from to delve more deeply into their research interests.

How does all this square with the main finding that respondents would allocate approximately half of the $100 of taxpayer money to teaching activities? In general, we believe that citizens would wish for faculty members to be spending at least half of their time in the classroom, a quarter of their time in conducting their research, and the remaining quarter of their time engaged with the community. An authentic dialogue with the public would include a narrative that points out that many more (nontenure-track) faculty members are spending close to 100% of their time teaching while a smaller portion of (mainly tenure-track) faculty members are more heavily involved in research activities. Of course, this means that university personnel involved in such a discussion with community stakeholders would also have to come clean on exactly what is happening in the realm of research, which is the next issue we wish to take up in terms of contextualizing our findings.

The Costs of Conducting Research

The impetus for the rather substantial upsurge in research activities within universities was the direct result of increases in federal funding directed toward university-based research following the Second

World War. This was prompted in large part by the release of a federal science policy guideline in 1945 authored by Vannevar Bush, the director of the wartime Office of Scientific Research and Development. This document, entitled *Science—The Endless Frontier: A Report to the President for Postwar Scientific Research*, formalized the relationship between the federal government and the institutions of higher learning that officials wished to use as research laboratories.[18]

The establishment of organizations such as the National Science Foundation (NSF) and the National Institutes of Health (NIH), federal agencies that were designed to administer over and direct research funding to universities, were created as the direct result of these science policy guidelines. Some thirty-five years later, the US Congress passed the Bayh–Dole Act. This congressional action in 1980 granted universities the right to patent the results of this federally funded research. As might be expected, this legislation created huge economic incentives for universities to conduct studies in close collaboration with business and industry partners, placing faculty members squarely at the center of the development of today's global knowledge economy.[19]

While the flow of dollars to research efforts within universities sounds like a surefire mechanism of support for higher education, all is not what it seems according to higher education critics. Take, for example, the writing of Christopher Newfield, who recently published a book with the provocative title *The Great Mistake: How We Wrecked Public Universities and How We Can Fix Them*.[20] Among other issues, Newfield made the assertion that tuition hikes, as often as not, have been caused by the fact that research endeavors—which are high status activities within many public and private universities—actually cost the university much more to operate than the total amount allotted to researchers through the grants they have received in support of their empirical efforts. Newfield's estimate is that public universities lose around $24 internally for every $100 gained in external grants. Simply put, the federal government is not providing as much money as it really takes to conduct the research they are purporting to support. So, where is the money coming to cover those losses? Tuition, as it turns out, is the main source of coverage for these shortfalls at public universities (large, private research universities also tend to use endowments).

Newfield argued that university leaders should come clean with internal and external stakeholders about the way that the money is flowing within our institutions of higher learning when it comes to the funding of research efforts. He writes:

> The first requirement is for universities to stop treating research accounting as though it involves commercial secrets and open the books. The principal investigators on major grants should be able to find out what happens to the indirect funds that come with their grants but are removed from them by the central administrators. The same is true for the university community, which lives in the dark about fund flows. Faculty should be able to see, understand, debate, and participate in setting research funding policy. Their tuition contributions to research should earn students a place at the table, where they can understand how their payments underwrite the overall academic operation. (315)

Of course, bringing this to light has the potential to generate "shock and anger," as Newfield predicted in his book, especially among those university employees and students who had no idea that this sort of cross-subsidization was going on within their institutions.

At the same time, however, Newfield also forecasted the potential for "reconciliation" as an outcome of this increased transparency, which seemingly would occur over time as those faculty and students better understood how their public universities operated. We were less certain about the average citizen's take on all of this. How angry would the public be about the cross-subsidization of research that had been taking place inside of universities? What would happen if university and citizen stakeholders got together in order to discuss such matters? In order to gain a better sense of the possibilities, we reached out to Newfield to gain his perspective on what such a campus-community dialogue might look like.

We asked Professor Newfield if he thought that citizens would have a negative reaction to the use of tuition dollars to subsidize research. Citizens and lawmakers certainly would not be surprised to hear that this was the case, he replied. "They have been told for years that science makes money, that it's a big profit center. Look at what research does for the state's economy, they are also told, and look what at what research is doing for our university budgets." So, the idea that you must spend money in order to make money would not be lost on citizens. What has happened more recently, Newfield went on to say, is that universities are now less aggressive in citing grant revenues as a reflection of fiscal health. However, they largely have not explained to the public that grants generate net losses for campuses, he said.

As to the question of how a campus-community dialogue about these sorts of issues might proceed, Professor Newfield noted that too many faculty members (to say nothing of staff and students) still do not understand how research monies flow within their universities. "There is an educational process that necessarily begins inside of the institution, so that people start to understand that 24 cents of institutional funds are spent on every grant dollar that is brought into a public university," he said. "But I don't know that critical scholars can make this kind of educational process happen without support. There needs to be senior people in administration who say this is true. There needs to be a 12-step program for universities to come clean and acknowledge these issues."

The power of an addiction metaphor to describe what universities must do here is not lost on us. After all, the goal of a 12-step substance abuse program is to experience a recovery from a set of choices (i.e., use of the substance) that has led to outcomes associated with individual damage (i.e., health, economic, and otherwise) and interpersonal dysfunction. Such a recovery includes the explicit admission of being powerless in the face of the substance, an overt declaration of self-responsibility, and a willingness to make amends. If the "substance" at issue here is external grant funding, we can think of administrators within many universities who seem to be displaying a sort of addictive behavior. At the very least, they have lost all perspective over the place of research in the overall mission of their university, they are reluctant to acknowledge the costs associated with research efforts, and they seem blind to the fact that the cross-subsidization of research means that other portions of the institutional mission are negatively impacted as a result.

Therefore, Newfield recommended that universities get their own houses in order before pursuing a dialogue with external stakeholders. Once that is accomplished, then campus leaders might begin a discussion with citizens about what is similar and what is different about the pursuit of a university degree in comparison to what occurs at the elementary and high school educational levels. In higher education, he goes on to say, we must be knowledge creators and not just knowledge consumers. A part of knowledge creation is how we, as a people, must adapt and evolve to new situations, and another portion of these higher education endeavors involves meaning making. Once we are able to lay these sorts of issues out on the table in a coherent manner, Newfield stated, then we can facilitate a discussion about how the organization of these knowledge creation activities within the confines of a university should be funded.

As we close out this section, we wish to note that we also discussed with Professor Newfield the findings regarding how citizens would allocate money to teaching, research, and community services. The figures—approximately half the money for teaching and the remainder split up relatively evenly between research and community services—were not far from the amounts of state support that Professor Newfield himself might assign, he told us. He did quickly point out, however, that the amount internally allocated to research should be reduced in direct proportion to the *federal* government stepping up and providing grant funding that covered the true costs associated with the research they were supporting through grants and contracts.

In turn, Professor Newfield expressed some ambivalence about the amount of funding that would be allocated toward community services. "So much of this feels like we are doing public relations work instead of doing more Extension-based activities. If it were more about going into communities, finding out what's on their minds, and then trying to design research or educational activities that would satisfy their needs, I would probably increase its share of the pie." He went on to lament that the implementation of efforts that would be viewed as remaining true to the original Extension mission was not what most universities were typically doing at present. This is the perfect lead-in to our next subject matter, which pertains to the current state of outreach and engagement activities more generally among all public universities and of the more specific work being conducted by Cooperative Extension Services in our nation's land-grant institutions.

Outreach, Engagement, and Cooperative Extension Services

In our land-grant universities book, we explained how higher education leaders sought to counter state budget cuts as far back as the 1990s by creating a narrative which highlighted the special set of visible and sustainable relationships that were maintained between their campuses and the communities they were designed to serve. As a result, several higher education organizations began to encourage this sort of community outreach and engagement work and to codify what these engagement-oriented activities looked like in practice. This included the call for more "engaged institutions" by the Kellogg Commission on the Future of State and Land-Grant Universities,[21] the Carnegie Foundation for the Advancement of Teaching Classification for Community Engagement,[22] and the Innovation and Economic Prosperity (IEP) Universities Designation[23] developed by the Association of Land-Grant and Public Universities (APLU).

These organizational efforts continue to have a significant impact in terms of underscoring the importance of university engagement with communities. While the Kellogg Commission had issued reports on a variety of topics that included the student experience,[24] student access,[25] learning environments,[26] and campus culture,[27] only the report on the engaged institution[28] seems to have withstood the test of time in terms of continued attention from university leaders. In turn, the Carnegie designation has been bestowed on over 350 universities to date and that designation has been portrayed as having "served as the tool that forced an institution to change direction" toward more rigorous and impactful engagement efforts.[29] Finally, the number of universities obtaining the IEP designation from APLU continues to grow as well, and the institutional commitment to gain this recognition has initiated the creation of a set of best practices surrounding innovation and economic prosperity activities.[30]

The origin story for all these outreach and engagement efforts begins with the Smith-Lever Act of 1914. This congressional action created what became known as the Cooperative Extension Services system, which was designed to take important lessons from university classrooms and findings from research laboratories and apply them directly to farms, fields, family homes, and related subjects.[31] This federal legislation thus created the very first impetus for institutions of higher learning to engage with members of the community, incentivizing university personnel to leave the confines of their campuses (the proverbial "ivory towers") and work among the public at large.[32]

By the early 1990s, however, there was trouble brewing for Extension efforts at the very same time these other outreach and engagement efforts were getting their starts. As we discussed in our previous book, a great deal of concern had been expressed by university leaders regarding the public's perception of Extension. So much so, it turned out, that the term "engagement" was coined and adopted in order to signify that something very different was being put forward in the Kellogg Commission report.

To be fair, a part of the difficulty with the "Extension" label was that, by federal statute, this was a specific land-grant endeavor, thus depriving non-land-grant institutions any sense of ownership. However, Extension was often viewed as providing services to primarily rural populations, and those services were decidedly unidirectional in orientation. In brief, this meant that the university provided resources directly to the community, but nothing of value necessarily was returned to the university. Engagement, in contrast, was a way of capturing campus-community partnerships that were bidirectional and thus related to activities that were both *mutually derived* and *mutually beneficial*, as well as not being portrayed as applicable to rural locations only.

There has been at least one report that directly employed elements of the Kellogg Commission reports in charting a future for Extension.[33]

Other scholars have written about the challenges facing Extension as well, including the necessary development of partnerships outside of the traditional Extension system,[34] the need to better use brand identity,[35] and dealing with audience erosion in the high tech information marketplace.[36] Most of these articles and reports are predicated on the notion that Extension can and will remain a vital and relevant part of the land-grant university's outreach and engagement efforts if certain singular issues are recognized and dealt with in a direct manner.

To us, the conceptual frameworks being employed by these and other writers are often as not calls for first order change within Extension, when a higher order change is required.[37] First order changes are incremental, and they involve modest shifts within a present organization's structure. Higher order changes (second, third, etc.) involve changes in the organizational structure itself. We bring this up here because we believe that the public's understanding of what Extension can contribute to the present and future development and well-being of our nation's citizens (and, therefore, if and how it should be supported through the use of taxpayer monies) directly hinges on a decidedly modern image of its offerings. Regrettably, our belief is that real life examples of how Extension are doing at a statewide (let alone systemwide) level are few and far between.

We have written about the fit of Cooperative Extension Services inside of the twenty-first-century land-grant mission. In one article, we engaged in a dialogue about this very topic with Roger Rennekamp, who at the time was the Extension director at The Ohio State University, and Steve Bonanno, who then was the Extension director at West Virginia University.[38] One clear takeaway from this conversation was the need for Extension to position itself as an independent *academic* unit within the university, not simply as a service-oriented group of professionals. Here, we developed an argument for a heightened focus on tenure-track faculty specialists and county agents who would create and maintain joint instructional experiences and research programs with non-Extension faculty members representing the widest spectrum of departments and colleges across campus.

In a second article, we focused on 4-H, one of Extension's most well-known and beloved program initiatives.[39] Joined by Jennifer Sirangelo, the president and CEO of the 4-H Council, and Karen Pittman, the president and CEO of the Forum for Youth Investment, we discussed some of the most promising new initiatives coming out of 4-H that aligned with the twenty-first-century land-grant mission. With the present 4-H network of over 3,500 professionals and 500,000 volunteers as a powerful backdrop, our conversation centered on youth programming activities that were aimed at raising up social and economic mobility in rural America, as well as 4-H's more recent efforts to intensify their programmatic impact on youth residing in more urbanized settings. With a new national goal of reaching one out of every five youths in America by 2025 (almost doubling their present capacity), Extension leaders will be forced to pay attention to some critical operational issues, including the reallocation of resources to areas most in need of services and professional development concerns, especially the expansion of cultural competency skills to better address the demands of typically underserved youth populations.

We have outlined some heavy lifts in this section so far, yet none of this compares to the efforts that must be undertaken to enhance the profile of Extension in the eyes of the public. We cannot exaggerate the number of times we have had to explain what Extension is to citizens we speak to on a regular basis. Thankfully, the public's recognition of 4-H itself is much greater, and yet there is a fundamental lack of awareness about its connection to Extension. If we are to expect our citizens to support the use of taxpayer money in support of community-based services, the ready identification of Extension-based activities must be increased in rather dramatic fashion.

As we shall see in our next chapter, which focuses primarily on survey participant perceptions of the role that public universities should play in meeting the needs of rural and urban communities, geographic location can play an important role in shaping people's beliefs and behaviors. We bring this up here because Cooperative Extension Services has historically excelled in meeting the needs of rural America and, in tandem, has struggled to find an urban foothold. We believe that until and unless Extension finds a way to balance its portfolio, to the extent that its programs and activities are known by the public, they will be perceived as "not me" by the 80% of the American population who are living in more urbanized settings.

Extension's historically rural foundation is a function of its longstanding ties to agriculture. What began as support in helping farm families with food preservation and preparation methods has more recently morphed into supporting the development and maintenance of community food systems.[40] At times, this seems to have created what we might term a "division of labor" that portrays land-grant universities and Cooperative Extension Services as "owning" engagement with rural communities, whereas the non-land-grant (and typically metropolitan-located) universities are the proprietors of services rendered to urban communities. Such a demarcation has given rise to the "urban grant university" concept that has reappeared at various times throughout the past half a century.[41]

Not one of the land-grant university presidents and chancellors that we interviewed for our land-grant universities book liked this division of labor. To a person, they believed that Cooperative Extension Services can and should be serving all citizens, not just those living in rural communities. At the same time, these academic leaders also recognized some significant challenges facing Extension, including the "zero sum" mindset that resources applied to services in more urbanized locations translated automatically into reductions in programming traditionally implemented in more rural locales. While significant cuts in funding over the years have fed this concern, some of the university leaders we interviewed indicated that the colleges of agriculture that house Extension Services have jealously guarded those rural-based programs and thus have been resistant to anything done outside of their traditional areas. This last point is consistent with the criticisms that have been lobbed in the academic literature at deans of agriculture for their failure to more systematically integrate Cooperative Extension Services into both university life and the community at large.[42]

Summary

We began this chapter with a discussion of how the study participants would distribute public funding across university activities associated with teaching, research, and community-based services. Overall, respondents expressed the desire to provide almost half of all public monies toward teaching efforts, with the remaining 50% of funds divided almost equally to research and community outreach programs and services. Next, we discussed the important lack of differences on these allocation amounts as a function of the politically oriented variables, most notable because it seems as if Democrats and Republicans find it hard to agree on anything these days. We also provided some rationale for the significant differences we uncovered in terms of three demographic characteristics: gender, age, and level of educational attainment.

The remainder of this chapter covered several topics that provided some contextualization of these findings, including teaching responsibilities and the growth in employment of nontenure-track faculty members, the true costs associated with conducting research, and the current and future state of Cooperative Extension Services. In each case, we asserted that greater public understanding of these issues would provide citizens with the increased opportunity to make informed decisions about where and how they would wish for taxpayer money to be spent by their public universities.

4

Focusing Attention on Rural and Urban Communities

But the chief use of agricultural fairs is to aid in improving the great calling of *agriculture,* in all its departments, and minute divisions—to make mutual exchange of agricultural discovery, information, and knowledge; so that, at the end, *all* may know everything, which may have been known to but *one,* or to but a *few,* at the beginning—to bring together especially all which is supposed to not be generally known, because of recent discovery, or invention.

Just as we started the third chapter with a quote from a September 1859 speech that Abraham Lincoln gave to the Wisconsin State Agricultural Society, so, too, do we begin this fourth chapter. In this same speech, Lincoln described agriculture as "the great calling," and, in so doing, he highlighted the tremendous importance of rural locations in terms of the health and well-being of our nation. This was a time when only 20% of American citizens lived in cities after all. Of course, it is exactly the opposite today, with approximately 80% of our nation living in more metropolitan locations. What then, we ask, is the role that our public universities should be playing in service to both rural and urban citizens?

This chapter examines the data collected on our second higher education-based survey question, which asked respondents to consider—in an ideal world—who should be prioritized by public universities in their state: rural or urban communities. As noted in earlier chapters, this question was predicated on the theme reported in the *Land-Grant Universities for the Future* book regarding "meeting the needs of rural communities versus the needs of a more urbanized America." As a reminder, the possible responses to this question included: (a) rural communities should be prioritized; (b) urban communities should be prioritized; or (c) there should be no difference between how rural and urban communities are prioritized. Based on our previous work regarding the formula for success, we believed that the preponderance of study participants would endorse the idea that there should be no difference between rural and urban counties when it comes to prioritizing public university activities.

Findings from the Overall Sample

A substantial majority of participants—595 individuals or 71%—in the entire sample reported that there should be no difference between how rural and urban communities are prioritized, thus confirming our hypothesis. Other respondents were evenly split between reporting that rural communities should be prioritized (112 individuals or 13%) or reporting that urban communities should be prioritized (108 individuals or 13%). The remaining 29 (3%) participants chose "I don't know" or skipped this question, and so were excluded from additional consideration of this item.

Further Analyses

In order to test for potential differences in how respondents wanted their public universities to prioritize rural and urban communities, we ran a series of chi-square tests using all demographic variables (gender, age, race/ethnicity, geographic location, and educational attainment) and politically-oriented variables (party affiliation, liberal/conservative orientation, actual voting behavior in 2016, and predicted voting behavior in 2020). The results regarding the demographic variables indicated significant effects for gender, age, educational attainment, and geographic location. We discuss those results in the demographics section below. In turn, the results regarding the political variables indicated significant effects for party, orientation, and predicted voting behavior in 2020. We report on those results in a separate section for politically oriented variables.

Demographic Variables and Prioritizing Rural and Urban Communities

The comparison of male and viewpoints regarding the prioritization of rural and urban communities by public universities yielded significant differences ($X^2 = 9.59$, df 2, p < .001) for gender. More specifically, 226 (67%) of males thought that rural and urban communities should be equally prioritized by public universities, 48 (15%) believed that rural communities should be prioritized, and 58 (18%) reported that urban communities should be prioritized. In turn, 369 (76%) of females thought that rural and urban communities should be equally prioritized by public universities, 64 (14%) believed that rural communities should be prioritized, and 50 (10%) reported that urban communities should be prioritized. In general, the gender differences resided in the fact that a greater percentage of males prioritized urban communities, whereas a greater percentage of females endorsed the notion that rural and urban communities should be treated equally.

The comparison of younger and older participant viewpoints regarding the prioritization of rural and urban communities by public universities yielded significant differences ($X^2 = 36.63$, df 2, p < .001) for age. More specifically, 254 (65%) of the 18- to 44-year-old participants thought that rural and urban communities should be equally prioritized by public universities, 57 (14%) believed that rural communities should be prioritized, and 81 (21%) reported that urban communities should be prioritized. In turn, 341 (81%) of the 45-year-old and older participants thought that rural and urban communities should be equally prioritized by public universities, 55 (13%) believed that rural communities should be prioritized, and 27 (6%) reported that urban communities should be prioritized. Overall, then, a greater percentage of older participants believed that rural and urban communities should be equally prioritized, whereas a greater percentage of younger respondents prioritized urban communities.

The comparison of rural and urban resident viewpoints regarding the prioritization of rural and urban communities by public universities yielded significant differences ($X^2 = 14.77$, df 2, p < .001) for geographic location. More specifically, 471 (73%) of urban residents thought that rural and urban communities should be equally prioritized by public universities, 75 (12%) believed that rural communities should be prioritized, and 95 (15%) reported that urban communities should be prioritized. In turn, 124 (71%) of rural residents thought that rural and urban communities should be equally prioritized by public universities, 37 (21%) believed that rural communities should be prioritized, and 13 (8%) reported that urban communities should be prioritized. Unsurprisingly, a greater percentage of rural participants prioritized rural communities and a greater percentage of urban participants prioritized urban communities.

Use of the educational attainment variable to examine potential differences regarding the prioritization of rural and urban communities by public universities yielded significant differences ($X^2 = 33.96$, df 4, p < .001). More specifically, 183 (81%) participants with a high school diploma or less educational attainment thought that rural and urban communities should be equally prioritized by public universities, 19 (9%) believed that rural communities should be prioritized, and 21 (10%) reported that urban communities should be prioritized. In turn, 185 (78%) of the participants with some college or an associate's degree thought that rural and urban communities should be equally prioritized by public universities, 35 (15%) believed that rural communities should be prioritized, and 17 (7%) reported that urban communities should be prioritized. Further, 227 (64%) of the participants with a four-year college degree or greater educational attainment thought that rural and urban communities should be equally prioritized by public universities, 58 (16%) believed that rural communities should be prioritized, and 70 (20%) reported that urban communities should be prioritized.

Overall, a greater percentage of those participants with a four-year degree or greater prioritized urban communities, whereas a greater percentage of respondents with some college or a high school diploma or less endorsed the idea that rural and urban communities should be treated equally.

Political Variables and Prioritizing Rural and Urban Communities

Use of political party to examine potential differences regarding the prioritization of rural and urban communities by public universities yielded significant differences ($X^2 = 38.39$, df 6, p < .001). More specifically, 120 (70%) participants claiming affiliation with the Republican party thought that rural and urban communities should be equally prioritized by public universities, 37 (22%) believed that rural communities should be prioritized, and 15 (8%) reported that urban communities should be prioritized. In turn, 246 (68%) of the participants reporting affiliation with the Democratic party thought that rural and urban communities should be equally prioritized by public universities, 46 (13%) believed that rural communities should be prioritized, and 69 (19%) reported that urban communities should be prioritized. Further, 150 (77%) of the participants with the Independent affiliation thought that rural and urban communities should be equally prioritized by public universities, 24 (12%) believed that rural communities should be prioritized, and 22 (11%) reported that urban communities should be prioritized. Finally, 79 (92%) of the participants claiming some other political affiliation thought that rural and urban communities should be equally prioritized by public universities, 5 (6%) believed that rural communities should be prioritized, and 2 (2%) reported that urban communities should be prioritized. In general, a greater percentage of Republican participants prioritized rural communities, a greater percentage of Democrats prioritized urban communities, and Independents and those with other party affiliations displayed the greatest percentage of respondents who endorsed the notion that rural and urban communities should be treated equally.

Use of the liberal-conservative continuum variable to examine potential differences regarding the prioritization of rural and urban communities by public universities yielded significant differences ($X^2 = 48.84$, df 6, $p < .001$). More specifically, 268 (72%) participants who described themselves as liberal in their political orientation thought that rural and urban communities should be equally prioritized by public universities, 42 (11%) believed that rural communities should be prioritized, and 63 (17%) reported that urban communities should be prioritized. In turn, 143 (64%) of the participants reporting a conservative political orientation thought that rural and urban communities should be equally prioritized by public universities, 56 (25%) believed that rural communities should be prioritized, and 25 (11%) reported that urban communities should be prioritized. Further, 138 (81%) of the participants claiming a middle of the road political orientation thought that rural and urban communities should be equally prioritized by public universities, 13 (8%) believed that rural communities should be prioritized, and 19 (11%) reported that urban communities should be prioritized. Finally, 46 (96%) of the participants claiming the "none of the above" label thought that rural and urban communities should be equally prioritized by public universities, 1 (2%) believed that rural communities should be prioritized, and 1 (2%) reported that urban communities should be prioritized. Mirroring the political party findings, a greater percentage of conservatives prioritized rural communities, a greater percentage of liberals prioritized urban communities, and middle-of-the-road citizens and those claiming the "none of the above" label displayed the greatest percentage of respondents who endorsed the notion that rural and urban communities should be treated equally.

The comparison of definite and non-definite 2020 voters regarding the prioritization of rural and urban communities by public universities yielded significant differences ($X^2 = 44.24$, df 2, $p < .001$) for this voting behavior variable. More specifically, 493 (78%) of the definite 2020 voters thought that rural and urban communities should be equally prioritized by public universities, 77 (12%) believed that rural communities should be prioritized, and 60 (10%) reported that urban communities should be prioritized. In turn, 102 (55%) of the non-definite voters in the 2020 presidential election thought that rural and urban communities should be equally prioritized by public universities, 35 (19%) believed that rural communities should be prioritized, and 48 (26%) reported that urban communities should be prioritized. Hence, a greater percentage of definite 2020 voters endorsed the idea that rural and urban communities should be treated equally, and a greater percentage of non-definite 2020 voters were split between prioritizing rural communities and prioritizing urban communities.

Initial Reactions to the Findings

The general findings related to the entire sample—where a substantial majority of participants reported that there should be no difference between how rural and urban communities are prioritized—was supported by the "formula for success" we discussed in earlier chapters and in our 2018 land-grant universities book. From our prior discussions with university leaders and other higher education experts, we were led to believe that the focus was less about the rural versus urban distinction and more about the need to focus on the needs of *communities*, regardless of geographic location.

Comparing Public Sentiment Against What We Know

Whether or not rural and urban communities are being prioritized by public universities would be best judged by who benefits most in terms of educational attainment. That is, do residents from rural and urban locations derive equal benefit from the college education offered by their public universities? There are any number of ways that we might approach this question, but one way that stands out most is to compare the rates by which rural and urban residents are attaining a four-year diploma.

While the number of people from rural areas who have attained a college degree has risen over the past 15 years, the growth in diplomas earned by rural citizens was not as large as the increase in attainment rates among urban dwellers. Reports utilizing figures from 2000 and 2015 indicated that the number of four-year degrees earned by urban residents grew from 26% to 33%, whereas those residents from rural areas only increased from 15% to 19%. This rising rural-urban gap in educational attainment also extended to the differential impact of a college degree on economic well-being, such that completing a four-year degree was associated with significantly increased income levels for urban residents in comparison to their rural counterparts.[1]

College admissions rates immediately following high school graduation show similar discrepancies, especially when the suburban distinction is taken into account. Overall, 67% of graduates from suburban schools enrolled in college in 2016, compared to 62% of urban school graduates and 59% of rural school graduates.[2] This is not from a lack of preparedness, as rural students display graduation rates at or above that of urban students[3] and tend to score as well on tests of college preparedness.[4] Instead, it has been posited that a rising sense of hopelessness in rural America has been contributing to a dampened set of expectations about the use of higher education as a vehicle for getting ahead.[5] For example, a recent Pew survey reported that 40% of rural white males (and a third of all rural adults) thought that their children will experience a lower standard of living than they did compared to 23% of adults in cities.[6]

Access to an institution of higher learning also matters here, especially regarding geographic proximity. Nicholas Hillman has written that "to truly understand students' college choices, we must understand the environment in which their choices occur. However, traditional theories of college choice focus on the process of opportunity instead of the geography of opportunity" (990).[7] This higher education scholar described what he termed "education deserts" that exist where the nation's most impoverished citizens live. All too often, those deserts are located within more rural areas, creating a very simple formula for college attendance: as distance between a rural resident and an institution of higher learning increases, the chances of attending and completing a college degree decreases.[8]

Demographic Differences as Related to the Findings

The significant differences that were found regarding the demographic variables of gender, age, level of educational attainment, and geographical location are interesting, if somewhat unsurprising. Of course, most predictable of all the results would be the finding that a greater percentage of rural participants prioritized rural communities and a greater percentage of urban participants prioritized urban communities. Plain and simple, this is a self-serving attitude toward resource allocation within the roughly one-third of the sample that did not report a desire for public universities to place equivalent emphasis on rural and urban communities.

Another foreseeable finding was related to educational attainment, where a greater percentage of those participants with a four-year degree or greater prioritized urban communities, while a greater percentage of respondents with some college or a high school diploma or less endorsed the idea that rural and urban communities should be treated equally. There, clearly, is some self-serving attitude being displayed here as well within that smaller portion of the survey participants who were not calling for equal treatment, as many more college graduates reside in urban areas.[9] This extends to the finding that a greater percentage of younger respondents prioritized urban communities in comparison to a greater percentage of older participants who reported that rural and urban communities should be equally prioritized. In general, urban residents are younger than rural residents[10] and, if those younger residents earn a college degree, they are more likely to move to an urban area.[11]

Finally, the significant differences as a function of gender were not anticipated. A greater percentage of females than males aligned with the majority within entire sample in reporting that public universities should place equivalent emphasis on rural and urban communities. In contrast, significantly more males within the one-third of the sample not calling for equivalent treatment indicated that public universities should prioritize urban communities. We were not able to couch this finding in any of the literature we reviewed, nor did the vast array of experts with whom we were in contact during this study have anything further to offer by way of explanation. So, we will leave this finding without further elucidation. As Sigmund Freud reportedly once quipped, sometimes a cigar is just a cigar.

Political Variable Differences as Related to the Findings

The significant differences that were found regarding our politically oriented variables seemed to point in a uniform direction. Within the smaller portion of survey participants who were not calling for equal treatment, a greater percentage of Republican participants wished for public universities to prioritize rural communities, and a greater percentage of Democrats in contrast prioritized urban communities. Independents and those with other party affiliations continued to display the greatest percentage of respondents who endorsed the notion that rural and urban communities should be treated equally by public universities. In turn, a greater percentage of conservatives wished for public universities to prioritize rural communities, a greater percentage of liberals prioritized urban communities, and middle-of-the-road participants displayed the greatest percentage of respondents who endorsed the notion that rural and urban communities should be treated equally.

We are conversant with issues pertaining to the rural and urban divide that we believe have contributed to some of the differences in opinion among our survey respondents regarding the prioritization of rural and urban communities by public universities. Our previous book opened with a discussion of a conceptual framework we referred to as the capital and the countryside, based on an op-ed article penned by Michael Barone.[12] The "capital" was associated with more urbanized areas and with cultural elites who live on the coasts of our country, who have greater educational attainment levels, and who are more heavily populated by immigrants and persons of color. The "countryside," in contrast, represents the heartland of the country, which is more rural, and whose people are less educated and less culturally and ethnically diverse.

Barone had used this framework to explain the results of the 2016 US presidential election. In tandem, we believed that the capital and countryside labels layered quite nicely onto "blue state" and "red state" terminology in strictly political terms and, in turn, were going to be directly applicable to urban and rural geographic distinctions. The fact that our politically oriented findings lined up so well with this sort of conceptual framework was unsurprising but hardly comforting. There is a real polarization in our nation that includes geographical features, and this political divide has had unquestionable consequences for America. As but one example of how much geography becomes part of our destiny as citizens in the most vibrant democracy in the world, the 2016 presidential election were described as "the year that the white rural voter roared" quite loudly.[13] Those citizens residing in the countryside may not have been as numerous as those in the capital, but their opinions ended up mattering greatly as voters. This rural and urban divide clearly remained on display in our most recent 2020 presidential election as well.[14]

There are many and varied ramifications of these political and geographic schisms for our public universities. To us, it is easy to see how the mentality and thus the political leanings of those who work and study on our nation's college campuses are thought to be associated with the "capital" variety of voters. Among other things, this perception has contributed to suspicion and angst about certain left-slanted viewpoints being used to teach students inside of our American institutions of higher learning (more about this in chapter 8). In turn, such beliefs have served to underscore the notion that our public universities are not aligned with the "countryside" point of view associated with "Middle America" or perhaps "Flyover Country" as rural areas have been labeled more recently.[15] As a result, students from more rural backgrounds who may hold more traditional values and beliefs may not feel welcomed by our public universities[16] and, as a result, may come to feel alienated when they arrive on campus,[17] if they come at all.[18]

And yet, we are heartened by the larger finding that a solid majority of our citizens see no difference in how public universities should focus on rural and urban communities, even as we recognize that they are not always experiencing similar challenges. The message from the preponderance of our survey respondents seems to be that we are as one people, regardless of the reality that most Americans live in more urbanized locations. This is consistent with the message we heard from higher education thought leaders as reported in our land-grant universities book. In other words, the message seems to be this: stop thinking in terms of rural and urban, and instead start thinking in terms of the higher-level variable of community.

The last of the significant differences that we found in our analyses regarding the political variables concerned the predicted 2020 voting behavior of our survey respondents. Here, we found that a greater percentage of definite 2020 voters endorsed the idea that rural and urban communities should be treated equally, whereas a greater percentage of non-definite 2020 voters were split between prioritizing rural communities and prioritizing urban communities. We translate this directly as a set of matched instructions for university administrators and state lawmakers alike: those citizens who are most active politically wish for public universities to be equally focused on rural and urban issues.

Contextualizing Rural and Urban Differences

The implications of the findings reported in this chapter seem relatively straightforward and, in some very important ways, are consistent with previous work we have helped to advance. For example, your senior author (Gavazzi) has written previously about the need for public (and especially land-grant) universities to lead the way in creating geographical representation on their campuses, if for no other reason than to provide for another form of diversity.[19] In turn, Gavazzi also worked with several analysts who had access to the *Wall Street Journal* and the *Times Higher Education* college rankings database to examine the degree to which land-grant universities have lost touch with rural America and, in so doing, have lost touch with their historical roots.[20] Our main point here has been that, while a focus on the needs of urban *and* rural communities is essential, our public universities have largely been out of balance on this front.

The fact that public sentiment is so strongly geared toward a more evenhanded prioritization of rural and urban community needs would seem to allow public universities an ability to escape from the sorts of discussions that have been portrayed as damaging to rural communities. Critical rural theorists,[21] conceptual cousins to both critical race theorists[22] and critical feminist theorists,[23] have asserted that the "binary" nature of such discourse (White/Black and male/female, or rural/urban in the present case) defines the marginalized group primarily in reference to the dominant group. This sort of binary narrative portrays the "out group" as deficient in comparison to the "in group"—for example, depicting rural citizens as less literate than urban residents[24]—thus using language that serves to reproduce the power imbalance.[25]

A central issue within this perspective is something that has been termed *urbanormativity* or the tendency to see the urban experience as the standard by which all other practices are evaluated.[26] Within the realm of higher education, this sort of bias has had the effect of excluding rural populations from participation in university life. Kathleen Gillon wrote:

> While it has been documented that rural students enroll in post-secondary education at rates lower than their urban counterparts, urbanormativity as a social structure has allowed not only college access and equity to be framed primarily as an urban matter, but participation in higher education to be framed as a practice reserved for urban people and communities. This framing has resulted in the silencing or the complete absence of rural students and communities from higher education scholarship and practice. (44)[27]

Urbanormativity may also have the effect of denying any value to plans for the rural citizen to return home after completing a college degree, instead promoting a set of ideals concentrated on the value of moving and settling into a more urbanized location.[28]

We had the opportunity to speak to three of the authors of the book *Critical Rural Theory*, including Alexander Thomas, Brian Lowe, and Gregory Fulkerson.[29] We were particularly interested in their views about the impact of urbanormativity on higher education, starting with their own home institution of SUNY College at Oneonta, which is located in one of the most northern counties of the Appalachian region.

We were also interested in how the urbanormativity concept extended to the position of their institution within the larger SUNY public university system that their campus is connected to administratively.

To kick things off, Dr. Thomas noted that their group considered the campus and surrounding community as a "sandbox for research" regarding the urbanormativity concept. The campus is situated in a rural and Appalachian area. However, it is only three hours from New York City and about an hour and a half from its suburbs, and approximately 80% of their students come from the New York combined statistical area. "Ironically, when you talk to a student who comes from a more rural community, there is almost a sense of shame and timidity that they have in admitting that they grew up locally." Examples of this sort of casual urbanormativity extended to SUNY College of Oneonta faculty members as well, many of whom choose to live a significant distance away from campus because they say they don't want to live "in the middle of nowhere." Instead, they are electing to commute from the suburbs of Albany, Utica, or Binghamton, thus reinforcing the urban (or at least suburban) ideal.

To the credit of the SUNY system, these scholars did not report any sort of marginalization as a function of their more rural location in comparison to other SUNY campuses. Instead, there was more of an awareness of the relative clout of some of the other SUNY campuses that held the Carnegie I doctoral granting designation and thus projected a strong research mission. In comparison, SUNY Oneonta is categorized as an M2 master's degree granting (medium) program, which translates into a greater emphasis on their teaching mission. That said, there was also some sensitivity to the fact that schools even more rural than their campus—and farther away geographically from New York City proper—did perhaps carry some sort of stigma. Where the urbanormativity was much more easily seen by these researchers, however, was in the number of fellow faculty members who used the campus as a steppingstone to other positions in "better" locations, again meaning more urban.

We were interested in their reactions to the findings of our study, especially in light of the work these scholars have been doing with the urbanormativity concept. There was no surprise among these scholars regarding our finding that 70% of the survey respondents wished for rural and urban communities to be treated equally by public universities. In the hypothetical, they stated that this sort of sentiment seemed distinctly American. Going a step further, however, Dr. Fulkerson also thought this finding fit quite well within the "rural mystique" literature.[30] He stated to us: "There are several studies that have looked at the public's opinion of rural people, and the findings have indicated an overwhelmingly positive viewpoint. It's almost like a paradox, though, because you have these very positive assessments of rural citizens on the one hand, and on the other hand, you have this underbelly of stereotypical thinking, similar to the way the 'noble savage' concept gets applied to Native American peoples."

We return now to our primary objective in writing this book, which centers on the promotion of campus-community dialogue about the findings from our survey efforts. This sort of conversation would necessarily involve a redoubled effort to raise awareness of the public's desire for a more evenhanded approach to urban and rural communities, while simultaneously recognizing and owning the more lopsided approach that our public universities have taken so far. It does seem to be the case that higher education has adopted a decidedly urban slant in much of its work, or perhaps even more specifically, a suburban bias.[31]

Happily, there are sprigs of hope that some sort of shift may already be afoot in this regard. Some universities seem to have rediscovered the value of recruiting and retaining students from more rural backgrounds, and at least some of this reawakening has been attributed to the results of the 2016 US presidential election.[32] There is the explicit recognition that a significant portion of Americans have grown to mistrust our public universities, especially in terms of not offering an education that reflects the value system of working-class citizens.[33] Hence, we must do all that we can to make certain that urban, suburban, and rural students all feel welcome and valued by our nation's public institutions of higher learning. Especially for those rural students, we must intentionally let them know not only that they are welcome to come to our campuses, but also that we will help prepare them to go back home—if that is what they wish to do—with a set of skills that will help them to build better circumstances for those communities from which they have come.

Summary

We began this chapter with a discussion about how study participants responded to our second higher education survey question, one that asked participants to consider—in an ideal world—who should be prioritized by public universities in their state: rural communities, urban communities, or if both rural and urban communities should be treated equally. Over 70% of respondents reported that public universities should place equivalent emphasis on rural and urban communities. Next, we presented rationales regarding the significant differences that were found regarding the demographic variables of age, educational attainment, and geographic location. For these variables, we posited that self-serving attitudes toward resource allocation were the primary drivers of these differences. Regarding the significant gender differences that were found, however, we did not offer any solid conclusions.

Further, we reported on the significant differences found on political variables involving party, orientation, and predicted voting behavior in 2020. Consistent with our previous work, we witnessed a split between Republican and conservative participants being more likely to want their public universities to prioritize rural communities, whereas Democratic and liberal respondents wishing that urban communities would be prioritized. Independent and middle-of-the-road participants remained most likely to have endorsed the notion that rural and urban communities should be treated equally.

The remainder of this chapter covered several topics that provided some contextualization of these findings, including our previous work on the capital and countryside conceptual framework, the introduction of critical rural theory, and the inclusion of the concept of urbanormativity. In each case, we asserted that greater public understanding of those issues—which tend to place urban and rural needs at odds with one another—would provide citizens with the increased opportunity to make informed decisions about where and how they would wish for public universities to prioritize efforts to provide assistance to communities. Within such an expanded intellectual environment, we hoped to stimulate a more balanced appreciation for the idea that public universities, by design, were meant to provide for the needs of *all* communities, regardless of their geographic location.

5

Global Footprint versus Closer to Home

I do not mean to say that this government is charged with the duty of redressing or preventing all the wrongs in the world; but I do think that it is charged with the duty of preventing and redressing all wrongs which are wrongs to itself.

We begin this fifth chapter with a quote from a September 1859 speech that Abraham Lincoln gave in Cincinnati, Ohio. The event itself may well have yielded the most widely read oration of Lincoln's pre-presidency, and at least one historian has declared that this speech was most responsible for his nomination as the head of the Republican ticket.[1] While this speech was not purposefully international in flavor, it focused specifically on the world's biggest curse of its time: slavery in all its forms. Lincoln's specific focus was on preventing the westward expansion of slavery into the western states. Hence, the future president was seen and heard calling forth a nation to remedy a truly global challenge by rejecting its growth at the local level.

The dynamic tension between international and local issues has been felt by members of public universities since the time of their inception in the United States. On the one hand, our land-grant universities were founded in part to address the specific and localized needs of each state.[2] On the other hand, the rise of the global knowledge economy has placed enormous pressures (while offering enormous incentives) on universities to become more inclusive, more expansive, and more involved in matters of the world.[3] This chapter examines the data collected on our third higher education-based survey question, one that asked survey respondents to consider—in an ideal world—whether public universities in their state should place more of their emphasis on global/international issues, more emphasis on those issues closer to home that more directly impacted the communities in which they lived, or if the public universities of their state should emphasize international and local issues equally.

As noted in earlier chapters, this question was predicated on the theme reported in our *Land-Grant Universities for the Future* book regarding the dynamic tension between "global reach versus closer to home impact." As a reminder, the possible responses included: (a) global/international concerns should be emphasized more than issues impacting my community; (b) issues impacting my community should be emphasized more than global/international concerns; or (c) there should be no difference in emphasis between global/international concerns and issues impacting my community. Based on our previous work regarding the formula for success, we hypothesized that participants were most likely to report that local issues should trump more global-based activities.

Findings from the Overall Sample

Contrary to our hypothesis, the most frequent response to this question was that there should be no difference in emphasis between global/international concerns and local issues, endorsed by 366 (43%) participants in the sample. Even more surprising to us, the next most frequent response was that global/international concerns should be more greatly emphasized, endorsed by 280 (33%) of the respondents. As it turned out, only 150 (18%) of the participants reported that local issues should be more greatly emphasized. The remaining individuals (48 individuals or 6%) chose "I don't know" or skipped this question and so were excluded from this specific analysis.

Further Analyses

In order to test for potential differences in how respondents wanted their public universities to emphasize global concerns and local issues, we ran a series of chi-square tests using all demographic variables (gender, age, race/ethnicity, geographic location, and educational attainment) and politically oriented variables (party affiliation, liberal/conservative orientation, actual voting behavior in 2016, and predicted voting behavior in 2020). The results regarding the demographic variables indicated significant effects for gender, race/ethnicity, age, and educational attainment. We discuss those results in the demographics section below. In turn, the results regarding the political variables indicated significant effects for party, orientation, and predicted voting behavior in 2020. We report on those results in a separate section for politically oriented variables.

Demographic Variables and Emphasizing International Concerns and Local Issues

The comparison of male and female viewpoints regarding the emphasis on international concerns and more localized issues yielded significant differences ($X^2 = 15.93$, df 2, p < .001) for gender. More specifically, 121 (38%) of male participants thought that international and local issues should be equally emphasized by public universities, 122 (38%) believed that global concerns should be emphasized, and 76 (24%) reported that local issues should be emphasized. In turn, 245 (51%) of female participants thought that international and local issues should be equally emphasized by public universities, 158 (33%) believed that global concerns should be emphasized, and 74 (16%) reported that local issues should be emphasized. In general, a greater percentage of females believed that global concerns and more localized issues should be equally emphasized, whereas a greater percentage of males reported that more localized issues should be emphasized.

The comparison of White/Caucasian and non-White/Caucasian viewpoints regarding the emphasis on international concerns and more localized issues yielded significant differences ($X^2 = 7.61$, df 2, p < .02) for race/ethnicity. More specifically, 290 (46%) of White/Caucasian respondents thought that international and local issues should be equally emphasized by public universities, 209 (33%) believed that global concerns should be emphasized, and 129 (21%) reported that local issues should be emphasized. In turn, 76 (45%) of non-White/Caucasian respondents thought that international and local issues should be equally emphasized by public universities, 71 (42%) believed that global concerns should be emphasized, and 21 (13%) reported that local issues should be emphasized. Hence, a greater percentage of White/Caucasian participants (by percentage) believed that local issues should be emphasized, whereas a greater percentage of non-White/Caucasian respondents reported that global issues should be emphasized.

The comparison of younger and older viewpoints regarding the emphasis on international concerns and more localized issues yielded significant differences ($X^2 = 15.77$, df 2, p < .001) for age. More specifically, 148 (38%) of 18- to 44-year-old participants thought that international and local issues should be equally emphasized by public universities, 155 (41%) believed that global concerns should be emphasized, and 79 (21%) reported that local issues should be emphasized. In turn, 218 (51%) of 45-year-old and older participants thought that international and local issues should be equally emphasized by public universities, 125 (30%) believed that global concerns should be emphasized, and 71 (17%) reported that local issues should be emphasized. In general, a greater percentage of the younger participants believed that global issues should be emphasized, whereas a greater percentage of the older participants believed that global and local issues should be equally emphasized.

Use of the educational attainment variable to examine potential differences regarding the emphasis on international concerns and more localized issues yielded significant differences ($X^2 = 24.55$, df 4, p < .001). More specifically, 118 (56%) of the participants with a high school degree or less educational attainment thought that international and local issues should be equally emphasized by public universities, 63 (30%) believed that global concerns should be emphasized, and 30 (14%)

reported that local issues should be emphasized. In turn, 121 (51%) of the participants with some college thought that international and local issues should be equally emphasized by public universities, 76 (32%) believed that global concerns should be emphasized, and 39 (17%) reported that local issues should be emphasized. Further, 127 (36%) of the participants with a four-year college degree or greater educational attainment thought that international and local issues should be equally emphasized by public universities, 141 (40%) believed that global concerns should be emphasized, and 81 (23%) reported that local issues should be emphasized. Hence, a greater percentage of those respondents in both of the educational attainment groups that had not achieved a four-year college degree believed global concerns and local issues should be equally emphasized, whereas a greater percentage of the participants having attained at least a four-year college degree believed that global concerns should be emphasized.

Political Variables and Emphasizing International Concerns and Local Issues

Use of political party to examine potential differences regarding the emphasis on international concerns and local issues yielded significant differences ($X^2 = 25.28$, df 6, p < .001). More specifically, 82 (49%) participants claiming affiliation with the Republican party thought that global concerns and local issues should be equally emphasized by public universities, 40 (24%) believed that global concerns should be emphasized, and 45 (27%) reported that local issues should be emphasized. In turn, 145 (41%) of participants reporting affiliation with the Democratic party thought that global concerns and local issues should be equally emphasized by public universities, 154 (43%) believed that global concerns should be emphasized, and 57 (16%) reported that local issues should be emphasized. Further, 99 (51%) of participants with the Independent affiliation thought that global concerns and local issues should be equally emphasized by public universities, 60 (31%) believed that global concerns should be emphasized, and 35 (18%)

reported that local issues should be emphasized. Finally, 40 (51%) of participants claiming some other political affiliation thought that global concerns and local issues should be equally emphasized by public universities, 26 (33%) believed that global concerns should be emphasized, and 13 (17%) reported that local issues should be emphasized. In general, a greater percentage of Republican participants emphasized local issues, a greater percentage of Democrats emphasized global concerns, and Independents and those with other party affiliations displayed the greatest percentage of respondents who endorsed the notion that global concerns and local issues should be equally emphasized.

Use of the liberal-conservative continuum variable to examine potential differences regarding the emphasis on global concerns and local issues by public universities yielded significant differences ($X^2 = 27.74$, df 6, p < .001). More specifically, 155 (42%) participants who described themselves as liberal in their political orientation thought that global concerns and local issues should be equally emphasized by public universities, 159 (43%) believed that global concerns should be emphasized, and 57 (15%) reported that local issues should be emphasized. In turn, 96 (45%) of participants reporting a conservative political orientation thought that global concerns and local issues should be equally emphasized by public universities, 60 (28%) believed that global concerns should be emphasized, and 58 (27%) reported that local issues should be emphasized. Further, 90 (53%) of participants claiming a middle-of-the-road political orientation thought that global concerns and local issues should be equally emphasized by public universities, 50 (30%) believed that global concerns should be prioritized, and 29 (17%) reported that local issues should be emphasized. Finally, 25 (60%) of participants claiming the "none of the above" label thought that global concerns and local issues should be equally emphasized by public universities, 11 (26%) believed that rural communities should be emphasized, and 6 (14%) reported that local issues should be emphasized. Mirroring the political party findings, a greater percentage of conservatives emphasized local issues, a greater percentage of liberals emphasized global concerns, and middle-of-the-road citizens and those claiming the "none of the above" label displayed the greatest percentage of respondents who endorsed the notion that global concerns and local issues should be equally emphasized.

The comparison of definite and non-definite 2020 voters regarding the emphasis on global concerns and local issues by public universities yielded significant differences ($X^2 = 14.39$, df 2, p < .001) for this voting behavior variable. More specifically, 295 (48%) of definite 2020 voters thought that global concerns and local issues should be equally emphasized by public universities, 219 (36%) believed that global concerns should be emphasized, and 98 (16%) reported that local issues should be emphasized. In turn, 71 (39%) of non-definite voters in the 2020 presidential election thought that global concerns and local issues should be equally emphasized by public universities, 61 (33%) believed that global concerns should be emphasized, and 52 (28%) reported that local issues should be emphasized. Hence, a greater percentage of definite 2020 voters endorsed the idea that global concerns and local issues should be equally emphasized by public universities, while a greater percentage of non-definite 2020 voters reported that local issues should be emphasized.

Initial Reactions to the Findings

The general findings related to the entire sample—where over 40% of participants reported that there should be no difference in emphasis between global/international concerns and local issues, and an additional one-third of the sample that believed global/international concerns should be more greatly emphasized—took us completely by surprise. We hypothesized the exact opposite response; that is, participants would report that local issues should be emphasized more than global-based activities.

Of course, we were aware of the strong motivation that public universities have had to expand their global reach as the world economy became more internationalized.[4] In fact, our previous land-grant universities book dealt directly with the longstanding call for universities to adopt a more international presence. This included our recognition of writing done by those individuals who were attempting to reimagine and reinvigorate the land-grant mission in terms of helping to create a more globally connected society.[5] This included the concept of the "world-grant ideal," which held that the Morrill Act's stipulation for land-grant universities to be responsible for their "own backyard" necessarily should be extended to include a more "worldwide backyard" focus as well.[6]

Our analysis of the qualitative data gleaned from interviews conducted with university leaders led us to believe that the dynamic tension fostered between local and global priorities created a number of counterproductive pressures, including the viewpoint that global engagement was an "either/or" proposition.[7] The idea that these local versus global issues could be viewed as part of a zero-sum framework was echoed and amplified by the higher education thought leaders we subsequently interviewed. What we heard distinctly from this group of individuals was that, although your university's activities might be global, they better look and sound as if they have a local application.[8] Hence, we had come to expect that public sentiment would be weighted heavily toward an emphasis on more homegrown sensibilities.

Comparing Public Sentiment Against What We Know

Because we were so flummoxed by our findings, we decided to reach out to colleagues who might help us to better understand the dynamic tension between global and local issues and how public sentiment might be so strongly supportive of the international dimension of higher education. We immediately looked to William Brustein, the vice president for global strategies and international affairs and Eberly family distinguished professor of history at West Virginia University. Because he served previously as the vice provost for global strategies and international affairs at The Ohio State University, he was quite well-known to both of your authors. It is important to note here that Dr. Brustein is also renowned by colleagues the world over for his work on international education, including formal recognition for his outstanding service to the field of international education administration by the Association of International Education Administrators.

The first thing Dr. Brustein pointed out was that most premier international programs with which he was familiar did contain explicit and ongoing recognition of the impact that these global efforts had on local interests and issues. Given the fact that a significant portion of funding for public universities comes from state legislatures, he pointed out that international education personnel took great pains to work with lawmakers to understand and appreciate the ways in which the university's global programs had a positive impact on the state's economy. These benefits would include the establishment of overseas markets for goods produced within the state, especially through university-corporate partnerships that were established as a result of the international outreach. Underscoring the power of alumni networks, Dr. Brustein also pointed out that the return of recent graduates to their home countries who subsequently were hired by companies participating in these university-corporate partnerships often cemented these international economic connections.

Dr. Brustein was quick to point out that local stakeholders in various industries within a given state were also likely to serve as witnesses to the powerful impact that international higher education programs could have on the local economy. He stated that "through the exchange of knowledge, and the exchange of expertise, universities and their partners—both home and abroad—quickly recognize the reciprocal benefits that accrue from these sorts of activities. There are countless examples where universities were pivotal in the development of economic connections between local businesses and international companies." It may be the case that the knowledge of such partnerships and their benefits are more widely known and appreciated by citizens than we had imagined, according to Dr. Brustein. He indicated that international student contact with various stakeholders in communities through internships and cultural exchange program offerings may further solidify these positive sentiments as well.

The conversation then pivoted to any literature, scholarly or otherwise, that would provide supportive evidence of this phenomenon. The writing is just not there, Dr. Brustein told us, unequivocally. "This is a neglected area because it's not the sexiest aspect of university work on the global stage. It is not the place where revenue is generated right away, as it is when you talk about international student tuition and fees. You do not experience these same economic benefits right away. Instead, you must be able to see the potential of the partnerships that will evolve over time." It is precisely this rather mundane and future-forward component of the work surrounding the translation of international efforts into local gains, Dr. Brustein said, that has prevented more scholars from studying and writing about this specific aspect.

Dr. Brustein also stated that university leadership mattered a great deal in terms of remaining focused on the local impact of international higher education programs. For such programs to attend to the positive influence of global activities on those communities served by the university, he went on to say, presidents, provosts, and other senior administrators had to be oriented toward that sort of outcome. Importantly, this meant having someone specifically assigned to the task of creating and maintaining those relationships with local stakeholders, which is not something that many universities seem to do, according to Dr. Brustein. When no one is given that set of responsibilities, he went on to say, then it is a great deal less likely that the university without such a position would be generating publicity about such efforts. So, if there is no such information being produced, then there is nothing about which to write.

Demographic Differences as Related to the Findings

The significant differences that were found regarding the demographic variables of gender, age, level of educational attainment, and geographical location are interesting, and some of these findings make more sense than others. The fact that a greater percentage of males believed local issues should be more emphasized in comparison to females, who were more likely to report that global and local issues should be equally emphasized, is a bit confounding. So, too, is the finding that younger participants believed that global issues should be emphasized, whereas a greater percentage of the older participants believed that global and local issues should be equally emphasized. There simply is not much in the way of literature that would have supported a hypothesis that gender or age would have mattered here.

The finding that a greater percentage of non-White/Caucasian respondents reported that global issues should be emphasized in comparison to the greater percentage of White/Caucasian participants who believed that local issues should be emphasized is more understandable to us. It is reasonable to assume that persons of color might be more likely to have a sense of connectedness to international people and places, a sentiment that would translate into greater support for global efforts within higher education. In turn, the fact that more participants who attained a four-year college degree or greater believed that global concerns should be emphasized is plausible simply because the experience of university life would greatly increase an individual's exposure to international students and study aboard opportunities.

Political Variable Differences as Related to the Findings

The significant differences that were found regarding our politically oriented variables seemed to point in a uniform direction. Not surprisingly, a greater percentage of Republican participants emphasized local issues and a greater percentage of Democrats emphasized global concerns, with Independents and those with other party affiliations right in the middle endorsing an equal emphasis on global and local issues. Mirroring the political party findings, a greater percentage of conservatives emphasized local issues and a greater percentage of liberals emphasized global concerns, with middle-of-the-road citizens again taking a central position by endorsing global and local issues equally. Almost by definition, the populist flavor of Republican and conservative messaging tends to favor more local and nativist issues,[9] whereas Democrats with more liberal and progressive platforms are now viewed as being more supportive of global and international concerns.[10]

In turn, the finding that a greater percentage of definite 2020 voters endorsed the idea that global concerns and local issues should be equally emphasized by public universities appears to be an avenue for higher education leaders to strike some sort of balance between Democratic and Republican (and liberal and conservative) platforms. That is, regardless of political affiliation, those citizens who bother to vote in elections tend to be those who wish their public universities to remain involved in both global concerns and local issues. Said a bit differently, this finding may grant permission for universities to ignore the increasingly shrill aspects of positions taken by the extreme left and the extreme right when setting policies in this area.

Contextualizing Global and Local Issues

The literature makes it abundantly clear that there has been a dramatic increase in international activities undertaken by universities, seen as part of a "global academic revolution" that has taken place over the past fifty years.[11] The "big business" aspect of internalization has been estimated at $100 billion globally.[12] These significant financial incentives for involvement in international education rests largely on the recruitment and retention of international students, who invariably are seen as "cash cows" because they pay much larger amounts of tuition and fees as compared to American (and especially in-state) students.[13]

There certainly has been plenty of media coverage surrounding the increased involvement of universities in global activities. One of the most widely recognized forms of international involvement revolves around study abroad programs, many of which have shown a marked increase in student participation over the years.[14] To support American students wishing to study overseas, as well as to recruit international students into educational programs back at home, universities have increasingly been setting up "gateways" or "embassies" in other countries.[15] Curricular changes aimed at increasing student "global competence" have become more widely implemented[16] and now include significant internship experiences and co-op models for both studying and working abroad.[17]

Of course, all the publicity for these activities has not been uniformly positive. One of the biggest pushbacks against the influx of international students was the perception that these students were taking "spots" that were formerly more freely available to American students.[18] Similarly, faculty members have opined about the ways in which the focus on preparation to enter the global marketplace has drowned out the importance of student involvement in studies and projects that have more local impact and meaning.[19] One more recent article even declared the "golden age" of international higher education to be over, the result of a shift in American politics and sensibilities.[20]

We had the good fortune of being able to talk about the state of international higher education with Philip Altbach, a research professor of educational leadership and higher education at Boston College who is also the founding director of the Center for International Higher Education and the author of *Global Perspectives on Higher Education*.[21] We began our discussion with a focus on our survey results, with special attention given to the finding that 76% of respondents believed either that there should be no difference in emphasis between global/international concerns and local issues or that global/international concerns should be more greatly emphasized. This was as much of a surprise to Dr. Altbach as it was to us, although he provided a more nuanced way of discussing his own predictions about what the public thought about international efforts. He shared that it was not so much that he thought the public was against global activities per se as much as the issue did not matter to them. Instead, he thought that what was more important to the average citizen were issues surrounding career preparation and workforce development, which, by nature, are more local in orientation.

Our conversation with Dr. Altbach took place in early April 2020, right in the middle of the nationwide shutdown occurring as a result of the COVID-19 pandemic. So, of course, we were interested in his thoughts about the impact that the coronavirus would have on international higher education. He responded by reminding us that international efforts were already on a downward trajectory prior to the pandemic, particularly regarding student mobility and the enrollment of international students in American universities. Dr. Altbach went on to say: "Several things are going on here that are unrelated to COVID-19. First, the China bubble is about finished. Chinese students will not stop coming here to study, but the percentage gains are going to stop. That may be made up for to some degree by students from India, but those students are very price sensitive so the offset may not be as great. Second, the adverse rhetoric coming out of the Trump administration about immigration certainly has had an impact on the attractiveness of coming to the United States. The broader trends more recently have not been wholly negative, but they have not been as gung-ho as they had been for the previous twenty years."

Regarding the COVID-19 pandemic's impact more specifically, Dr. Altbach thought it would take some time to rebuild the international focus and mobility patterns of students coming to study in America. He said, "I don't think we are going to go back to the status quo right away, but American students are still going to be interested in study abroad, and international students are still going to be interested in coming to study at our nation's universities." Interestingly, Dr. Altbach reported that some higher education thought leaders believe that distance education is going to play a major role in how international higher education will move forward. "I don't believe that at all. We are getting more experience with distance education, and it will be a bigger part of the picture, but students want to study at a university, not on a computer." We will be covering more of what Dr. Altbach and his colleagues believe will be happening in the post-pandemic world. For now, we end by recognizing that international higher education already was experiencing significant disruptions to what had been a pattern of steady growth over the past several decades.

Summary

We began this chapter with a discussion about how study participants responded to our third higher education-based survey question, one that asked survey respondents to consider—in an ideal world—whether public universities in their state should place more of their emphasis on global/international issues, more emphasis on those issues closer to home that more directly impact the communities in which they lived, or if the public universities of their state should emphasize international and local issues equally. Contrary to our hypothesis, the most frequent response to this question was that there should be no difference in emphasis between global/international concerns and local issues, and an additional one-third of the sample indicated that global and international concerns should be more greatly emphasized. Surprising to us, slightly less than one-fifth of the respondents reported that local issues should be more greatly emphasized.

Next, we presented rationales regarding the significant differences that were found regarding the demographic variables of gender, race/ethnicity, age, and educational attainment. While there was scant literature that supported the idea that gender or age would have mattered on this topic, we did believe it was reasonable to expect that non-White/Caucasian respondents and those individuals with a four-year college degree or greater would be more supportive of global activities. Further, we reported on the significant differences found on political variables involving party, orientation, and predicted voting behavior in 2020. Here, we thought that the pattern of results made a great deal of intuitive sense. Republicans and conservatives would tend to favor more local issues through their populist leanings, whereas Democrats and liberals would seem to be more supportive of global activities as part of their more progressive agendas.

The remainder of this chapter covered several topics that provided some contextualization of these findings, including the dramatic increase in international activities undertaken by universities over the past 50 years that had been discussed as part of a "global academic revolution." We also covered the "big business" aspect of internalization, including most significantly the enrollment of international students in programs on American campuses. Media coverage of these issues also was discussed, including the examination of study abroad programs and gateway initiatives set up in other countries. Finally, we reported on a variety of issues that may have contributed to what has been described as the end of the "golden age" of international higher education.

6

Merit-Based Aid and Needs-Based Aid for Students

Mr. Clay's lack of a more perfect early education, however it may be regretted generally, teaches at least one profitable lesson; it teaches that in this country, one can scarcely be so poor, but that, if he *will*, he *can* acquire sufficient education to get through the world respectably.

O ur sixth chapter begins with a quote taken from Abraham Lincoln's eulogy remarks regarding the life of Henry Clay, the Kentucky politician known as "The Great Compromiser" that the future president admired more deeply than any other individual.[1] Speaking on July 6, 1852, Lincoln extolled the man who served in both the US House of Representatives and the US Senate as well as having been secretary of state during the administration of President John Quincy Adams. In this homage, we again witness the future president making the connection between education and achievement of the "American Dream."

Who should pay for these educational pursuits, however? And who should be the beneficiaries of whatever largesse is freed up to provide such support? These sorts of vexing questions have taken a front burner position in discussions about the doling out of student aid.[2] During the 2015–2016 academic year, 77.1% of all students attending four-year public universities received some form of financial aid from federal, state, institutional, and employer sources (up from 69.2% during the 2003–2004 academic year).[3] The historically strong bipartisan support for this rather copious amount of overall public support provided to those who would seek a college degree may be eroding, however. Evidence of ideological splits among the left and the right about who should have access to different forms of financial aid are especially noticeable in more recent political discussions about free college and debt forgiveness, among other issues.[4]

This chapter examines the data collected on our fourth higher education-based survey question, an item which asked survey respondents to consider—in an ideal world—what should be prioritized for student-directed funding by the public universities of their state: needs-based aid (based on family income) or merit-based aid (based on student academic performance). As a reminder, possible responses included: (a) needs-based aid should be prioritized for funding over merit-based aid; (b) merit-based aid should be prioritized for funding over needs-based aid; (c) there should be no difference in funding provided for needs-based aid and merit-based aid; or (d) none of the above (I do not believe public universities should provide either needs-based or merit-based aid).

This survey question was predicated on the theme presented in the *Land-Grant Universities for the Future* book regarding "the focus on rankings versus an emphasis on access and affordability." Based on our previous work regarding the formula for success, we believed that study participants would endorse the idea that needs-based aid should be prioritized for funding over merit-based aided when it came to prioritizing public university activities, or at least subscribe to the statement that there should be no difference between needs-based aid and merit-based aid.

Findings from the Overall Sample

Contrary to our hypothesis, the most frequent response to this question was that merit-based aid should be prioritized for funding over needs-based aid, endorsed by 416 (49%) participants in the sample. The next most frequent response was that there should be no difference in funding provided for needs-based aid and merit-based aid, endorsed by 311 (37%) of the respondents. As it turned out, only 100 (12%) of the participants reported that needs-based aid should be prioritized for funding over merit-based aid. Nine of the individuals (1%) chose none of the above and the remaining 8 individuals (1%) chose "I don't know" or skipped this question. These latter 17 respondents were excluded from this specific analysis.

Further Analyses

In order to test for potential differences in how respondents wanted their public universities to fund needs-based and merit-based aid for students, we ran a series of chi-square tests using all demographic variables (gender, age, race/ethnicity, geographic location, and educational attainment) and politically oriented variables (party affiliation, liberal/conservative orientation, actual voting behavior in 2016, and predicted voting behavior in 2020). The results regarding the demographic variables indicated significant effects only for the age variable. We discuss that singular finding in the demographics section first. In turn, the results regarding the political variables indicated significant effects for party, orientation, and predicted voting behavior in 2020. We report on those results in a separate section for politically oriented variables.

Demographic Variables and Needs-Based and Merit-Based Aid

The comparison of younger and older participant viewpoints regarding the funding of needs-based and merit-based aid for students yielded significant differences ($X^2 = 17.62$, df 2, p < .001) for age. More specifically, 137 (35%) of the 18- to 44-year-old participants thought that needs-based and merit-based aid should be equally funded by public universities, 188 (48%) believed that merit-based aid should be prioritized, and 67 (17%) reported that needs-based aid should be prioritized. In turn, 174 (40%) of the 45-year-old and older participants thought that needs-based and merit-based aid should be equally prioritized by public universities, 228 (52%) believed that merit-based aid should be prioritized, and 33 (8%) reported that needs-based aid should be prioritized. In general, a greater percentage of younger respondents prioritized needs-based aid, whereas a greater percentage of older participants believed that needs-based and merit-based aid should be prioritized equally.

Political Variables and Needs-Based and Merit-Based Aid

Use of political party to examine potential differences regarding the funding of needs-based and merit-based aid by public universities yielded significant differences ($X^2 = 20.76$, df 6, p < .002). More specifically, 51 (29%) participants claiming affiliation with the Republican party thought that needs-based and merit-based aid should be equally prioritized by public universities, 109 (62%) believed that merit-based aid should be prioritized, and 16 (9%) reported that needs-based aid should be prioritized. In turn, 145 (40%) of participants reporting affiliation with the Democratic party thought that needs-based and merit-based aid should be equally prioritized by public universities, 160 (44%) believed that merit-based aid should be prioritized, and 58 (16%) reported that needs-based aid should be prioritized. Further, 78 (39%) of the participants with the Independent affiliation thought that needs-based and merit-based aid should be equally prioritized by public universities, 103 (51%) believed that merit-based aid should be prioritized, and 20 (10%) reported that needs-based aid should be prioritized. Finally, 37 (43%) of the participants claiming some other political affiliation thought that needs-based and merit-based aid should be equally prioritized by public universities, 44 (51%) believed that merit-based aid should be prioritized, and 6 (7%) reported that needs-based aid should be prioritized. Hence, the greatest percentage of Republicans, Independents, and participants with other political affiliations prioritized merit-based aid, whereas Democrats displayed the largest percentage of respondents who prioritized needs-based aid.

Use of the liberal-conservative continuum variable to examine potential differences regarding the funding of needs-based and merit-based aid by public universities yielded significant differences ($X^2 = 40.50$, df 6, p < .001). More specifically, 164 (43%) participants who described themselves as liberal in their political orientation thought that needs-based and merit-based aid should be equally prioritized by public universities, 154 (41%) believed that merit-based aid should be prioritized, and 60 (16%) reported that needs-based aid should be prioritized. In turn, 56 (25%) of participants reporting a conservative political orientation thought that needs-based and merit-based aid should be equally prioritized by public universities, 147 (65%) believed that merit-based aid should be prioritized, and 22 (10%) reported that needs-based aid should be prioritized. Further, 68 (39%) of participants claiming a middle-of-the-road political orientation thought that needs-based and merit-based aid should be equally prioritized by public universities, 90 (52%) believed that merit-based aid should be prioritized, and 16 (9%) reported that needs-based aid should be prioritized. Finally, 23 (46%) of the participants claiming the "none of the above" label thought that needs-based and merit-based aid should be equally prioritized by public universities, 25 (50%) believed that merit-based aid should be prioritized, and 2 (4%) reported that needs-based aid should be prioritized. Mirroring the findings related to political party, the greatest percentage of conservatives, middle of the road, and participants claiming "none of the above" status prioritized merit-based aid, whereas those with a liberal orientation displayed the largest percentage of respondents who prioritized needs-based aid.

The comparison of definite and non-definite 2020 voters regarding the funding of needs-based and merit-based aid by public universities yielded significant differences ($X^2 = 37.13$, df 2, p < .001) for this voting behavior variable. More specifically, 265 (41%) of definite 2020 voters thought that needs-based and merit-based aid should be equally prioritized by public universities, 319 (50%) believed that merit-based aid should be prioritized, and 56 (9%) reported that needs-based aid should be prioritized. In turn, 46 (24%) of non-definite voters in the 2020 presidential election thought that needs-based and merit-based aid should be equally prioritized by public universities, 97 (52%) believed that merit-based aid should be prioritized, and 44 (24%) reported that needs-based aid should be prioritized. Hence, definite 2020 voters displayed greater percentages of respondents who believed that needs-based and merit-based aid should be equally prioritized, whereas non-definite voters displayed the greatest percentage of participants who believed that merit-based aid should be prioritized.

Initial Reactions to the Findings

The general findings related to the entire sample—where almost half of all participants reported that merit-based aid should be prioritized over needs-based aid—was exactly the opposite finding that we expected. We had predicted that more respondents would prioritize needs-based aid over merit-based aid, or at the very least would have chosen the response that equally weighted needs-based aid and merit-based aid. Our hypothesis was based on an extrapolation of earlier findings from our interviews of university presidents and higher education thought leaders, who spoke of the great amount of emphasis that was being placed on affordability in the nation's conversation about the state of higher education. We had assumed that this public pressure was designed to help those who were least able to afford to go to college, rather than to lower costs for those who were most prepared academically to take advantage of a university education. In fact, only slightly more than 10% of the study respondents reflected that line of thinking.

Comparing Public Sentiment Against What We Know

How does the public's desire to allocate funding toward merit-based and needs-based aid stack up against the current reality of the situation? Data on 2016–2017 expenditures from the National Center for Education Statistics (NCES) indicated that public four-year institutions spent 5% of their total budgets on student aid.[5] In turn, the NCES reported that 14% of students attending four-year public universities received needs-based aid from their institutions during the 2015–2016 academic year (collecting an average of $3,600 in aid), compared to 13.4% of those same students who received merit-based aid from their universities (collecting an average of $5,200 in aid).[6]

While the percentages of students who receive merit-based and need-based aid is quite similar, there is about a $1,600 difference in the amount of aid, or approximately 20% more funding designated as merit-based aid. Further, while the number of students receiving both forms of institutional aid appears to have been growing over the past decade, the difference between the amounts of merit-based and needs based-aid has remained relatively constant. For purposes of comparison, the NCES reported that 9.3% of students attending four-year public universities received needs-based aid during the 2003–2004 academic year (collecting an average of $2,800 in aid), compared to 9.2% of those same students who received merit-based aid (collecting an average of $4,200 in aid).

Although beyond the budgetary control of public universities, it is important to note that both merit-based and needs-based aid are typically made available to students from state government sources. The NCES reported that 22% of students attending four-year public universities received needs-based aid from state governments during the 2015–2016 academic year (collecting an average of $3,400 in aid), compared to 4.4% of those same students who received merit-based aid from state government (collecting an average of $2,700 in aid). Here, then, we see a rather significant skew toward needs-based aid from state governments both in terms of the number of students receiving such aid and the amount of that financial assistance.

One additional large source of needs-based aid for college students—again, completely distinct from the budgets of public universities—comes from the federal government through completion of the Free Application for Federal Student Aid (FAFSA) form.[7] This source of financial assistance for US citizens (and certain eligible noncitizens) is entirely needs-based, although it does require that the student maintain adequate academic progress, remain in good standing with other federal student loan programs, and be enrolled in an accredited academic program. All told, the federal government provides approximately $120 billion in the form of grants, work-study opportunities, and subsidized loans each year to over 13 million students attending all forms of public and private institutions of higher learning and career schools.[8] Approximately $30 billion of that federal money is needs-based aid, the majority of which is handed out through Pell Grants.

Demographic Differences as Related to the Findings

The only significant difference that was found regarding the demographic variables was related to age. Here, a greater percentage of younger respondents prioritized needs-based aid, whereas a greater percentage of older participants believed that needs-based and merit-based aid should be prioritized equally. We would place this finding alongside the age-related differences reported in chapter 3 regarding the allocation of public funding toward teaching, research, and community-based programs and services. Readers will recall that younger citizens put more public money toward community services as compared to older citizens, who allocated more funds to teaching. We believe our use of the same adage to explain those results applies equally here. If you are not a socialist when you are young you have no heart, and if you are not a conservative when you are older you have no head. In this case, younger citizens have a greater stake in lifting up those people in the community who are least able to afford a college degree, whereas older citizens are a bit more circumspect, wishing to have universities balance their distribution of internal funding more equally between those who most need it and those who have demonstrated the greatest abilities.

Political Variable Differences as Related to the Findings

The significant differences that were found regarding our politically oriented variables all seemed to point in a uniform direction. The greatest percentage of Republicans, Independents, and participants with other political affiliations prioritized merit-based aid, mirrored by the finding that the greatest percentage of conservatives, middle of the road, and participants claiming "none of the above" status also prioritized merit-based aid. In contrast, Democrats displayed the largest percentage of respondents who prioritized needs-based aid, echoed by the findings that those respondents with a liberal orientation prioritized needs-based aid.

These findings fit squarely within current discourse surrounding higher education. On the one hand, the progressive (more Democratic, more liberal) higher education agenda certainly has built a more needs-based aid platform, which typically has been headlined by the push for "free college." Inserted into the national conversation by President Barack Obama during his 2015 State of the Union address, the no-cost availability of a higher education experience has been touted as one particularly powerful way to reduce all sorts of economic and racial disparities.[9] In contrast, the more conservative (and more typically Republican) stance is to rail against the lack of merit as a centering criteria within higher education activities, which has been blamed for everything from ballooning student debt to the recent college admission scandals.[10]

The other significant finding was related to predicted 2020 voting behavior. Here, definite 2020 voters displayed greater percentages of respondents who believed that needs-based and merit-based aid should be equally prioritized in comparison to non-definite voters, who believed that merit-based aid should be prioritized. This finding matches the finding reported in chapter 4 regarding the endorsement of definite 2020 voters regarding idea that rural and urban communities should be treated equally. Once again, we view this as a set of harmonized instructions for university administrators and state lawmakers; to wit, those citizens who are most active politically want their public universities to be equally focused on needs-based and merit-based aid.

Contextualizing the Findings Related to Merit-Based and Needs-Based Aid

During the first inaugural address ever to be given on January 20 (instead of March 4 as originally set in the US Constitution),[11] Franklin Delano Roosevelt stated in 1937, "The test of our progress is not whether we add more to the abundance of those who have much; it is whether we provide enough for those who have too little." Some fifty years later, President Ronald Reagan quipped the following in remarks made to the National Governors Association: "[I]f you serve a child a rotten hamburger in America, Federal, State, and local agencies will investigate you, summon you, close you down, whatever. But if you provide a child with a rotten education, nothing happens, except that you're liable to be given more money to do it with. Well, we've discovered that money alone isn't the answer."[12] We bring up these two presidential quotes here because it sets a context for the remainder of this chapter. Essentially, the story of student financial aid seems to have reverberated between these two poles of progressive and conservative political tendencies.

During that period of fifty years in between Roosevelt and Reagan, our nation witnessed the creation and rapid expansion of student aid, beginning with the GI Bill in the aftermath of World War II. This support for armed services veterans in the 1940s was followed three decades later by the development of a slew of government financial assistance programs in the early 1970s, including most prominently the Basic Educational Opportunity Grant (renamed the Pell Grant), the State Student Incentive Grant, and the Supplemental Educational Opportunity Grant. Taken together, these student aid programs represented a "golden age" that allowed colleges and universities to expand their campuses in service to the ever-growing numbers of students seeking a higher education degree.[13]

The original intent of the financial aid programs developed in the 1970s was to increase access to colleges and universities for those who could least afford to attend. As such, the aid was largely needs-based in orientation. While this sort of aid continues to flow toward eligible students, many critics have called for a drastic overhaul of the rather burdensome application and distribution processes.[14] There are those who have stated, in plain and simple fashion, that financial aid as it currently exists is broken.[15] So damaged, in fact, that the entire student-based system must be replaced with arrangements that are focused more on the institution at large instead of the student as an individual recipient.

More recently, however, institutions of higher learning have increasingly offered merit-based aid "to recruit the best, the brightest, and the most likely to contribute to the capital campaign" (75).[16] This growth in merit-based aid has raised questions about whether or not needs-based aid has been hampered in the process.[17] Fortunately, at present, it seems to be the case that, at least at the state level, the growth in merit-based aid has not coincided with a decrease in needs-based aid.[18]

That said, there is no way of knowing how much of that state funding would have been directed toward needs-based aid if the merit-based mechanisms did not exist. There is evidence to suggest that the increased availability of merit-based aid is creating greater inequities inside of the university in terms of the underrepresentation of race/ethnicity and socioeconomic class.[19] Additionally, within the university, it certainly is the case that one more dollar spent on merit-based aid translates into one less dollar spent on needs-based aid. After all, there is only so much money that is doled out in scholarships. It may also be getting worse as the "merit-aid arms race" continues to widen the gap between merit-based aid and needs-based aid.[20] Further, there is some evidence to suggest that universities tend to shift more of their internal allocations toward merit-based scholarships when state appropriations are decreased.[21]

Some caution is warranted here as there is a "blurring line" between merit-based aid and needs-based aid.[22] That is, students who receive a merit scholarship also may qualify for needs-based aid, and, of course, the reverse is true as well. That said, at least one study has indicated that needs-based aid has a more pronounced effect on student success (defined as persistence and on-time graduation) than does merit-based aid.[23]

We would also be remiss if we did not point out that, at least at the federal level, loans have overtaken grants in terms of the primary mechanism for distributing needs-based aid. This metamorphosis of aid has coincided with a shift in "generational responsibilities" in terms of paying for college (from earlier attitudes that parents would pay toward the expectation that the burden fell on the offspring instead), which has been seen as a primary driver of student debt accumulation more recently.[24] Further, it is important to remember that "free college" does not translate into a lack of debt following graduation. Many students who have already received a "free" degree—having paid zero tuition or fees—still borrowed money to pay for room and board, books and supplies, and other living expenses during their college years.[25]

Some conversations about student aid for higher education purposes have employed the concept of deservingness,[26] which is part of a larger set of perceptions among our citizens regarding how a variety of benefits should (or should not) be distributed to those who are less financially secure.[27] A fascinating dissertation was completed in 2018 by Jacob Hester, a doctoral student in political science at the University of Alabama, who used the concept of deservingness to explain differences in state-level decisions about merit-based and needs-based aid.[28] Among other results, Hester reported findings indicating that states with more negative viewpoints about students of color and students from lower socioeconomic backgrounds (referred to as "negative social constructions" in the text to imply a lack of deservingness) tended to apportion fewer taxpayer dollars toward needs-based aid. This same dissertation also provided a thorough discussion of the way that state lawmakers doled out more merit-based aid to students who typically came from more advantaged groups, who are seen in a more positive light and hence are "more deserving."

Clearly, deservingness is in the eye of the beholder. In 2016, the American Talent Initiative (ATI) was launched with the following mission statement: "Talented students from every zip code and income level *deserve* the opportunity to access an excellent college education" (emphasis ours).[29] Created through initial funding from Bloomberg Philanthropies and coordinated by the Aspen Institute, ATI was designed to enroll an additional 50,000 low- and middle-income students by 2025 in those colleges and universities that had the greatest resources and highest graduation rates. In the simplest of terms, this effort was undertaken because these well-endowed institutions of higher learning have overwhelmingly been attended by students from more advantaged families.

Three years into the work of ATI, a report was released that provided an update on this initiative. From the 2015–2016 academic year to the 2017–2018 academic year, progress across all 320 ATI-eligible institutions in the United States was pegged at just over 20,000 new students, or about 40% of the original objective.[30] The 120 institutional members of ATI accounted for 62% (12,837 students) of this increase. By the 2018–2019 academic year, however, continued (albeit modest) gains among some ATI members were offset by declines in the other ATI members, resulting in a net gain of only eight students that year (results from the other ATI-eligible institutions were not accessible at the time of this report's writing).

Clearly, there was worry being expressed about a plateauing effect among ATI members. The report went on to recount four characteristics of those universities that were able to maintain momentum in their enrollment of additional low- and middle-income students. Those features included: (1) a strategic commitment of resources to the ATI objective by senior leaders and board members; (2) not relying solely on "traditional pipelines" to attract new student enrollments; (3) focusing on recruitment and retention efforts with these low- and middle-income students; and (4) making needs-based aid a *top priority*. So, we again come back to the dynamic tension that exists between the provision of needs-based aid and the standard financial models employed at most universities, which, traditionally, are ways of financing higher education through a reliance on tuition dollars and/or the privileging of merit-based aid.

Similar points have been made by other higher education writers who have been paying attention to the more recent plateauing of the ATI numbers. These critiques have including the writing of Michael Nietzel, president emeritus of Missouri State University and former provost at the University of Kentucky. Among other pieces, Dr. Nietzel penned an article that argued for the conversion of merit-based aid into needs-based aid, as well as holding presidents and other senior administrators more directly accountable through specific performance goals and annual evaluations conducted by board members.[31] This scholar also published a book in 2018 entitled *Coming to Grips with*

Higher Education that, among other things, called for a major overhaul of financial aid, again with an emphasis on reducing income disparities in college-going populations.[32]

We had the opportunity to speak to Dr. Nietzel at some length about his work as a senior academic administrator, as well as his experience as a senior policy advisor to then Missouri Governor Jay Nixon. Our conversation began with his policy work, in large part because of his reaction to some of our study's findings. Dr. Nietzel expressed little surprise regarding the significant support for prioritizing merit-based aid, based largely on his familiarity with issues experienced inside of the governor's office. During his tenure as policy advisor, Dr. Nietzel explained, Missouri provided its needs-based financial aid to more than 50,000 students, and merit-based aid to in excess of 6,000 students. He stated that "during difficult financial times, when we cut back on those scholarship programs, the outcry you would hear from the families of those 6,000 students dwarfed what you would hear from the families of students receiving needs-based financial aid. It's a very powerful political audience, because they are largely middle- and upper-class families who have solid connections with their state legislators." In fact, Dr. Nietzel explained, there were at least two instances where the political clout of this relatively small number of constituents was able to hold harmless the merit-based funding while other higher education appropriations were cut.

Moving back to his experience inside of academic institutions, we asked Dr. Nietzel about the flattening out of the ATI statistics. In a nutshell, why are the institutions pledged to increasing the numbers of low- and moderate-income students not able to meet their goals? While not professing to know the exact answer to this question, Dr. Nietzel provided us with some hunches. For starters, he stated his belief that these institutions of higher learning were still fighting against indicators of "so-called quality" that mitigate against the ATI goals. "The easiest thing for these universities to do is to simply accept more students. But they don't do that because they want to maintain things like smaller class size averages and amount of dollars spent per student.

There are far too many ratings-derived indicators of quality that are serving as barriers to the very goals they profess to be seeking."

Another hunch that Dr. Nietzel shared with us was that many senior administrators still see initiatives like ATI as a zero-sum game. In essence, the thinking goes, if they took in more low- and moderate-income students, they fear those admissions would diminish how many "good students" they could accept. As cynical as that may seem, Dr. Nietzel states, the fact remains that universities who pledged their participation in the ATI initiative may have had mixed motives. "It's one thing to sign a letter of intent to get involved because it looks good to do so. It's quite another thing to say that we are going to spend five or ten or fifteen million dollars a year for this purpose. I think there are institutions that didn't want to be viewed as not wanting to make the commitment, but yet are still being pretty cautious and tight with the amount of money they put behind the initiative."

So, we end this chapter where we began. The dynamic tension between needs-based and merit-based aid continues unabated. President Lincoln made clear his understanding of the connection between education and achievement of the "American Dream." And yet, we as a people seem to be ensnared in a very complex set of issues that revolve around who should pay for these educational pursuits, and who should be the beneficiaries of whatever financial aid is offered in support of a college degree.

Summary

We began this chapter with a discussion about how study participants responded to our fourth higher education-based survey question, an item which asked survey respondents to consider—in an ideal world—what should be prioritized for student-directed funding by the public universities of their state: needs-based aid (based on family income) or merit-based aid (based on student academic performance). The general findings related to the entire sample—where almost half of all participants reported that merit-based aid should be prioritized over needs-based aid—was exactly the opposite finding that we had expected. Next, we presented a brief rationale regarding the significant difference that was found regarding the demographic variable of age, equating it to similar findings reported on the first survey item regarding the allocation of taxpayer monies. We also discussed the significant differences found regarding the political variables involving party, orientation, and predicted voting behavior in 2020. We noted that these results were consistent with the progressive and conservative positions situated within the national dialogue currently taking place on higher education topics.

The remainder of this chapter covered several topics that provided some contextualization of these findings, including a comparison of the original intent of the financial aid programs—to increase access to colleges and universities for those who could least afford to attend—versus the growth in merit-based aid; the evidence suggesting that the increased availability of merit-based aid is creating greater inequities inside of the university in terms of race/ethnicity and socioeconomic class underrepresentation; and the more pronounced effect of needs-based aid on student success in comparison to merit-based aid. Further, we also discussed how loans have overtaken grants in terms of distributing needs-based aid, the use of the concept of deservingness to explain differences in state-level decisions about merit-based and needs-based aid, and the initiation and progress of the ATI. Taken together, we hoped that the public's greater understanding of the dynamic tension that exists between needs-based and merit-based aid would provide citizens with the increased opportunity to make informed decisions about where and how they would wish for public universities to prioritize efforts to provide financial assistance to students.

7

National Rankings

The Scourge of Higher Education

You can fool all the people some of the time, and some of the people all the time, but you cannot fool all the people all the time.

Our seventh chapter begins with a quote that may or may not have been said by Abraham Lincoln, but is nonetheless widely attributed to him.[1] Our intention here is to bring attention to an issue that has long vexed a great many people in higher education: the national rankings of our colleges and universities. Focusing on undergraduate education and initiated largely in the 1980s by the likes of periodicals such as *U.S. News and World Report*—there were attempts to rank graduate programs as far back as the 1920s—such attempts to provide a hierarchical ordering of institutions of higher learning seem to have taken on a life of their own.[2] That is, these national rankings have become a big business and as such have been driving many of the most important decisions that leaders of colleges and universities are making about themselves and their futures.[3] All too regrettably, it is a textbook example of the tail wagging the dog.

This chapter begins by examining the data collected on our fifth higher education-based survey question, which asked survey respondents to agree or disagree with the following statement: When it comes to university rankings like *US News and World Report*, it matters a lot to me where the public universities of (my state) are ranked. Possible responses on a five-point Likert-like scale ranged from "strongly agree" to "strongly disagree," with an anchor point in the middle labeled "neither agree nor disagree." Akin to the fourth survey item covered in the previous chapter, the fifth question was based on the theme presented in the *Land-Grant Universities for the Future* book regarding "the focus on rankings versus an emphasis on access and affordability." At the simplest level, we predicted that study participants would endorse the idea that national rankings did not matter, meaning that more respondents would be neutral or would not care (disagree or strongly disagree) about university rankings.

At a more complex level, we hypothesized additionally that *if* respondents endorsed the idea that needs-based aid should be prioritized for funding over merit-based aid in item four, *then* those same participants would be more likely to disagree or strongly disagree about the importance of national rankings. We thought that the opposite case would be equally likely. That is, *if* respondents endorsed the idea that merit-based aid should be prioritized for funding over needs-based aid in item four, *then* those same participants would be more likely to agree or strongly agree about the importance of national rankings. Finally, *if* respondents endorsed the idea that there should be no difference in funding provided for needs-based aid and merit-based aid, *then* those same participants would be more likely to remain neutral about the importance of national rankings.

We made this last more complex set of predictions based on some facts and hunches we had about the relationship between student aid and national rankings. First, we know that one of the levers that universities can pull in order to rise in those rankings is to increase the standardized test scores of their incoming freshman class.[4] In order to attract those students with high SAT and ACT scores, university admissions offices must offer more merit-based aid to those students. In fact, often as not, universities engage in bidding wars, plain and simple. If it is known that your competitors are offering a 50% scholarship for students scoring in the ninetieth percentile on the ACT, for example, then the temptation exists to begin offering a 75% scholarship to your own prospects.

Second, we know there is a bias in these standardized test scores that is tilted toward families with more resources. Students coming from more wealthy school districts, and from more well-to-do families, generally do better on ACT and SAT examinations.[5] As we know from our previous chapter, these are the students who have been privy to more of the merit-based aid that has been offered by universities. Third, and cumulatively, we also suspected that the individuals paying the most attention to national rankings are those individuals who are most in the position to "window shop" the universities their family members will attend, often as not making their final decision based on the combination of the amount of merit-based scholarship being offered from the university with the highest national ranking.

In our initial analyses, we will report on the findings regarding the fifth survey question, as well as testing for potential differences using our demographic and political variables. Once these preliminary analyses are conducted, then we combined the responses from both the fourth and fifth survey questions in order to test our additional hypothesis. All of this was done in preparation for some closer scrutiny we wished to give regarding the impact that national rankings have had on America's public universities.

We will have plenty to say about national rankings following our reporting out on the survey data and analyses we conducted. However, before delving into these results, we do wish to share one story that provides some strong clues about where we are headed with this. Shortly after your second author (Gee) took over the helm of Brown University as its seventeenth president in 1998, his office received a letter of congratulations from one of the ranking firms. The rankings of law schools recently had been compiled, Gee was told in the correspondence, and the College of Law at Brown University had been ranked eighth in the nation. Gee had to write back to let them know that Brown University did not have a law school. You see, when you run a popularity contest that is based largely on reputation (something that was heavily emphasized by these national rankings in earlier days), stubborn facts sometimes get in the way.[6]

Findings from the Overall Sample

The most frequent response to our fifth survey question was that national rankings mattered (agree or strongly agree), endorsed by 400 (47%) participants in the sample. The next most frequent response was the neutral response (neither agree nor disagree), endorsed by 269 (32%) of the respondents. As it turned out, only 162 (19%) of the participants reported that national rankings did not matter (disagree or strongly disagree) when it came to their state's public universities. The remaining individuals (13 individuals, or 2%) chose "I don't know" or skipped this question, and so were excluded from this specific analysis. Hence, we were only marginally correct in our original hypothesis that national rankings would not be important to citizens. To be certain, a full 51% of the sample was neutral or disagreed/strongly disagreed with the statement about the importance of national rankings. However, 47% of the sample had agreed or strongly agreed with that statement.

Further Analyses

In order to test for potential differences in how respondents viewed national rankings, we ran a series of chi-square tests using all demographic variables (gender, age, race/ethnicity, geographic location, and educational attainment) and politically oriented variables (party affiliation, liberal/conservative orientation, actual voting behavior in 2016, and predicted voting behavior in 2020). The results regarding the demographic variables indicated significant effects for gender and educational attainment. We discuss those results in the demographics section below. In turn, the results regarding the political variables indicated significant effects for party and voting behavior in 2016. We report on those results in a separate section for politically oriented variables. Finally, we ran one additional analysis that included responses from both the fourth and fifth survey questions. A significant finding emerged that indicated an interesting and somewhat contradictory (at least to us) pattern of responses whereby those participants who least valued national rankings also were most likely to endorse the provision of merit-based aid over needs-based aid. We discuss those findings and their implications as well below.

Demographic Variables and National Rankings

The comparison of male and female viewpoints regarding the importance of national rankings yielded significant differences ($X^2 = 11.24$, df 2, p<.004) for gender. More specifically, 167 (49%) of males thought that national rankings mattered (agreed or strongly agreed), 91 (27%) were neutral about the importance of national rankings, and 81 (24%) reported that national rankings did not matter (disagreed or strongly disagreed) when it came to their state's public universities. In turn, 233 (47%) of females thought that national rankings mattered (agreed or strongly agreed), 178 (36%) were neutral about the importance of national rankings, and 81 (17%) reported that national rankings did not matter (disagreed or strongly disagreed) when it came to their state's public universities. Hence, although relatively equal percentages of males and females thought that national rankings mattered, those that did not and were male by percentage were more likely to be against national rankings, whereas females by percentage were more likely to be neutral.

Use of the educational attainment variable to examine potential differences regarding the importance of national rankings yielded significant differences ($X^2 = 36.32$, df 4, p < .001). More specifically, 90 (40%) participants with a high school diploma or less educational attainment thought that national rankings mattered (agreed or strongly agreed), 97 (43%) were neutral about the importance of national rankings, and 39 (17%) reported that national rankings did not matter (disagreed or strongly disagreed) when it came to their state's public universities. In turn, 98 (41%) of the participants with some college or an associate's degree thought that national rankings mattered (agreed or strongly agreed), 91 (38%) were neutral about the importance of national rankings, and 52 (21%) reported that national rankings did not matter (disagreed or strongly disagreed) when it came to their state's public universities. Further, 212 (58%) of the participants with a four-year college degree or greater educational attainment thought that national rankings mattered (agreed or strongly agreed), 81 (22%) were neutral about the importance of national rankings, and 71 (20%) reported that national rankings did not matter (disagreed or strongly disagreed) when it came to their state's public universities. Therefore, respondents with a four-year college degree by percentage were more likely to report that national rankings mattered, whereas participants in the lower educational attainment categories by percentage were more likely to be neutral about the importance of national rankings.

Political Variables and National Rankings

Use of political party to examine potential differences regarding the national rankings yielded significant differences ($X^2 = 17.31$, df 6, $p < .008$). More specifically, 78 (44%) of the participants claiming affiliation with the Republican party thought that national rankings mattered (agreed or strongly agreed), 58 (33%) were neutral about the importance of national rankings, and 40 (23%) reported that national rankings did not matter (disagreed or strongly disagreed) when it came to their state's public universities. In turn, 203 (55%) of the participants reporting affiliation with the Democratic party thought that national rankings mattered (agreed or strongly agreed), 100 (27%) were neutral about the importance of national rankings, and 65 (18%) reported that national rankings did not matter (disagreed or strongly disagreed) when it came to their state's public universities. Further, 89 (44%) of the participants with the Independent affiliation thought that national rankings mattered (agreed or strongly agreed), 74 (37%) were neutral about the importance of national rankings, and 38 (19%) reported that national rankings did not matter (disagreed or strongly disagreed) when it came to their state's public universities. Finally, 30 (35%) of the participants claiming some other political affiliation thought that national rankings mattered (agreed or strongly agreed), 37 (43%) were neutral about the importance of national rankings, and 19 (22%) reported that national rankings did not matter (disagreed or strongly disagreed) when it came to their state's public universities. Here, respondents claiming a Democratic affiliation, by percentage, were most likely to report that national rankings mattered, whereas participants claiming any of the other three political affiliations, by percentage, were more likely to be neutral or report that national rankings did not matter.

The comparison of voting behavior in the 2016 presidential election regarding the importance of national rankings yielded significant differences ($X^2 = 14.60$, df 2, $p < .001$) for this political variable. More specifically, 357 (51%) of those respondents who voted in the 2016 election thought that national rankings mattered (agreed or strongly agreed), 214 (31%) were neutral about the importance of national rankings, and 129 (18%) reported that national rankings did not matter (disagreed or strongly disagreed) when it came to their state's public universities. In turn, 43 (33%) of those participants who did not vote in the 2016 election thought that national rankings mattered (agreed or strongly agreed), 55 (42%) were neutral about the importance of national rankings, and 33 (25%) reported that national rankings did not matter (disagreed or strongly disagreed) when it came to their state's public universities. Hence, the greatest number by percentage of participants who voted in the 2016 election thought that national rankings mattered, whereas those who did not vote in the 2016 election were more likely to be neutral or report that national rankings did not matter.

Combining Responses to the Student Aid and National Rankings Items

Combining the student aid and national ranking responses yielded significant differences ($X^2 = 14.63$, df 6, $p < .006$). More specifically, 196 (48%) participants who prioritized merit-based student aid thought that national rankings mattered (agreed or strongly agreed), 133 (32%) were neutral about the importance of national rankings, and 83 (20%) reported that national rankings did not matter (disagreed or strongly disagreed) when it came to their state's public universities. In turn, 134

(44%) of participants who thought that public universities should equally prioritize merit-based and needs-based aid thought that national rankings mattered (agreed or strongly agreed), 112 (37%) were neutral about the importance of national rankings, and 59 (19%) reported that national rankings did not matter (disagreed or strongly disagreed) when it came to their state's public universities. Further, 65 (65%) of participants who prioritized needs-based student aid thought that national rankings mattered (agreed or strongly agreed), 20 (20%) were neutral about the importance of national rankings, and 15 (15%) reported that national rankings did not matter (disagreed or strongly disagreed) when it came to their state's public universities. Therefore, respondents prioritizing needs-based student aid, by percentage, were most likely to report that national rankings mattered, whereas participants prioritizing merit-based aid or reporting that both merit-based and needs-based aid should be equally prioritized, by percentage, were more likely to be neutral or report that national rankings did not matter.

Initial Reactions to the Findings

The general findings related to the entire sample—where just over half of all participants reported that national rankings did not matter—only marginally supported our initial hypothesis. We say this because this majority group was comprised of respondents who were neutral *in combination with* those who reported that they disagreed or strongly disagreed with the statement about university rankings being important. Compare this to the largest single group of respondents, who were those who agreed or strongly agreed with the statement that national rankings mattered. It seemed to be the case that a great many more people cared about national rankings in contrast to what we had assumed.

Comparing Public Sentiment Against What We Know

How does the relatively even split in public support for effort to rank universities found in our present study compare against what we know from other sources? To answer this question, we must begin by recognizing that rankings developed by the mainstream media represent only one of three sets of tools available to indicate differential performance among universities. The other two performance indicators include quality assurance measures developed by accreditors and accountability measures created by governmental agencies. Whereas quality assurance measures are more responsive to university purposes and accountability measures more amenable to policymakers, rankings are viewed as inherently "student friendly" in their orientation.[7]

In terms of public sentiment, then, this "three-legged stool" of performance measures is quite unbalanced in favor of the rankings systems when it comes to how students and their families attempt to discern quality. Some scholars have discussed this as a byproduct of the massification of higher education—that is, the making available to the masses of what was once marketed solely as a luxury item.[8] As we shall see below, however, there are some distinct demographic and political differences that exist within this reverence for national rankings of universities.

Demographic Differences as Related to the Findings

The significant differences that were found regarding the demographic variables of gender and level of educational attainment were interesting. Regarding gender, we must first state that relatively equal percentages of males and females thought that national rankings mattered (agreed or strongly agreed with the statement about rankings). However, males were more likely to be against national rankings (disagree or strongly disagree with the statement about rankings), whereas females by percentage were more likely to be neutral. On the one hand, there seems to be nothing inherently masculine about believing national rankings do not matter. On the other hand, however, being more neutral about a topic area may have some of the hallmarks of a more feminine style of decision-making, at least in terms of not wanting to commit to a stance until all facts are known.[9]

The differences in terms of educational attainment levels were much more explainable in terms of previous literature. In our study, respondents with a four-year college degree were more likely to report that national rankings mattered, whereas participants in the lower educational attainment categories were more likely to be neutral about the importance of national rankings. Educational attainment levels served as our proxy variable for socioeconomic status, and there are studies indicating that national rankings matter more to more affluent students and their families.[10] These individuals are more likely to use the rankings to select the "best schools" that, in turn, will lead to the "best jobs," placement in the "best graduate schools," and other higher outcome quality indicators,[11] even though available research indicated that rankings such as U.S. News and World Report have been shown to be notoriously poor predictors of such outcomes.[12]

Political Variable Differences as Related to the Findings

The significant differences that were found regarding our politically oriented variables were twofold. First, in terms of political party, respondents claiming a Democratic affiliation were most likely to report that national rankings mattered, whereas participants claiming any of the other three political affiliations were more likely to be neutral or report that national rankings did not matter. We make sense of this finding by viewing the item itself as a "vote of confidence" about the value of higher education more generally. That is, we know that recent national polls have found large and growing differences between Democrats and Republicans on the topic of higher education. As but one example, a 2017 Pew Research Center poll indicated that Republicans expressed decidedly more negative views in comparison to their Democrat counterparts when asked if colleges and universities were having a positive impact on the way things were going in our country.[13] In this light, it makes sense to us that participants with Democrat leanings would place higher value on a quality indicator such as national rankings in comparison to respondents with other political affiliations.

Second, the greatest number of participants who voted in the 2016 election thought that national rankings mattered, whereas those who did not vote in the 2016 election were more likely to be neutral or report that national rankings did not matter. Here, we believe that being more politically active would also lend itself to the placement of a higher value on a performance measure of higher education. Voter apathy, on the other hand, would seem to translate readily into a more complacent attitude about such a quality indicator.

Combining the Items Regarding National Rankings and Student Financial Aid

We hypothesized that larger numbers of respondents would not care about national rankings because they would care more about access and affordability as per the theme presented in our *Land-Grant Universities for the Future* book. In hindsight, there are several critical mistakes that we made in formulating this hypothesis. First and foremost, we now know from the previous chapter that we were wrong about the comparatively small amount of public support that was voiced for needs-based aid. Clearly, more substantial numbers of our respondents espoused the prioritization of merit-based aid than we had imagined would be the case. Second, and perhaps more importantly, we made the erroneous assumption that citizens would understand how increases in national ranking tend to hinge on the use of merit-based aid to attract students who scored well on their standardized tests. This lack of knowledge was on display most pointedly within the finding that respondents who prioritized needs-based student aid by percentage were most likely to report that national rankings mattered to them.

Contextualizing the Findings Related to National Rankings

The implications of the findings reported in this chapter are a bit less straightforward than the results we have discussed in previous chapters. We recognize that national rankings are the most "student- and family-friendly" performance indicators available to the public, while at the same time acknowledging (and lamenting, really) that there is likely a scarcity of knowledge among citizens about how colleges and universities move up and down in the national rankings. We would like to use the remainder of this chapter to increase the public's comprehension of exactly what is at stake regarding these university ranking systems.

We begin here by repeating what we believe to be the most scandalous of all difficulties associated with the national rankings. One of the few levers that colleges and universities can exert control over when it comes to their rankings is raising the average standardized test scores of their incoming freshman class. To boost those averages as a strategy for moving up in the rankings, institutions of higher learning throw gobs of merit-based aid at students who have achieved the highest scores on the ACT and SAT examinations. These students tend to be from families that are relatively well off financially, and thus are least likely to require any sort of needs-based aid to attend college.

That last fact is what bothers us so much about the finding that those participants who are most in favor of prioritizing needs-based aid are also those individuals most likely to believe that national rankings matter. You simply cannot have it both ways. If you are in favor of more needs-based aid, you must stand against the importance of those national rankings that place value on the average standardized test scores of the incoming freshman classes (and they virtually all weight these scores rather heavily).[14] If, on the other hand, you are a proponent of more merit-based aid going to students, then go ahead and love those national rankings to your heart's desire!

There are some additional issues that we believe the public should become more knowledgeable about regarding these national rankings. We cannot improve upon the way that Jung Cheol Shin laid out the core problems that have been inherent to these sorts of activities since they first were created: "There have been two challenges to media-led rankings. Their first challenge is in relation to data reliability and the validity of measures. Secondly, ranking does not provide information on how to improve institutional quality because it simply provides ranking information" (27).[15] These are no small challenges, to be certain. If the data are neither reliable nor valid, then the resulting information contained within the rankings are essentially worthless from a scientific standpoint, akin to being a "Mickey Mouse" evaluation system as described by the dean of Harvard's law school.[16] Despite this, at least one scholar[17] has noted the negative correlation between the quality and popularity of a given ranking system (i.e., the less reliable and valid the ranking, the more the public accepts it). Further, even supposing that the data has some reliability and validity claims, the fact that there is no practical connection to any sort of plan for improvement on the factors used in the evaluative formulas renders those rankings inoperative to the colleges and universities being evaluated.

Worse yet is the fact that these dubious rankings increasingly are being adopted by governments and other agencies for quality assurance purposes. Grant Harmon wrote about this concern by stating the following:

> While national quality assurance agencies have generally been critical of ranking systems, pointing to doubtful methodologies, arbitrariness in choice of indicators, lack of transparency and bias towards larger and English speaking research-intensive institutions, both global and national rankings appear to be satisfying public demand for information and are influencing prospective students' choices. Rankings have become new forms of 'super' quality assessments that have considerable attraction for Ministers and the public, especially since quality is expressed in simple numerical scores or league tables. (36)[18]

What this means as a bottom line is that the media-led rankings are supplanting the other forms of performance measures we discussed above that are more amenable to the responsiveness of universities and policymakers. And the ramifications of the rankings affect not only where students decide to attend college, but also how funds flow to universities in the form of research dollars from the government and industry partners and development dollars given through alumni donations.[19] Couple all of this with the fact that these rankings typically change the criteria used within the formulas they employ on an annual or semi-annual basis, rendering year-to-year comparisons moot.[20]

At the end of the day, the leaders of our public universities have permitted media-driven rankings to drive the discussion about what counts as a quality indicator in higher education. Julie Carpenter-Hubin, who has served both as president of the Association for Institutional Research and as chair of the Association of American Universities Data Exchange, does not mince her words when it comes to the present state of feeding university data into these ranking systems. This coeditor of the 2019 book *The Analytics Revolution in Higher Education*[21] recently wrote an essay on this subject matter, stating,

> By complying with the demands of these publishers, colleges and universities have allowed themselves to be evaluated and graded through their rankings, which are more numerous than ever. We have ceded evaluation of our work to entities that have little interaction with us, and whose primary motivation is profit rather than student success. We have allowed them to grade our work without determining first whether they have any qualifications to evaluate us, or whether their metrics are aligned with our purpose. (222)[22]

This is hardly a recipe for understanding how universities compare against one another, let alone how well any single institution of higher learning is doing when it comes to providing a meaningful college degree.

Summary

We began this chapter with a discussion about how study participants responded to our fifth higher education-based survey question, which asked survey respondents to agree or disagree with the statement "when it comes to university rankings like *US News and World Report*, it matters a lot to me where the public universities of my state are ranked." We were only marginally correct in our original hypothesis that national rankings would not be important to citizens, such that 51% of the sample was neutral or disagreed/strongly disagreed with the statement about the importance of national rankings, while 47% of the sample had agreed or strongly agreed with that statement. Additionally, we reported that participants who least valued national rankings were also most likely to endorse the provision of merit-based aid over needs-based aid, the exact opposite of what we had expected.

Next, we presented rationales regarding the significant differences that were found regarding the demographic variables of gender and educational attainment. While we were genuinely puzzled about the impact of gender, we were much more comfortable in making sense of the fact that respondents with a four-year college degree were more likely to report that national rankings mattered. This was so because educational attainment levels were serving as our proxy for socioeconomic status, and the literature was quite clear that more affluent students and their families cared more about national rankings.

Further, we reported on the significant differences found on political variables involving party and voting behavior in 2016. We thought the finding that participants with Democrat leanings were more supportive of national rankings indicated that they were placing a higher value on higher education overall in comparison to respondents claiming any other political affiliation. Regarding the finding that those participants who voting in the 2015 US presidential election were more likely to believe that national rankings mattered, we offered the thought that being more politically active also lent itself to the placement of a higher value on a performance measure of higher education.

The remainder of this chapter covered several topics that provided some contextualization of these findings. We recognized that national rankings are the most "student- and family-friendly" performance indicators available to the public at present. At the same time, we also lamented the scarcity of knowledge among citizens about how colleges and universities move up and down in these national rankings, and thus we laid out several of the main challenges surrounding the information and formulas used to derive these rankings. This included the fact that one of the few levers that colleges and universities can exert control over when it comes to their rankings is raising the average standardized test scores of their incoming freshman class, which typically is accomplished through use of merit-based aid (and all too often at the expense of needs-based aid). We also noted the problems associated with the reliability and the validity of measures used within the formulas of these national rankings, as well as the fact that the factors being employed in these rankings typically were divorced from any sort of steps that universities could take to better themselves (and thus their rankings). Finally, we also made mention of the fact that these media-led rankings have been supplanting other forms of performance measures over time, even while these rankings changed their evaluative criteria from year to year.

We began this chapter with Lincoln's (likely apocryphal) statement that you cannot fool all the people all the time. Unfortunately, to date it seems to be the case that a great number of people have been and currently are being hoodwinked into thinking that national rankings do matter, at least in terms of their serving as a reliable and valid way to compare one university against another. Absent any display of leadership on the part of university administrators and governing board members alike, the citizens of our nation seem destined to have their public universities driven by some rather foolish notions about what performance in higher education looks like in America.

8

Jobs and Politics and Sports, Oh My!

Our government rests in public opinion. Whoever can change public opinion, can change the government, practically just so much. Public opinion, on any subject, always has a "central idea," from which all its minor thoughts radiate.

O ur eighth chapter begins with a quote from a speech that Abraham Lincoln gave in 1856 to a Republican banquet in Chicago. In many ways, this focus on public opinion was a foreshadowing of the attention the future president would give to the power of public sentiment. In fact, historians see this specific speech as having laid the foundation for the remarks Lincoln would later give in his debates with Stephen Douglas,[1] which provided us with the related quote that we used to begin our second chapter. We will get back to this idea of a "central idea" in a moment.

The present chapter reports on responses made to the sixth and final survey item, which asked participants to respond to the following open-ended question: If there was one thing that the public universities in your state could do that would make you feel more comfortable about how taxpayer money was being used to support higher education, what would it be? As noted earlier, we predicted that participants would provide open-ended responses that would fall into several categories related to the seven themes presented in the *Land-Grant Universities for the Future* book. Based on our work on the formula for success contained in our previous writings, at the very least, we anticipated that the greatest amount of attention would be paid to how universities were spending the money that was provided by public tax dollars, as well as issues surrounding how much time faculty members were teaching in the classroom as compared to other activities in which they were engaged (and especially those efforts related to research and the provision of services to communities). That said, we readily acknowledged the fact that we interviewed only those individuals connected to higher education in our previous study. Hence, we were open to the possibility of other, as-yet-to-be identified themes developing out of this open-ended question.

The Data

We decided to use our first 600 respondents (100 from each of the six states we targeted) in our qualitative data analyses to provide equal probability of citizens from different locales having their views represented in the output. As such, a total of 488 (81%) participants used for this portion of our analyses had typed something in the text box provided for the sixth and final survey item. All 100 citizens (100%) from Ohio provided a response. In descending order of participation, there were 92 New Yorkers, 79 Californians, 79 Texans, 77 Floridians, and 61 West Virginians who also provided some sort of open-ended response.

The Analysis Strategy

The open-ended responses were deconstructed into themes and emergent patterns that matched the purposes of this study. Our strategies for analyzing the qualitative data included both open coding[2] and axial coding.[3] A file of the open-ended responses was merged into a qualitative data analysis software package known as NVivo[4] and coded using an interactive process. Our colleague, Deanna Wilkinson, an expert in qualitative methods, began the data analysis process by reading through all open-ended responses in order to create our initial set of categories. Each code was explicitly defined by Dr. Wilkinson (and where appropriate, she assigned multiple codes), and the initial categories subsequently were grouped together as an organized family of ideas (also referred to as "tree nodes").

From there, your authors read through all the same open-ended responses as a consistency check, as well as to explore alternative interpretations. Where necessary, we discussed anomalies until we reached consensus regarding the best interpretation of each open-ended response. Mirroring other qualitative research, our final coding structure for the open-ended responses emerged from an iterative process that fit the data to themes that were relevant to our study.[5]

Overall Findings

In total, there were five themes that contained 100 or more open-ended responses (figure 1). In descending order, those categories included access and affordability (259 open-ended responses), financial stewardship (174 open-ended responses), faculty and the teaching mission (148 open-ended responses), community focus and outcomes (146 open-ended responses), and student-centered experiences (101 open-ended responses). In addition, there were four additional themes that contained less than 100 but more than 10 open-ended responses. Those categories included campus climate issues (76 responses), communicating with the public (75 open-ended responses), college sports (39 open-ended responses), and research (26 open-ended responses).

There also were two categories with less than 10 open-ended responses containing items that did not fit well inside of any of the other themes, including diversity issues (seven open-ended responses) and one single item that advocated for every university to have a garden that supplied meals for students (figure 2). While we will not be attending to these open-ended responses any further in this chapter, we include notation of their existence here because our plans to conduct additional quantitative and qualitative analyses with the data

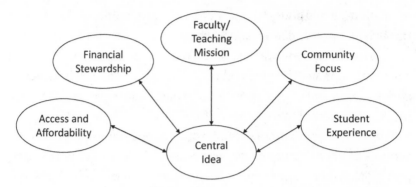

Figure 1. Five "Central Idea" Themes as Related to the Open-Ended Reponses

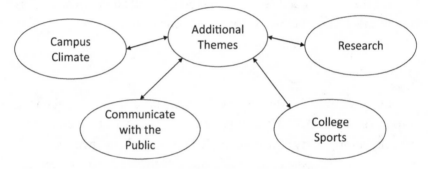

Figure 2. Emergent Themes from the Open-Ended Responses

generated by the eventual inclusion of citizens from additional states may increase the salience of these (and other heretofore undiscovered) themes. That said, we will deal with the issue in a much more significant manner in our last chapter.

As Lincoln noted in the quote that began this chapter, public opinion is based on a central idea. We believe we have uncovered a central idea that has five spokes in terms of paths to helping citizens feel more comfortable about how taxpayer money is being used to support higher education. Each of those spokes, which largely fulfill our predicted outcomes, will be examined in more detail next. Following this, we also wish to dissect the four additional themes that, while not reaching the same level of frequency, nonetheless are thought to be worthy of further exploration. While they were not predicted by our previous work, we believe they may hold additional clues that may help improve the relationship between our public universities and the citizens they are supposed to be serving.

A Central Idea with Five Major Themes

The most frequently mentioned issue on the topic of increasing citizen comfort with the use of taxpayer money at public universities revolved around the issue of access and affordability (221 open-ended responses in total). As a reminder, this topic fits squarely inside of the themes that were developed in our previous land-grant universities book. More specifically in terms of that prior work (as well as reflecting issues covered in chapters 6 and 7 of the present book), we discussed this as a dynamic tension concerned with "the focus on rankings versus an emphasis on access and affordability."

The responses that came together to comprise this access and affordability theme can be divided further into several subcategories. The subcategory containing the most frequently mentioned open-ended responses were issues related to *reducing the burden of tuition and fees* (84 responses), represented by a response such as this: "Keep tuition and fees low for everyone." Comments related to *scholarships and other forms of aid* (55 open-ended responses) represent a second subcategory within this theme, characterized by this statement: "Make more money available for needs-based scholarships as long as they meet academic criteria. I also wish more work-study opportunities were available." Another subcategory might best be labeled *fair access to higher education* (52 open-ended responses), displayed in comments like this: "Help children from middle class families attend college. It's not fair that the wealthy get to go with no worries about finances and the poor get to go because the government caters to them." Finally, a smaller set of responses focused more specifically on *student debt reduction* (18 open-ended responses) such as this one: "More free grants given to students, so they are not left with so much debt after graduation."

Financial stewardship, the second most frequently mentioned theme (212 open-ended responses), was also predictable from our previous work. It is related to the most frequently mentioned topic reported in our previous book; that is, the dynamic tension surrounding "concerns about funding declines versus the need to create efficiencies." Unsurprisingly, the subcategory with the most open-ended responses was labeled the *need to reduce spending* (93 open-ended responses). Comments that encouraged public universities to reduce spending often as not were targeting administrative bloat, a perception represented well by this simple yet direct comment: "Eliminate the layers of administration." Interestingly, a second subcategory surrounding financial stewardship expressed the *need to increase spending* (44 open-ended responses). Those participants that urged greater expenditures were typically focused on resources flowing to the instructional mission, displayed in comments like "more money for teachers in order to attract more and better teachers" and "more basic learning facilities instead of these fancy buildings with lots of wasted space." One additional subcategory (55 open-ended responses) within this theme focused on *transparency in spending*, reflected in comments such as this: "Publish the financials showing where the money was spent in an easy to access location."

The 148 open-ended responses within the faculty and the teaching mission theme were also predictable from the work reported in our land-grant universities book, especially when we wrote about the need to balance research prowess against both teaching activities and community-based services. Responses largely fell into two prominent subcategories that corresponded closely to the name of this theme. Those participants commenting on the faculty members themselves (76 open-ended responses) were looking for a greater emphasis on *time spent on instruction*. Here is a representative quote in this regard: "Universities should specify the number of hours professors spend in the classroom compared to research hours. Decrease classroom instruction hours by graduate assistants while requiring at least 60% of instruction be done by professors." By extension, those participants who spoke about the teaching mission itself (72 open-ended responses) were largely advocating for more *practical and vocational coursework*. This latter subcategory contained a variety of comments such as "provide courses that will relate to real life issues" and "concentrate on making students ready for the real world with practical information such as managing finances and keeping a job."

The fourth theme involving community focus and outcomes (146 open-ended responses) is lodged within several themes reported in our previous work. For example, actions taken to meet the needs of communities is part of the closer-to-home impact that was juxtaposed against the desire for global and international reach discussed in our previous book. A community focus is also inherent to the dynamic tension between meeting the needs of rural versus urban citizens. Finally, our earlier writing also reported on the need to balance research prowess against both teaching activities and the provision of community-based services. Responses within this theme either fell into one coherent subcategory (32 open-ended responses) or became part of a rather lengthy list of activities and services desired by respondents. The subcategory took on the form of *understanding community needs*, and this topic is well-represented by the following quote: "Understand what this new generation of high school graduates needs/wants out of a University. Also understand what the older generation now needs/wants. It's all changing." The list of activities, on the other hand, spelled out exactly what these participants wanted to see from their public universities, including help for senior citizens, foster care youth, students in local school districts, adult learners, and so on.

The fifth and final spoke of the central idea we wish to develop in terms of paths to helping citizens feel more comfortable about how taxpayer money is being used to support higher education is the theme surrounding student-centered experiences (101 open-ended responses). Although we devoted an entire chapter to students in our *Land-Grant Universities for the Future* book, they are never referenced directly in any of the themes that were developed in that previous work. Indirectly, students are the reference point for the dynamic tension expressed between "the benefits of higher education versus the devaluation of a college diploma." That said, we wish to view this theme as the first significant expansion of our prior efforts.

There are two primary subcategories within the student-centered experiences theme. The first and largest subcategory (44 open-ended responses) concerns *career assistance*, and this is exactly what it sounds like. Here is a representative quote: "I would like to see more of an emphasis on job placement and job readiness for all degree programs. This could be accomplished through more company partnerships and sponsorships, intern programs, etc." The second subcategory involves the *provision of student support* (19 open-ended responses), much of which concerned the offering of services related to mental health, special needs populations, and nontraditional learners. For example, one participant stated, "I think more money could be used for those who are needy and need mental health services."

Four Additional Emergent Themes

As noted above, there were four additional themes generated from our analyses of the qualitative data, each of which contained less than 100 but more than 10 open-ended responses. The largest of these involved campus climate issues (76 open-ended responses), a theme that was not directly traceable to our previous work. Over half of these comments (46 open-ended responses) fell into a subcategory labeled *political views and indoctrination*, representing concern that students were being force fed a left-leaning political agenda in their classrooms. Here is a representative quote: "Prohibit socialist doctrine from being pushed by professors." A second subcategory that emerged was *free speech rights* (10 open-ended responses), exemplified as follows: "Ensure that all opinions are equally representative in public discussions. Stop biased repression of free speech." Two still smaller subcategories within this theme included *concern for equal rights* (8 open-ended responses) and *safety from violence* (7 open-ended responses). Examples of these latter two subcategories include "equal learning opportunities for all" and "zero tolerance for assault and bigotry" respectively.

Next in frequency is the communicating with the public theme (75 open-ended responses), another theme that was not directly traceable to our previous work. Remarks comprising this theme fell almost exclusively in one of two equally sized subcategories. The first of these subcategories is *proof of impact* (34 open-ended responses), which is represented by the following quote: "Communicate how taxpayer money is being spent and show a positive impact of taxpayer money." The second of these subcategories is *routine reports* (34 open-ended responses), exemplified by this statement: "Full, itemized public disclosure of teaching, research, and administrative expenses and payrolls, including individual salaries and benefits."

The third theme to be discussed here surrounds college sports (39 open-ended responses), yet another theme not directly traceable to our previous work. Responses here almost exclusively fell into the subcategory *reduce athletic expenditures* (37 open-ended responses), represented by the following quote: "Less athletics, more STEM. Does America want to be known for football?" There also were two responses that represented a subcategory labeled *pay student athletes*, which is exactly what it sounds like. The two statements here were "pay student athletes" and "paying athletes."

The fourth and final theme was centered on research (26 open-ended responses). We end with a theme that was predicated on our previous work reported in our land-grant universities book. Here, we point to the dynamic tension between "research prowess and excellence in teaching and community-based services." Within this theme, almost half of the comments (12 open-ended responses) are contained in a subcategory labeled *research as a priority*. The representative quote is this: "Research to solve/cure medical and psychological issues would be great." The other responses were not categorizable into another subcategory, but rather reflected a variety of opinions about what research efforts should entail, such as "more reputable research publications" and "publicize the efforts and successes of research."

Contextualizing the Central Idea Thematic Findings

The five themes forming the "central idea" of public sentiment regarding what colleges and universities could do to make citizens more comfortable about how taxpayer money was being used to support higher education all covered material that would be familiar to readers of our previous book. Each theme was readily identifiable as related to earlier themes we had elucidated from interview data or, in the case of the student experience category, could be lodged in the contents of a previous book chapter.

On the surface, then, we seem to have generated some evidence regarding the dependability of these themes. That is, we found the open-ended responses of citizens mirrored many of the same issues found in our conversations with university leaders. At the same time, the results of our present thematic analysis allowed us to gain a much greater in-depth understanding of citizen perceptions of these themes. We also recognized how the qualitative data allowed for a deeper understanding of the quantitative results generated from our other survey questions.

For example, let us begin with the central idea theme that garnered the greatest amount of open-ended responses: access and affordability. There were four subcategories that emerged within this theme: reducing the burden of tuition and fees, scholarships and other forms of aid, fair access to higher education, and student debt reduction. Of these, we dealt most extensively with issues surrounding scholarships and other forms of aid in our quantitative survey questions, especially in terms of the results that were presented in chapter 6 regarding merit-based aid and needs-based aid. In the beginning of that chapter, we reported that almost 80% of students attending four-year public universities received some form of financial aid. We also reported that only 1% of the sample from our survey endorsed the statement, "I do not believe public universities should provide either needs-based or merit-based aid."

Hence, an overwhelming majority of students receive financial aid, and almost every citizen surveyed believed they should be receiving some form of this aid. The only quibble was in the type of financial assistance—merit versus need—that public universities should be offering. If we couple this sentiment with the thematic subcategories surrounding the need to reduce the burden of tuition and subsequent debt that students carry as the result of the price tag on a college degree, we imagine that survey participants who mentioned these issues were of the belief that the amount of aid received by this overwhelming majority of students was simply not enough.

The final subcategory under the central idea theme of access and affordability dealt with fair access to higher education. Overlaying this topic on top of everything else within this theme leads us to the conclusion that universities seeking to increase the public's comfort in how taxpayer money is being used to support higher education must pay closer attention to the specific needs of working-class families. Ironically, this might help to explain why there was such robust support for merit-based aid in the sample. If needs-based aid is seen as unobtainable for a certain segment of society—those making just enough money to be disqualified for such financial assistance—then merit-based aid may be the only type of resource available for these families.

Financial stewardship, the second most frequently mentioned theme, included three subcategories: the need to reduce spending, the need to increase spending (on instruction), and transparency in spending. There are few surprises to be found here. University presidents and governing boards are very aware of the public's desire to see more efficient use of taxpayer dollars by institutions of higher learning, and they feel pressure to stem the rise of tuition costs. Similarly, the demand for transparency has been heard loud and clear by academic leaders. In response, many universities have followed the lead of companies in publishing employee salaries and other annual expenditures in their budgets.[6] The final subcategory in this thematic domain—increasing spending on instructional activities—is a perfect segue to our next theme. One gets the sense that many citizens are baffled by the complexity of the modern university's mission, and they wish for a simplified version of higher education that focuses mainly on teaching and learning activities.

Faculty and the teaching mission, the third central idea theme, was composed of two subcategories: time spent on instruction and practical and vocational coursework. In addition to connecting to the previously discussed theme, this focal area is firmly rooted in the findings we shared in chapter 3 regarding the distribution of taxpayer money in terms of expenditures on teaching, research, and community outreach programs and services. We reported that participants on average believed almost half of those public funds should be spent directly on teaching, with the remainder divided evenly between research and community engagement. In our third chapter, we also discussed the sentiment surrounding "the great disappearing teaching load," whereby faculty members were viewed as spending ever decreasing amounts of time in the classroom. What the qualitative findings added to these results is the sense that citizens believe that instructional activities should have a practical side, mostly in terms of being directly applicable to the world of work.

The fourth theme involving community focus and outcomes was comprised of one coherent theme—understanding community needs—and a list of specific activities related to meeting those community needs. In chapter 1, we focused quite extensively on the need to better understand the needs of the community, where we included a discussion of the principles surrounding a servant university mentality. We also took on the role of Cooperative Extension Services as a leading contributor to community outreach and engagement activities in chapter 3, explored urban and rural community issues in chapter 4, and, in chapter 5, we examined issues regarding the closer-to-home impact of the university. What the qualitative findings revealed was that, first, the survey participants viewed the university as necessarily being involved with citizens across the lifespan and, second, that a veritable laundry list of activities could be provided as examples of just how the public would like to have those connections made.

The fifth and final spoke of the central idea is the theme surrounding student-centered experiences and its two main subcategories: career assistance and the provision of student support. Here, again, we see the survey participants' preference for the more practical aspects of the educational process in terms of job readiness and placement discussed in the fourth central idea theme. The provision of student support generated a different set of expectations, however. There was a tendency to identify specific services for college students who were faced with various challenges to degree completion, a nuance from the qualitative data that was not detected in any of our more quantitative findings. There is an explicit recognition that some students are disadvantaged in their pursuit of a college education, and citizens wish to see public universities take certain actions to level the playing field for them.

Contextualizing the Findings Related to the Emergent Themes

Most of the additional emergent themes related to public sentiment regarding what colleges and universities could do to make citizens more comfortable about how taxpayer money was being used to support higher education broke some new ground for us, at least in terms of taking us beyond the material we covered in our land-grant universities book. Campus climate issues, communicating with the public, and college sports were all brand-new topics to consider in terms of elaborating on issues mentioned by the university presidents and chancellors we interviewed for that previous work. On the other hand, research as a priority represented an extension of earlier comments raised by these higher education leaders.

Let us begin with the emergent theme that garnered the greatest amount of open-ended responses: campus climate issues. This theme contained four subcategories, which together presented a kaleidoscope tale of what is happening on America's campuses today. The subcategory concerning political views and indoctrination is nested in an ongoing debate about the ways in which universities impact the ideologies of college students. On the right, there is great concern about the promulgation of a leftist agenda.[7] In contrast, individuals from the left and center believe this worry is dramatically overblown.[8] Nevertheless, we see solid documentation of the public's apprehensions here, real or otherwise.

The second subcategory regarding free speech rights is a related topic. Political factions from the left and the right are seemingly of one mind on this issue, at least on the surface. The American Civil Liberties Union (ACLU)[9] discusses the need for campus free speech as a critical component of higher education just as vociferously as the Foundation for Individual Rights in Education (FIRE).[10] The cases these two organizations taken on, however, at least at times, would seem to have radically different underpinnings. Nevertheless, the comments of our survey participants regarding campus free speech tended to be more neutral in orientation.

The final two subcategories in this emergent theme provided further variations on similar subject matter. The concern for equal rights certainly is connected to free speech issues, but it is also grounded in topics surrounding basic human rights. So, too, is the focus on safety from violence. In both cases, the citizens polled in our survey are expressing the belief that one can say whatever they wish, without fear of physical harm, and without inciting the intimidation and injury of others.

The second emergent theme was communicating with the public, which contained the two equally sized subcategories of proof of impact and routine reports. Proof of impact was a call for evidence that supported the efforts of the university in its various and sundry activities. We imagined that citizens were asking to view documentation regarding the effectiveness of teaching efforts, the productivity of research activities, and the yield of actions undertaken to engage communities. While university personnel are used to seeing these sorts of reports, clearly those same materials do not reach citizens in a digestible form on any sort of regular basis. The second subcategory comes into the frame as a request to see how the taxpayer dollars are being applied to these efforts. In its most simple form, the university spent this much money on this activity, and this is what resulted.

The third emergent theme surrounded college sports, with the two subcategories of reducing athletic expenditures and paying student athletes. The big business aspect of college sports has been grabbing headlines for many years now. A variety of actions have been taken as part of a push to share some of the $14 billion dollars in total revenue generated each year with those athletes.[11] Class-action lawsuits have been brought by former collegiate players regarding the use of their names and likenesses,[12] and at least one university football team attempted to organize themselves in a union.[13] Despite setbacks, some form of revenue-sharing with athletes seems all but inevitable, and our survey participants reflect that sentiment.

In addition, however, the underbelly of college sports has also been exposed, in part as the result of scandals that have rocked universities such as Michigan State, Ohio State, and Penn State.[14] These ignominies have paralleled the closer inspection of athletics department budgets. The bigger programs have little motivation to show a profit on paper, which has been said to "incentivize wild spending" on coaching salaries and other administrative positions.[15] Other athletics programs, in contrast, are often making ends meet only through use of tuition dollars to subsidize the activities.[16] Either way, survey respondent comments about the expenditures reflect the fact that citizens are not pleased with the amount of money being spent on college sports, especially in comparison to other expenditures.

The fourth and final emergent theme centered on research, which contained the single subcategory of research as a priority. We find ourselves back on familiar ground here, as research was a component of two themes discussed in our previous book. The presidents and chancellors we interviewed believed that there was a need to balance research prowess with excellence in both teaching and community engagement, and they also understood there was a demand to balance the theoretical (basic research) with the practical (applied research). What we obtained from the qualitative data generated from the open-ended text question in our survey was some insight into the fact that first, research was valued by some citizens, and two, the various directions that citizens would wish for the public university's empirical efforts to be aimed for the most part were more pragmatic in orientation. In some respects, this connects us back to the second emergent theme discussed above. To paraphrase, the university has spent this much money on research, and this is what was produced as a result.

Summary

We began this chapter with a description of the methodology we used to analyze the qualitative data generated from our final survey question. From these efforts, we first described five themes that together formed a "central idea" that connected back to evidence generated in our previous work with higher education leaders. In brief, these themes replicated many of the topics we had uncovered in that earlier book, including access and affordability, financial stewardship, faculty and the teaching mission, community focus and outcomes, and student-centered experiences. Next, we described four additional themes that were more emergent in nature, at least from the standpoint of not having been previously raised by the higher education leaders we had interviewed. Those categories included campus climate issues, communicating with the public, college sports, and research.

The remainder of this chapter provided some contextualization of these findings. For the central idea themes, we discussed topics related to a variety of subcategories that included: reducing the burden of tuition and fees, scholarships and other forms of aid, fair access to higher education, student debt reduction, the need to reduce spending, the need to increase spending (on instruction), transparency in spending, time spent on instruction, practical and vocational coursework, understanding community needs, career assistance, and the provision of student support. In turn, for the emergent themes we examined issues related to subcategories that included: political views and indoctrination, free speech rights, concern for equal rights, safety from violence, proof of impact, routine reports to communities, reducing athletic expenditures, paying student athletes, and research as a priority.

9

Disdain the Beaten Path

The Year 2020 as a Turning Point
for the American Public University

Towering genius disdains a beaten path. It seeks regions hitherto unexplored. It sees no distinction in adding story to story, upon the monuments of fame, erected to the memory of others. It denies that it is glory enough to serve under any chief. It scorns to tread in the footsteps of any predecessor, however illustrious. It thirsts and burns for distinction.

O ur ninth and final chapter begins with a quote from one of Abraham Lincoln's earliest known speeches. Entitled "The Perpetuation of Our Political Institutions," it was an address given in January 1838 to a Springfield, Illinois, group called the Young Men's Lyceum of Springfield, Illinois. Lincoln was not yet 30 years of age at the time, yet he was serving his third term as a member of the Illinois House of Representatives. At one level, the future president was responding to a racially charged incident in St. Louis that had occurred a few weeks earlier. At yet another deeper level, however, Lincoln also was framing a discussion about the fragility of public institutions, especially when human passions overtake reason.[1]

Throughout this book we have been focused on America's public universities, a large set of public institutions of higher learning that have been educating our citizens for over 150 years. Is some fragility beginning to show within these institutions in ways that would have been familiar to Lincoln? Further, is the detection of any sort of instability a function of human passions overtaking reason? And if so, can the inhabitants of these universities disdain the beaten path and move toward a greater reimagination of their covenant with the citizens they are supposed to be serving?

The events of 2020 certainly have placed various stress tests on our public universities. Our country, and the world for that matter, had not seen a public health crisis like the COVID-19 pandemic in over 100 years. Additionally, the social unrest following the deaths of several African American citizens—coming amid the coronavirus outbreak—was a throwback to protests that had inflamed our nation over 50 years ago. In combination, these calamities had presented our public universities with a set of unique challenges. So much so, in fact, that we may have been forced off the beaten path with no discernable way back.

Further, many observers of the 2020 US presidential election's aftermath had also been fraught with concern about the fragility of other public institutions, including the foundations of our constitutional democracy itself.[2] Donald Trump's refusal to accept the fact that he lost both the popular vote and the electoral college—reacting instead by launching false claims of widespread voter fraud and other election irregularities—created widespread anxiety about the peaceful transfer of power the United States had enjoyed since the presidential election of 1800.[3] Truly, the year 2020 had been among the most unprecedented of times.

It is our belief that we are never going to return to what once was the slow and steady reality of higher education in this country. Instead, our public universities must be ready for the many and rapid changes that await us all, now and into the foreseeable future. Personally, we thirst and burn for this distinction, this "new normal" that we now face.[4] Hence, we welcome the demand to create different ways of approaching our mission to develop talent through our teaching and learning activities, to create innovation through our research efforts, and to become great stewards of and for the communities we were designed to serve.

With this spirit of adventure, we wished to apply our study's findings to the crossroads in which our nation's public universities now find themselves. To do so, we first took one more look at the overall theme of our book—the need to pay closer attention to public sentiment regarding higher education—and examined some of the difficulties associated with university leaders having limited access to the opinions of the public at large. We then moved to interpret some of the main findings of our study in the context of events that had occurred throughout the year 2020.

First, we described the results of another brief survey we conducted amid the twin pandemics of COVID-19 and racial injustice, with specific attention paid to the manner that higher education administrators could and should access this sort of information. Next, we selected several topics covered in our main study that deserved additional emphasis, including the ways that universities distributed funding across various activities, the future of international higher education, and the pursuit of national rankings. We then tackled several issues that were tied directly to the themes generated from the qualitative data reported in chapter 8, including access and affordability, community engagement, and college sports. We also discussed issues that specifically focused on diversity and inclusion concerns, even though this topical area was accorded less significant status in terms of the themes that were developed out of the qualitative data. Further thoughts were shared about student mental health concerns, especially as they had been aggravated by decisions made throughout the pandemic about in-person instruction and the residential experience of college life. We end this chapter and our book with some final thoughts about just how far higher education will find itself off the beaten path in the third decade of the twenty-first century.

Paying Closer Attention to Public Sentiment

In our first chapter, we provided an overview of various opportunities and threats that institutions of higher learning had been facing prior to those that would manifest themselves in the year 2020. More than anything else, this chapter underscored our rationale for paying closer attention to public sentiment on higher education issues. While we acknowledged various efforts undertaken by higher education leaders to better understand their institutional strengths and weaknesses in the eyes of the public, we provided ample criticism that these leaders had not bothered to ask community stakeholders directly what they wanted and needed from their public universities.

We do not believe that senior university administrators have displayed a complete lack of engagement with the public, of course. Rather, our critique centers first and foremost on the truncated audiences that typically are privy to having these sorts of conversations. As we recount below, the people who consistently have the ear of university leaders are not exactly a representative sample of those citizens who are supposed to be served by the institution. Second, there is a noticeable lack of strategy in place for acting on whatever public opinion is shared with university leaders. Presidents and their staff members tend to flit from one social gathering to the next (or in the age of coronavirus, from one Zoom meeting to the next), with next to nothing in place that assembles the opinions being shared in those encounters, nor with any set of processes that readies the university for possible response.

So exactly who does have the ear of the university? As is often said, follow the money and you will find your answer. For starters, higher education officials are in regular communication with their congressional and senatorial delegations at both the state and federal levels (and even more discussion ensues during those yearly of biennial budget hearings, as one might imagine). University presidents and government relations representatives listen very closely to the wishes of legislators—they hold the purse strings to a significant amount of state support for universities, after all—and, in turn, talk with them about higher education issues, both in general and regarding the challenges and opportunities facing their institutions more specifically. The savviest of these higher education leaders must explain the good works and good deeds of their universities to legislators with a keen political eye kept on how that information can be packaged in as apolitical a message as is possible.

To a certain degree, senior administrators have also gauged public opinion through their relationships with those individuals who donate their time and treasure to any number of development initiatives: student scholarships, new and renovated buildings, endowed chairs, medical treatments, among others. Obviously, there is an immense challenge within universities to not have donors drive the direction of universities simply because they have given money. On the other hand, listening to what donors have to say and understanding their own views of the world has been a very important source of information to presidents and other institutional leaders in gauging public opinion and its impact on the day-to-day functioning of the university. Universities, therefore, cannot ignore, nor should they, the views of those who invest in the institution, many of whom are alumni or immediate members of their families.

Beyond direct fiscal influence, senior university administrators have also gauged public sentiment through the careful monitoring of opinion pieces that are published in local newspapers and otherwise expressed over the airwaves and through social media. Effective university leaders engage with these more vocal constituencies by carefully, concisely, and vigorously communicating certain core principles of the university that should be held by all those who love and respect the institution, both external and internal. The most successful of these leaders recognize that they should not only listen to these expressions of sentiment, but also help to shape those opinions through the contributions of their own op-eds, as well as sitting for interviews and posting relevant information on their own social media accounts.

Finally, some university leaders have been practical enough to gauge public opinion through conversations they hold with their own faculty members. They, too, are members of the public, of course. While some may hold a more rarified view of the world from inside the ivory tower, many other faculty members regularly engage in a straightforward fashion with various public constituents through their teaching, research, and service efforts. Thus, these engaged faculty members are capable of effectively communicating the wants and needs of those stakeholders with whom they are working most directly. Special attention to the interactions that Extension faculty members have with the public (discussed in chapter 3) bear particular significance here, as these professionals are geographically located in each of the counties served by the land-grant university of each state and are thus involved in dialogue with state citizens on an almost daily basis.

So, we have given credit where credit is due. Higher education leaders do have access to public sentiment through the interactions they maintain with legislators, their donor relations activities, through monitoring traditional and social media, and within those conversations they choose to have with faculty members who are regularly engaging with community members through their work. Unfortunately, as we alluded above, these individuals by no means whatsoever can be thought of as a representative sample of the constituency served by the university. In fact, these people tend to be more affluent, more well-educated, and more technologically sophisticated, among other distinctive traits.

In addition, we have also asserted that there is no sense that university leaders are working to coordinate the messages being received among these many and varied discussions, save for one very constricted topical area: financial support for the institution. While attention to this self-serving issue is logical, it is both narrow-minded and, ultimately, counterproductive. If the only thing that universities are willing to regularly discuss in public are its own finances, that institution is not going to make most people's priority lists. As we will observe below, there are many potential strengths and glaring weaknesses regarding public perceptions of universities that have been exposed as the result of events occurring throughout 2020.

A Path Hitherto Untraveled

What kind of effort would it take to engage citizens in terms of getting feedback on how public universities are doing in responding to the needs of those communities they were designed to serve? As it turns out, not much, especially for institutions of higher learning that are chock full of researchers who know how to conduct opinion polls. To prove our point, we spent a relatively small amount of money to test our ability to engage approximately 5,000 citizens across the nation in a brief survey regarding the response of public universities to both COVID-19 and issues surrounding racial justice.[5] Going back to the same American Population Panel we utilized for the survey (discussed in more detail in chapter 2), but expanding our sample parameters to include citizens across the entire nation, we asked the following two questions:

1. How strongly do you agree or disagree with the following statement: The public universities of my state have responded to the COVID-19 pandemic in ways that have directly benefited my community.
2. How strongly do you agree or disagree with the following statement: Currently, the public universities of my state are playing a helpful role in dealing with racism directed toward African Americans.

More specifically, these questions were put to 4,967 participants who represented all regions of the continental United States (39% Midwest, 32% South, 15% West, and 14% Northeast). Using the same politically oriented variables we employed in our earlier study, we found that 48% of participants identified as Democrats, 31% Independent, and 21% Republican, while 54% of respondents described themselves as liberal, 26% as conservative, and the remaining 20% as moderate.

In terms of results, around 40% of the entire sample agreed or strongly agreed that the public universities of their state were having a positive impact on community needs surrounding COVID-19 and racism. In turn, approximately one-fifth of the respondents disagreed or strongly disagreed, another 25% neither agreed or disagreed, and the remainder selected "don't know" as their response. Unsurprisingly, political party affiliation mattered in that significantly more Democrat participants agreed with both statements in comparison to Republican and Independent participants. The results regarding political ideology largely mirrored the political party findings, whereby significantly more conservative respondents disagreed with both statements in comparison to liberal and moderate respondents.

What does this mean for the leaders of our public universities? On the surface, the differences regarding politically oriented variables reported here are not unanticipated given the national polls we have discussed in various places throughout this book, as well as our own findings. What the findings of this newest survey do make more obvious, however, is that such generalized views are mirrored in the much more specific sentiments regarding the ways that public universities are handling issues surrounding the COVID-19 pandemic and social justice.

Widening our lens to an observation of results reflecting the views of the entire sample provides further sobering information for higher education leaders to absorb. Regardless of political affiliation or ideology, less than half of *all* respondents agreed or strongly agreed that public universities were meeting the needs of communities regarding these twin public health issues. The genuinely bad news is that approximately 25% disagreed or strongly disagreed.

However, a slightly more hopeful reading of these results would indicate that the remaining 35% to 40% of citizens polled across our nation had yet to be convinced *one way or the other* about the effectiveness of actions taken by institutions of higher learning in both these realms. As such, a considerable portion of these individuals—Democrat, Republican, Independent, liberal, moderate, and conservative alike—remained open to persuasion regarding the value of efforts undertaken by universities in terms of community needs related to COVID-19 and social justice issues.

Higher education leaders should pause and think carefully about these findings. Over one-third of the national sample that participated in this survey did not have enough information about what the public universities of their state had been doing to deal with the two most critical public health crises of our time to render an opinion about these institutions' usefulness to communities. The situation is reminiscent of the line spoken by the road crew captain—"What we've got here is failure to communicate"—right before he thrashes Cool Hand Luke in the 1967 film classic of the same name that starred Paul Newman. The inability to get the university's message out regarding its community-focused efforts may result in damaged relationships with the public, now and in the not-too-distant future.

This brings us back to the words uttered by Abraham Lincoln during his first debate with Stephen Douglas as quoted at the beginning of our second chapter. The future president emphasized the importance of finding out (and acting upon) what citizens think about the issues of the day. For society in general and universities more specifically in 2020, the defining issues have been COVID-19 and racial justice. Every other single topic paled in comparison. And yet, how many universities have any handle on how many of their constituents believe they are doing a decent job in tackling these concerns?

Because power resides in the will of the people, universities ignore the public's opinion on these and other subjects at their own peril. It is our firm belief that the leaders of our public institutions of higher learning must not only pay attention to public sentiment and become more responsive to the wants and needs of citizens. They also must go out (and send out others) to actively seek this sort of information and, in turn, organize a coordinated and ongoing response to the needs and desires expressed by those community members they are supposed to be serving.

What would this look like in practice? Polling has its limitations, of course, as we have seen through the 2016 and 2020 presidential elections. There are many things that the pollsters got flat out wrong. This is not to say that public perceptions about higher education cannot be surveyed successfully, as the results discussed above indicated. Hence, we encourage universities to find out what their constituents are thinking through the use of the expert talent they retain on their campuses.

In addition, all the survey data and information that one can gather from an armchair or from social science, there is, and must continue to be, the most important fact gathering effort—particularly by university presidents and chancellors—and that is to leave the bubble and travel to visit those who are impacted daily by the virus, by social and racial injustice, and by other acts of defiance to the common good. One of the authors (Gee), as a university president, has consistently traveled to the corners of the state to meet with local leaders, school superintendents, teachers, members of the public, and, most importantly, children. The purpose of such travel is twofold. First, to gain and share knowledge about the university as an instrument of change and how that change best can be affected. Second, and more importantly, to better understand how people are thinking about the university and how it can best improve its service to the citizens of the state.

University presidents tend to live in gilded cages. The vast majority have their special parking places, plush offices, and live in subsidized public housing. The only way a president can truly get a sense of the dynamics that are impacting the institution, both internally and externally, is to see it through the eyes of others. No amount of reading, listening to the stories of others, nor conversations with people in one's office will substitute for the information gained in a coffee shop, restaurant, drug store, or some other meeting place where people gather, individually or collectively, to discuss the concerns of their communities and the issues of the day.

Further, when a president does make such visits, they must be done not just once, as if a box was being checked. Instead, these visits must be consistently undertaken. The first time Gee visited every county in the state of Ohio, people were amused, but the general belief was that they would never see him again. The second time caused a stir, the third time a bit of bewilderment. But, by the fourth or fifth time, people believed in his seriousness about the importance of those visits and, we believe, they took him more seriously as both a leader and a listener. Without a doubt, university leadership is much richer outside the boundaries of an office, and universities are much more attuned to the needs of people when citizens are given an opportunity to talk and tell rather than listen and be preached to by university administrators.

Do the Politics of Reopening Plans Foreshadow How Universities Will Spend Public Monies?

In our third chapter, we provided an in-depth discussion of how the participants in our study would distribute public funding across university activities. Our findings indicated that the overall sample expressed the desire to provide almost 50% of all public monies toward teaching efforts, with the remainder divided up almost equally to research and community outreach programs and services. What was most astounding to us was the lack of differences surrounding the politically oriented variables, such that it did not matter whether a respondent was a Republican, Democrat, or Independent, nor did it matter if that survey participant was a self-described conservative, liberal, or more "middle of the road." On average, they all believed that half of the money should go toward teaching, with the remainder to be evenly split among research activities and community-based services.

In general, this may not be such a surprising finding, as most people—regardless of political affiliation—think the main task of a university is to teach. However, what was astonishing to us was the fact that those who leaned democratic and those who subscribed to a more republican orientation would agree on *anything at all.* As we noted in chapter 3, the only thing that people on different sides of the political aisle seem to agree on is that the polarization in America is getting worse.[6] So, how do we make sense of our own findings, and do they provide any sort of direction to our public universities?

For us, the "glass is half empty" interpretation regarding the lack of political differences reflected in our survey data about public university expenditures devolves quickly into the more cynical observation that it is merely a matter of time before this, too, becomes a hot button issue. That is, politicians and pundits have not yet discovered a way to weaponize the issue of how funds are distributed across teaching, research, and community serving activities. Given enough time, to follow this line of thinking, democratic and republican lawmakers (and their most vocal constituents) surely will find a way to engage in conflict about this issue as well.

The most recent evidence supporting such a pessimistic viewpoint comes from observations of the way that politics played a role in the way that decisions were made about reopening college campuses in the fall of 2020. A fascinating study conducted by John Barnshaw, vice president of research and data science at Ad Astra, and Chris Marsicano, an assistant professor of educational studies at Davidson College and cofounder of the College Crisis Initiative, compared reopening decisions made by 3,500 institutions of higher learning against databases from the Centers for Disease Control and Prevention (CDC), the Integrated Postsecondary Education Data System (IPEDS), and indicators of the political leanings of each state.[7] While university officials claimed publicly they were attending closely to such variables as active COVID-19 case numbers and student opinions about how and when to return, the most predictive variable was whether the state they were located in was red or blue in terms of its political orientation. That is, colleges and universities in red states were significantly more likely to return to face-to-face instruction, regardless of the public health and student opinion data.

The effect size grew if there was a political trifecta, where the two legislatures and governorship were represented by a single party. In states like Alabama, where both legislatures and the governorship were controlled by Republicans, institutions had greater odds of in-person instruction. Oppositely, in states like California where the assembly and the governorship were controlled by Democrats, the universities had greater odds of being online.

Anyone paying attention to the politics of the moment would not find it too hard to believe that pressure was being placed on schools to reopen as quickly as possible. Then-President Donald Trump had made the reopening of K–12 schools a major component of his political platform, going so far as to threaten educators with the loss of federal funding if they did not comply with his administration's wishes.[8] Similarly, Trump also used the return of college football as a leverage point for universities to reopen and subsequently made political hay out of the issue in the first presidential debate.[9]

We had the pleasure of discussing our findings with Dr. Barnshaw, who was also a research affiliate at the College Crisis Initiative discussed above. We specifically asked Dr. Barnshaw to comment on what it would take to politicize the distribution of funds directed toward teaching, research, and service. He told us that he thought the politicizing of teaching, research, and service-related activities was already underway. More specifically, Dr. Barnshaw stated:

> There are likely many origin stories of how these funds are being politicized, but in 2016, political consultant Frank Luntz stated his belief that

the Republican party had already lost the millennial generation because millennials have been "pushed to the left by their professors." Later that week, the 2016 Republican platform adopted language urging colleges and university trustees to avoid "political indoctrination." That framing had an effect. In 2015, only 37 percent of Republicans believed that colleges and universities have a negative effect on the way things are going in the country, but just two years later, that number jumped 21 points to 58 percent. Among Democrats, the percent of respondents that felt colleges had a negative effect on the way things are going in the country was virtually unchanged.

We also asked Dr. Barnshaw to comment on how certain issues specific to the situation our nation found itself in December 2020—including a pandemic that likely was going to get worse before it got better, a contested presidential election, and continued calls for racial justice—might affect the way the public viewed the distribution of funds by universities. He focused our attention on higher education's ability to demonstrate value. For example, Dr. Barnshaw pointed to the fact that a slight majority of Americans (51%) at the beginning of 2020 believed that a college education was very important.[10] However, he also noted that majority had dropped 19 points in just six years, with the greatest decline among adults aged 18–29 (down 33% during that same period).

Dr. Barnshaw went on to say that younger adults were increasingly skeptical of the value of a college degree, especially with rising tuition costs. He pointed to a *Gallup* poll that found only 34% of undergraduates strongly agreed with the statement that they will graduate with the knowledge and skills they need to be successful in the job market.[11] However, if students had a professor who cared about them, and there was experiential learning, like an internship or project, that number jumped to 76% of students that felt college would help them be successful. Dr. Barnshaw went on to say:

The most rewarding research undertaken by Ad Astra and the College Crisis Initiative has been to help students gain those research skills, or, to highlight to faculty what skills are most in-demand. When faculty teach those skills, and they remind the students that these are the skills employers are looking for in the workforce, we have seen students become more competitive in the labor market. Minor adjustments are making a difference in positively impacting the future for students and effectively demonstrating the value of higher education to students, employers, and the public. In pockets, these changes are occurring, but it is not yet scalable and systematic. Consequently, higher education runs the risk that the majority of citizens will not see the full value of higher education, which could negatively affect the way the public values the distribution of higher education funds for years to come.

Updating the Crystal Ball on International Higher Education

In our fifth chapter, we reported that over 40% of our sample believed there should be no difference in emphasis between global/international concerns and local issues by public universities and, much to our surprise, another third of the sample had endorsed the idea that global concerns should be more greatly emphasized. Our astonishment was born out of the belief that citizens most valued the local impact of their public institutions of higher learning. Clearly, our survey participants were quite receptive to the notion that their universities should have a more global footprint.

Of course, one of the most conspicuous ways that universities had taken on a more international flavor was through their efforts to serve international students while concurrently offering study abroad experiences for their domestic students. The COVID-19 pandemic triggered largescale shutdowns on international travel, however, placing severe restrictions on these sorts of activities. Our conversation in chapter 5 with Dr. Philip Altbach led us to believe that it would take a significant amount of time to rebuild the international focus and mobility patterns of students coming to study in America. That said, Dr. Altbach also believed that the demand for study abroad experiences and the desire for international students to enroll in American universities would pick up again in the aftermath of the pandemic.[12]

Our first conversation with Dr. Altbach was in April 2020, just as the coronavirus infection rates were beginning to rise in many of our nation's large urban locations. We decided to recontact Dr. Altbach in November 2020, following both the announcement of several promising COVID-19 vaccines, as well as the election of Joe Biden as the 46th president of the United States. We wished to know how much more understandable the situation regarding international higher education had become in the six months since we had last connected on this topic.

The most recent statistics certainly supported Dr. Altbach's original contention that international higher education was going to take a hit. There was a drop of over 20% in visa applications from international students in the fall of 2020, for example.[13] This translated into a decline in international student enrollment of over 40% in that same period.[14] All told, the economic damage to universities and the economy as a whole was startling, estimated to have cost the United States approximately $1.8 billion in cash and a total of 42,000 jobs.[15]

Echoing these sorts of figures and trends, Dr. Altbach told us in our second conversation that "the just released US international mobility figures have shown a significant decline in new international students. I continue to think that the short- and medium-term declines in international mobility to the United States will be quite significant. In the longer run, four to five years from now, these numbers will increase again, but there will not be the consistent growth that has been evident over the past two decades. The interest of students from the United States in study abroad activities also will take time to return, but in the medium term will do so."

Dr. Altbach also pointed out the ramifications for international university-based research. "While disrupted in the short-term, issues relating to collaboration with China in research and other areas will continue. The academic community has been and will continue to favor collaboration. Hence, the broader situation will become a bit more normalized in the post-Trump administration era," Dr. Altbach stated. In fact, the race for a COVID-19 vaccine has already generated exactly that sort of large-scale cooperation among the world's university-based scientists. As noted in a recent article cowritten by Dr. Altbach and his Boston College colleague Hans de Wit: "If one looks at the approximately 30 initiatives currently working on a vaccine, all depend on international partnerships of researchers—located in multinational companies, research institutes and universities that all need access to the best minds, sophisticated equipment and testing opportunities in different parts of the world. The effort is truly global and illustrates the necessity of the globalisation of science and scholarship."[16]

We close this section with some final words from Dr. Altbach on this subject matter. He stated that "for the United States, the era of significant annual increases in international student numbers is probably at an end, although the US, assuming that Donald Trump or a similar xenophobic nationalist does not return to the White House in 2024, will remain one of the top preferences for international students and faculty. Outward mobility for American students will also rebound." Dr. Altbach then summed up his thoughts by noting that "American colleges and universities are committed to an international approach, and globalization, perhaps modified and even made humanistic, is here to stay."

The Folly of Pursuing National Rankings

In our sixth chapter, we reported our surprise in finding that almost half of the sample endorsed the idea that merit-based aid should be prioritized for funding over needs-based aid, and, in our seventh chapter, we discussed our additional astonishment in terms of almost half of the sample endorsing the idea that national rankings mattered in terms of their state's public universities. Even more shocking to us was the pattern of responses we discovered when we combined the responses to these two survey questions. This action revealed that those participants who prioritized needs-based student aid were, by percentage, the ones who were most likely to report that national rankings mattered. We labeled this as at least somewhat contradictory because a rise in national rankings is typically accomplished by an increase in the standardized scores of incoming freshmen, who are attracted to enroll in a university when they are offered merit-based aid.

In our opinion, the onset of the COVID-19 pandemic laid bare the biased nature of college entrance exams and the patent absurdity of chasing national rankings. Expressing a near identical viewpoint, no less than the editor-in-chief of *Science*, H. Holden Thorp, published an op-ed in May 2020 that called for the immediate suspension of both college rankings and standardized exams.[17] In the piece he wrote, Dr. Thorp expressed great concern about the plight of undergraduate students amid the COVID-19 pandemic, especially those who already were predisposed to disadvantages in accessing a quality higher education experience. His worry was that a persistent focus on national rankings, such as *U.S. News and World Report*, and continued reliance on college entrance exams, such as the SAT and ACT, would only aggravate these inequities. Specifically addressing the rankings conducted by *U.S. News and World Report*, Dr. Thorp wrote:

> To any logical scientific observer, the fine distinctions of where schools show up on this list are statistically meaningless—but try telling that to a roomful of alumni or parents. Countless hours of trustee meetings are spent going over the minute details of the formula and setting institutional goals. Achieving these goals usually means doing things that make the college or university less accessible, like admitting more students with high standardized test scores.

Thus, we see college rankings and standardized test scores as being inextricably bound together. The rankings of colleges and universities have become a big business, selling access to information that is supposed to tell readers something about the quality of the schools being ranked. As such, these same rankings have been driving many of the most important decisions that leaders of colleges and universities are making about themselves and their futures. In essence, their strategic plans are focused most heavily on one goal: moving up in the rankings.

We believe that this is a textbook example of the tail wagging the dog. One of the few levers that universities can pull for the sake of rising in the *U.S. News and World Report* rankings is to increase the standardized test scores of their incoming freshman class.[18] Further, to attract those students with high SAT and ACT scores, university admissions offices must offer more merit-based aid to those students. In fact, often as not universities engage in bidding wars. If it is known that your competitors are offering a 50% scholarship for students scoring in the 90th percentile on the ACT, for example, then the temptation exists to begin offering a 75% scholarship to your own prospects.

To be fair, it has been reported that *U.S. News and World Report* was reportedly reviewing strategies for signs that their educational rankings had been affected by the public health crisis and its aftermath.[19] What was not addressed, however, were the underlying issues that Dr. Thorp pointed toward in his *Science* editorial. That is, the rankings are scientifically meaningless at best and, at worst, they contribute to further inequities among college students which would only be amplified by the COVID-19 pandemic.

Dr. Thorp called for a suspension of both the tests and the college rankings, but his editorial also appealed for a "more progressive form" of rankings to take the place of what *U.S. News and World Report* now offers. We asked the editor-in-chief of *Science* exactly what such a progressive rankings system would that look like in practice.[20] He told us that "a more progressive rankings system would be one that measured whether students are achieving better outcomes. This means that someone could look at those rankings and select the university that provided the best outcomes for students they most resembled. No ranking system allows you to do that right now." When we pushed this idea further and asked if such a ranking system was even possible at this moment in time he replied: "Yes, but this is up to universities and their governing boards. If you allow the people in the ranking business to continue with business as usual, they will. At the end of the day, this is an issue of leadership, plain and simple."

A short time after we had this conversation with Dr. Thorp, one candidate for a different sort of progressive ranking system appeared on the scene. A report entitled *Advancing University Engagement* was released as a direct response to the criticism that universities had become disconnected from societal needs.[21] Penned by the vice-presidents of three universities—Derek Douglas (University of Chicago), Jonathan Grant (King's College London), and Julie Wells (University of Melbourne)— the document provided readers with a framework for ranking universities according to their level of engagement with communities. The effort has been described as an attempt to simplify previous work launched in 2019 by the *Wall Street Journal* and *Times Higher Education College Rankings* using the United Nations' Sustainable Development Goals (known as Impact Rankings).[22]

A total of eight engagement indicators were employed in the *Advancing University Engagement* work, including university commitment to engagement; community opinion of the university; student access; volunteering; research reach outside academic journals; community engaged learning within curriculum; socially responsible purchasing; and carbon footprint. One of the report's authors, Jonathan Grant, described the value of these engagement indicators in the following manner: "A new system that recognizes these benefits would reassure the public and students that they are getting value for money, as well as incentivizing institutions to do more for communities and societies around the world."[23]

We believe that this sort of ranking system is indeed more progressive in orientation. The use of community engagement indicators would also go a long way toward emphasizing purpose over prestige, a particular hallmark of America's public and land-grant universities.[24] As one of us (Gee) quipped in an op-ed for *USA Today*:

> We have to learn how to be elite without being elitist, which means not impressing and intimidating each other with our academic credentials but helping each other to grow better educated, better prepared and better attuned to each other's needs. As Honest Abe knew well, that's the spirit that had always helped this nation thrive; it's also the spirit very much alive in the places he had built for this purpose, our land-grant universities.[25]

Hence, university leaders would do well to think about investing more time and energy in exactly this sort of progressive ranking system and how it might better serve the interests of their institutions of higher learning. Opting into such a ranking system would also have the added benefit of positively impacting public opinion by allowing universities to better articulate the contributions they are making to the well-being of society.

Will Economic Uncertainty Impact Access and Affordability?

In our eighth chapter, we reported on the sixth and final higher education survey question that asked participants to consider the following statement: If there was one thing that the public universities in your state could do that would make you feel more comfortable about how taxpayer money was being used to support higher education, what would it be? The most frequently mentioned issue on the topic of increasing citizen comfort with the use of taxpayer money at public universities revolved around the issue of access and affordability. The responses that came together to comprise this access and affordability theme were divided further into several subcategories, including issues related to reducing the burden of tuition and fees, scholarships and other forms of aid, fair access to higher education, and student debt reduction.

We have no doubt that the onset of the COVID-19 pandemic had a profound impact on the way that higher education was viewed by college-age students in terms of their ability to access an affordable university experience. Consistent with our belief, the fall 2020 survey of over 18,000 college-bound students conducted by *Niche.com* revealed strong evidence that the public health crisis had a profound impact on the decisions they made about their educational plans.[26] Mirroring other reported findings, lower-income students reported that they were more directly impacted by the spread of the coronavirus.[27] For example, they were 50% more likely to stay closer to home to attend college in comparison to students from higher income families. Often, these decisions were connected to the need for students to take care of other family members or to supplement the income of their households. The results of this study were foreshadowed by findings from an earlier poll conducted in the spring of 2020 by *Niche.com*, when over 36,000 seniors were asked if the public health crisis was affecting their thinking about college.[28] Almost 45% of these seniors said they were reconsidering their college choices, including 38% who indicated that they had considered staying closer to home.

In the fall 2020 survey, it was clear that financial issues had been creating more anxiety for college-bound students. Looking as far back as the 2016 survey conducted by *Niche.com*, almost 50% of students at that time believed they would be able to afford the college in which they had enrolled. Fast forward to 2020, and less than one-third of students held that same belief. On the other hand, these 2020 college students as a group were more satisfied with the financial aid package they received from their chosen school. So, even if these students expressed more concern about affordability, they ended up feeling better about the support they were offered.

As might be expected, lower-income students were much less likely to be confident they could afford their school of choice. Unexpectedly, however, even those low-income students who were the most prepared to attend college—including those with GPAs at or above a 4.0—remained deeply concerned that scholarships and other forms of tuition assistance would not be enough to help them completely pay for their education.

Uncertainties about going to college extended to student confidence in the degree to which they were adequately prepared for success. Here, student confidence in their level of preparedness has been showing a slight decline over the past three years: dropping from 82% who felt confident in 2017 to 79% in 2019. However, in 2020, the *Niche.com* survey split out academic preparedness from social preparedness. While 78% of the 2020 students believed that they were academically prepared, only 62% thought that they were socially prepared for college life. Hence, the drop in confidence levels seemed to have more to do with psychological and emotional readiness rather than pure academic abilities per se.

Another bright spot in the reported findings included the fact that most students were able to enroll in the school they most wanted to attend. In fact, just under 80% of all students participating in the

Niche.com survey reported that they were accepted to their first-choice college. Interestingly, there were no significant differences between those students who attended public and private high schools in terms of getting into their choice of schools.

One final piece of good news: less than 5% of all students participating in the survey reported that their family was not supportive of their decision to attend college. While the lack of family support was reported by a higher percentage of students from low-income families (7.5%) and first-generation students (7.1%) in comparison to the total sample, those numbers were relatively low. Hence, while the families of low-income and first-generation students may need extra attention in terms of understanding exactly *how* to provide encouragement and assurance, there seems to be little evidence that these family members are not supportive of their sons and daughters as they pursue a college degree.[29]

University leaders would do well to heed this most up-to-date information about the public's perceptions of higher education. Financial anxieties among potential college-bound students will only increase as a function of continued economic uncertainty, and this will especially be the case for those students whose families were more economically disadvantaged prior to, during, and in the immediate aftermath of the pandemic. At the same time, the recognition of the value of a college degree has largely remained constant, and, therefore, leaders must think carefully about what sets their institutions apart from the others in the eyes of their prospective students and families.

Focusing on Communities Through the Lens of Innovation and Economic Prosperity

A second theme from the qualitative data discussed in chapter 8 revolved around community focus and outcomes. This was a topic we had covered extensively in our *Land-Grant Universities for the Future* book. There, we had highlighted the efforts of public universities to rigorously document various community engagement efforts being undertaken across a broad spectrum of impact factors, especially including work that directly impacted the economic well-being of communities. Special mention was made of actions taken by the Association of Public and Land-Grant Universities to begin awarding what they termed the Innovation and Economic Prosperity (IEP) designation. This designation was bestowed upon universities that had "demonstrated a meaningful, substantial, and sustainable commitment to university economic engagement" with the communities they serve.[30] Institutions of higher learning undergo an intensive assessment process and, if they receive a positive review from the program review panel, are given the IEP designation.

The IEP designation is based on a set of metrics described as "four simple ideas": know, measure, tell, and engage.[31] That is, economic engagement activities are thought to have meaningful impact when universities *know* what they do well and what they need to improve on, when they *measure* their engagement levels, and when they are able to *tell* the story of their economic contributions. Universities are then better positioned to *engage* collaboratively with their campus and community stakeholders to promote economic prosperity. To date, only 66 universities have earned the IEP designation by demonstrating sufficient commitment to economic development through university-community partnerships.

It cannot be overstated that the COVID-19 pandemic had profoundly impacted the financial circumstances of communities across the nation. So, our question was this: did these "four simple ideas" from the IEP designation make any difference in terms of innovation and recovery from the economic damages wrought by this public health crisis? We asked this question of Shalin Jyotishi, who oversaw the IEP designation process as part of his portfolio of responsibilities as APLU's assistant director of economic development and community engagement.[32] Mr. Jyotishi, who had been tracking many of the stories emerging out of universities throughout the early months of the pandemic, told us that "it's no small feat for a university to implement a comprehensive strategy for maximizing its economic and societal impact. Nearly all IEP designees have leveraged our 'Economic Engagement Framework' to achieve this goal. Whether it's to educate a

21st century workforce, foster innovation ecosystems, or support resilient communities, IEP designees leverage the framework to strengthen how they support the regions they serve."

We agreed with this assessment and wished to provide some commendable examples of this sort of work being undertaken by public universities amid the pandemic. Our first exemplar is the work done at Kansas State University, a land-grant institution that has been portrayed as a leader in the battle against pandemics, largely because of the Biosecurity Research Institute it houses.[33] Activities surrounding the IEP designation had already connected experts in biosecurity, food security, and infectious disease prevention with the Manhattan, Kansas, business community, dubbed "the Silicon Valley of Biodefense" by former US Senate Majority Leader Tom Daschle.[34] With the onset of the pandemic, these university-community partnerships had started to yield licensed technology surrounding treatments for COVID-19 that reached both preclinical and clinical trials at the time this book was written.[35]

We spoke to Peter K. Dorhout, vice president for research at Kansas State, who noted that his university's use of the IEP process in response to the pandemic went beyond direct medical treatment. "Vaccines and treatments are one dimension of how we can impact the current situation, but ensuring adequate and safe food supplies is an additional dimension of our engagement. Whether through community pandemic planning and training developed by our National Agricultural Biosecurity Center or through engagement with the meat packing industries and cattle and hog producers through our Extension offices to help prevent food shortages when COVID-19 closes local processing facilities, K-State talent is assisting in stabilizing the state's multi-billion dollar agriculture economy."

Our second example involves efforts undertaken by the University of North Carolina at Chapel Hill. Again, work accomplished to achieve the IEP designation had put into place a variety of partnerships that allowed university personnel to respond rapidly to the needs of communities battling the COVID-19 pandemic. This included the manufacturing of personal protective equipment (PPE), which had not only connected faculty and staff with collaborators in the business community and UNC Health System, but also with colleagues at other universities such as Duke and North Carolina State University (another IEP designee).[36]

We spoke with Michelle Bolas, the associate vice chancellor of innovation strategy and programs at UNC-Chapel Hill, about these interrelated activities. She told us that "universities excel at research and generating new knowledge and discoveries, but they aren't traditionally positioned to manufacture products and get them into the market. Because UNC-Chapel Hill had already engaged in the IEP process, we had a strategy and data-driven framework in place before the pandemic hit that allowed us to support the programs who were ready to assist, activate partnerships, and ramp up in-house manufacturing of PPE in just a few weeks. The data systems that we've strengthened because of the IEP process give us real-time impact metrics that show Carolina's response to the needs of our state's health care providers."

Of course, the final chapter on the economic consequences of the COVID-19 pandemic is far from being written at the time our own book is being completed in December 2020. The story line at present indicates continued economic pain through significant portions of 2021. That said, we believe those universities that became centrally involved in just these sorts of innovation and economic prosperity activities will be the ones who help to create some of the more positive passages within this narrative and, as a result, will earn the gratitude of the public.

The Pleasures and Pains Associated with College Sports

The issue of college sports arose as another theme from the qualitative data discussed in chapter 8. Survey participants who mentioned this topic commented on one of two basic issues. One more dominant group discussed the need to reduce athletic expenditures by universities, while the second smaller group thought that universities should begin to share revenue with student-athletes. We will comment on the attention (fiscal and otherwise) that universities give to athletics first, followed by the issue of revenue sharing.

The success of university presidents and the triumphs generated from college sports are, often as not, viewed as intertwined, even if they are somewhat disconnected in truth.[37] We believe that, while fans and supporters of the university believe they are simply watching a football game, university leaders see their budget running up and down the field.[38] In many ways, that is the reality of intercollegiate athletics, which do have a significant impact on the way that people view a university.

Athletic budgets are, comparatively, a very small part of the overall budget of a university. However, the reality is that they have an outsized way of forming people's opinions of the institution. There is not a chemistry page in the local newspaper, nor a page on anthropology; but there is a sports section which is read avidly by so many people who support the university, as well as those who have only an interest in sports.

Similarly, no one has ever been successful in getting 100,000 fans to show up for a psychology lecture. They will visit the campus if there is an exciting athletic event, of course, and so that is where universities must be able to meet and greet those citizens who otherwise would not see any value in what is offered by institutions of higher learning. Hence, a thriving athletics program does bring distinction to the university and does allow the university to tell its story if it uses the athletic program as a vehicle through which information can be developed. In short, that is in the bailiwick of good management of the university and its athletic department.

We now move on to the topic of revenue sharing issues surrounding college athletics. Undoubtedly, college sports are a big business, with annual revenues that now exceed $14 billion by some estimates.[39] The emergence of the COVID-19 pandemic may have set in motion a game-changing situation for athletes and the departments that run college sports, however. In the spring of 2020, the National Collegiate Athletic Association (NCAA) announced over $375 million in payout reductions to schools due to the cancellation of the Division I basketball tournament.[40] Revenue stream reductions next came from delays associated with the fall 2020 football season. In the land of college sports, football is king. As the largest revenue generating unit of any athletics department, what happens to college football reverberates throughout the remainder of the sports programs.[41] While the $4 billion loss predicted by a total wipeout of college football did not materialize, the losses due to game cancellations resulting from player and staff COVID-19 infections are still being calculated.[42]

Amid this financial turmoil, a bill was introduced in the US House of Representatives that would allow college athletes to capitalize off their name, image, and likeness, something that has been vigorously opposed in the past by the NCAA and many university officials.[43] This congressional action was presented jointly by two former student athletes: Emanuel Cleaver, a Democratic representative from Missouri who played football for Murray State University, and Anthony Gonzalez, a Republican representative from Ohio who was a standout receiver for The Ohio State University football team.

In a press release, Congressman Cleaver stated that "I want to be unequivocally clear: This is a civil rights issue. For far too long college athletes across the country, many of whom are people of color, have been denied the basic right to control their name, image and likeness."[44] Added Congressman Gonzalez in a press release of his own, "I am proud to introduce bipartisan legislation with Rep. Cleaver today that delivers meaningful reforms and will make a difference in the lives of student athletes of all levels of competition across the country,"[45]

The introduction of this bill came with the significant backing of congressional colleagues from across the political spectrum, including Colin Allred (D-TX), Rodney Davis (R-IL), Josh Gottheimer (D-NJ), Jeff Duncan (R-SC), Marcia Fudge (D-OH), and Steve Stivers (R-OH). Officially named the Student Athlete Level Playing Field Act, this bipartisan bill[46] would seem to stand a very good chance of becoming law. Among other actions, the Student Athlete Level Playing Field Act would do the following:

1. Grant student athletes the right to capitalize off their own name, image, and likeness and engage in agent contracts.
2. Establish one federal standard for this sort of activity, thus pre-empting any existing or prospective state law.

3. Providing congressional oversight through the establishment of a commission that would include student athlete representation.

4. Ensure that student athletes would not be considered employees of universities, thus sparing the athletes from actions that might affect their scholarships or financial aid status.

Although the NCAA was working on its own guidelines to deal with name, image, and likeness standards, it has been reported that federal lawmakers believed those actions would "likely be incomplete."[47] The official response of the NCAA to the Student Athlete Level Playing Field Act was as follows: "We greatly appreciate U.S. Reps. Gonzalez and Cleaver's collaboration to sponsor bipartisan legislation to strengthen the college athlete experience. We look forward to working together with both representatives, their co-sponsors and other members of Congress to further establish a legal and legislative environment where our schools can continue to support student-athletes within the context of higher education."[48]

What has become known as the issue of Name, Image, and Likeness (NIL) now has been transformed into one of the major discussion points and legal hot spots in intercollegiate athletics. Of course, this is an issue fraught with a large set of concerns. Are student-athletes to be thought of as students first or athletes? As the word "student" is placed first, one might hope that college classes would take priority. Unfortunately, given the enormous pressures placed on participants in large revenue sports such as football and basketball, the more realistic hope has been that these students would be able to balance their school and athletic activities.[49]

One must also ask a related question: is intercollegiate athletics an amateur effort? Many student-athletes receive scholarships and fee allowances as well as an opportunity for an education and degree in return for the contribution of their athletic talents. One might ask the same about the tuba players in the marching band or the violinists in the university orchestra. Are they not equally worthy of recognition because they are displaying their talents as are athletes? And, once one goes down the slippery slope of "paying" athletes for their name, image, or likeness, does this not create yet another way for significant mischief and mismanagement in intercollegiate athletics?

There is no doubt in our minds that the present situation opens up the possibility of "pay for play" schemes which harkens back to the 1930s and one of the major reasons that the University of Chicago and its president at the time, Robert Hutchins, dropped college football altogether.[50] Of great interest to us is the fact that the Knight Commission on Intercollegiate Athletics put forth a series of recommendations in December 2020 as to how, if NIL becomes a reality, some boundaries can be developed.[51] We applaud them for their efforts, but we believe that this will fundamentally change the character of athletics in higher education. In the end, these sorts of activities may well lead to the professionalization of college sports or their ultimate demise.

It Is Getting Worse for Students of Color

Readers will remember that the issue of diversity did appear in the qualitative comments reported in chapter 8. However, because there were less than ten open-ended responses (in fact, there were only seven individual comments in total), we did not believe the topic of diversity met criteria in terms of its identification as a significant theme in our analyses. That said, we were convinced by the events of 2020 that there may be no more salient an issue than diversity and inclusion at this moment in time, especially on the campuses of our public universities.

The news about efforts to create a more diverse higher education environment is not good, at least in terms of our nation's most selective public institutions. The dire situation is described in detail by the Education Trust, which released a report entitled "Segregation Forever?" in July 2020.[52] This account presented extremely discouraging news regarding the number of Black and Latino students who enroll in America's premier public colleges and universities. Using letter grades to indicate the relative diversity of each institution's student body, the report gave an F to a large majority of institutions it evaluated.

Sadly, in many cases the enrollment of Black and Latino students was reported to be *lower* than it was 20 years ago.

The Education Trust is a nonprofit organization that works to close opportunity gaps disproportionately affecting students of color, students from low-income families, and other historically underrepresented students. As it has done in the past, the Education Trust examined enrollment figures from the 50 public "flagship universities" across the nation,[53] described by higher education scholar Alex Usher[54] as those "world class universities with a commitment to teaching top undergraduate students, to providing top-level professional education and to a mission of civic engagement, outreach and economic development." The flagship university of each state was typically founded first and often receives the most support in terms of tax dollars. Think University of California-Berkeley, University of Nebraska-Lincoln, Penn State University, and the University of Georgia.

In the present report, however, the Education Trust added another 51 institutions that were equally as selective and exclusive when compared to the flagships. In all, these 101 universities were graded according to how well each institution's enrollment reflected the racial and ethnic demography of the state in which it is located. The findings in this report made it clear that, despite some marginal gains in access for Latino students over the past two decades, both Black and Latino students continue to be shamefully underrepresented within these universities. In many instances, their representation in enrollment figures has actually declined. More specifically, over half of the selective institutions earned Ds and Fs in terms of their enrollment of both Black and Latino students. That said, the numbers were clearly worse regarding Black students, in that more than 75% of the universities received failing grades.

How does this happen in an era when so many university leaders have been so outspoken about racial injustice? A big part of the problem appears to be a profound disconnect between what administrators say out loud and what they do in practice. From the authors of the Education Trust report,

Improving access for Black and Latino students at the 101 institutions included in this report is a matter of political will and institutional prioritization. With larger endowments and more funding, these institutions have the resources to do so, but their leaders must make a conscious commitment to increasing access. Below are several actions that institutional leaders can take to improve access for Black and Latino students at selective public colleges and universities. We also offer a few actions policymakers should take to help institutions become more accessible.

In all, there were 10 recommendations provided in the Education Trust report:

1. Adopt goals to increase access
2. Increase access to high-quality guidance counselors
3. Use race more prominently in admissions decisions
4. Rescind state bans on affirmative action
5. Increase aid to Black and Latino students
6. Alter recruitment strategies
7. Improve campus racial climates
8. Use outcomes-based funding policies equitably
9. Leverage federal accountability
10. Reduce the role of standardized testing and/or consider making tests optional

A *Chronicle of Higher Education* article quoted Andrew Howard Nichols, the senior director of research at the Education Trust who authored this report, as saying, "It is past time for public-college presidents to take substantive anti-racist action that matches their soaring anti-racist rhetoric."[55] Indeed, positive change in the enrollment numbers of Black and Latino students is only going to happen when these university leaders stop talking about diversity and start taking concrete action. We must emphasize here that such work should be undertaken immediately and without thought given to the popularity of such activities with the public at large.

Student Mental Health Concerns:
Post COVID-19 Traumatic Stress Disorders?

Throughout the pandemic, colleges and universities had continually adjusted their plans to provide in-person, hybrid, and full online courses in response to fluctuating COVID-19 cases. As well, students were forced out of their campus residences when the coronavirus first took hold in the spring of 2020, and many more students experienced a second wave of campus closings in the fall. We continue to worry about how well college students have been adjusting to these rapidly shifting environments.

Some research studies that have been published throughout the earlier months of the pandemic regarding the impact of COVID-19 on college students this past semester have provided us with some important clues about their mental health status. Unfortunately, the available information has pointed toward a rough road ahead for many of these young adults. One particularly innovative study conducted by a group of Dartmouth researchers used smartphone data alongside self-reported symptoms of mental health distress generated from a group of undergraduate students both prior to and amid the COVID-19 outbreak.[56] Their findings indicated that college students were significantly more anxious and depressed during the pandemic. Similar increases in mental health distress have also been reported in a study of college students residing in Switzerland.[57]

Instead of mental health issues, however, what had captured a great deal of attention during the onset of the pandemic was the interpersonal behavior of college students as they returned to campuses. Everyone knew that students were going to socialize at parties—despite the presence of a public health crisis—as they have done so for the past 600 years.[58] The fact that they would gather in close quarters, however, was seen as a direct threat to the reopening strategies of colleges and universities, as those plans largely depended on students adhering to rigorous social distancing guidelines. Such expectations had been roundly criticized as delusional, futile, and in opposition to everything we know about the behavior of college students.[59]

We believe the research findings about typical young adult activities—combined with the data on negative mental health trajectories experienced by college students during the outbreak of the COVID-19 pandemic—are a warning sign that points to even greater problems ahead. Within the mental health field, it is widely known that individuals who are anxious and depressed can often turn to alcohol and other drugs to "treat" their symptoms.[60] Unfortunately, this form of "self-medication" may have the opposite effect over time. That is, while substance use may offer temporary relief to the individual, in the long run those symptoms of depression and anxiety typically increase.

One can imagine the vicious cycle that forms within this context. To wit, college students experiencing mental health symptoms could increase their partying behavior as a coping response to the distress that they are feeling. Continued changes to the opening (and reopening) plans of colleges and universities may have added even more fuel to the fire. That is, students who may have been somewhat anxious about their return to campus—or for freshmen, their first ever experience of living on their own—had all those plans upended by one or more alterations to what they were told to expect. As a result, they became even more anxious, and perhaps even a bit depressed, about the circumstances in which they now found themselves. It is easy to see how some of these students may become even more vulnerable to increased substance use of one form or another over time.

There had been an upsurge of interest in the mental health issues of college students prior to the COVID-19 pandemic, largely because clinicians had been warning of an emerging "epidemic" of mental health problems.[61] As we move toward the end stages of this viral-based public health crisis, now is exactly the right time to press even harder on this issue, as even more college students are likely to be suffering from various forms of psychological distress. The effects of some sort of "post-COVID stress disorder" may be with us for some time to come.[62]

The Great Reset of Public Higher Education

We end this final chapter and thus our book by telling a quick story. In the year 1665, the Great Plague was decimating London, England. As a result, Cambridge University sent its students home to study alone, mirroring what present-day universities had done (except, of course, without the benefits of online technology). One of those students was Isaac Newton, who used this alone time to pioneer the work that we now call calculus, as well as furthering his theory of gravitation. In fact, Newton was so productive during this time that historians have labeled this period in his life as the Annus Mirabilis, or Year of Wonders.[63]

When the plague subsided and Newton returned to Cambridge, however, the world as it was known at the time had fundamentally changed. Obviously, the point of this story is that disruptions can vary in scope by geography, by political or social sectors and, certainly, on the personal level. What is common to almost all periods of human history, however, is that these disruptions coincide with significant and *positive change* at the societal level.

So, as we contemplate the disturbances we are witnessing now in so many different areas of the university—including those topics we have covered in this chapter and book—what we realize here is that fundamental and positive change is about to occur once again. While we understand the disruptive forces we have been facing have been both frightening and demoralizing, we believe steadfastly that the lessons to be learned from this period of time will be largely productive in the long run.

Therefore, what we cannot do is hope to go back to the lives we knew previously. In fact, one of us (Gavazzi) has forecast that such efforts to return to "business as usual" will guarantee the failure of the public university as we now know it. Particularly alarming has been the "all-too-slow pace of change taking place in the academic realm right now."[64] Therefore, we believe that university leaders must embrace what we would like to term "The Great Reset of Public Higher Education." While we cannot claim to know exactly where such readjustment will take us, we are willing to point out some of the clues we have observed so far.

The possibilities inherent to this "Great Reset" center first on the ways that disruptions have spurred great innovation throughout 2020 and in much shorter timeframes than anyone thought possible. When our former ways of doing things were no longer possible, we invented new ways of doing those things that remained important to us. Going online with our instructional activities certainly is one leading example here. We believe these new ways of conducting business will result in permanent approaches to working effectively and living efficiently after the disruptions of 2020 have subsided. While we will not ever wish to teach 100% of our classes online, we are certain that our universities will be providing such remote instruction at levels not thought possible even a few years ago.

We also would hazard a guess that the Great Reset has been trigged by a keener awareness of the value of various interpersonal relationships that connect members of the university community together. Many of us have seem to have realized that—as a university family—our defined and nurtured values are much more meaningful that we might have once thought. We truly have a greater appreciation of those who are now not so present in our lives, both at a personal and collegial level. Further, believe it or not, we think that many of us have grown to become more kind and caring, both at an institutional level and as individuals. Such acts of compassion, especially within and despite the very toxic political environment in which we find ourselves, have helped renew people's faith in society at large and the value of universities more specifically because of this renewed state of grace.

That said, we think that the hardest part is now upon us. The vaccine is arriving, and the pandemic will either burn itself out through inoculation, through herd immunity, or some combination thereof. So, what is next? How do we look beyond the moment and toward the horizon? How do we now start helping everyone within our university community to embrace the faith that things will be better as the pandemic subsides? How do we change people's mindsets by getting them to move from fear to thinking of possibilities? How do we help people, particularly within our university, prepare themselves for an unfolding future that will very likely be different from anything that we have experienced up to this point? And because of that, how do we make certain that we generate hope for a brighter future when it has been in such short supply as of late?

We urge university leaders to approach these fundamental questions both with the lens of optimism and the spirit of collaboration. Optimism will carry the day in a higher education world that shakes out into four categories: (1) those that do not survive or are consolidated; (2) those that barely survive but remain vulnerable; (3) those that survive but not without significant setbacks; and (4) those that remain thriving institutions, now and into the foreseeable future.[65] Candidly, we believe that most institutional leaders are mired in the minutia of the moment and not thinking about a thriving strategy. They had best begin to think as thrivers soon, and that sort of mindset begins with the realization that disruption, ultimately, will have been our friend.

Finally, we assert that the leaders of *thriving* institutions of higher learning will be those that most skillfully understand and respond to the wishes and desires of the communities they have been designed to serve. Returning to one of our favorite quotes from President Lincoln, public sentiment is indeed *everything*: "Without it, nothing can fail; against it, nothing can succeed." It is worth noting that the final line in that specific passage from Honest Abe stated that "whoever molds public sentiment goes deeper than he who enacts statutes or pronounces judicial decisions." We would humbly revise that last quote to state that whoever molds public sentiment creates more thriving public universities than those who are deaf to the voices of community stakeholders.

You are invited to participate in a short research survey being conducted by The Ohio State University to look at people's political attitudes and their views of higher education. We believe this survey can provide useful information to researchers and others about the degree to which different university activities may be supported by the public.

To participate, you must be 18 or over and must reside in the U.S. Your participation in the survey is voluntary. There are no right or wrong answers and you may refuse to answer any question or questions. You may refuse to participate or stop the survey at any time without penalty or loss of benefits to which you are otherwise entitled. The main risk in your participation would be a breach in data confidentiality, a risk we believe is extremely low due to our institution's strong security measures. We do not foresee any other risks or discomforts from this research.

It takes 10 minutes, on average, to take the survey. You may skip any questions you do not wish to answer. The online survey can be taken independently on a computer, laptop, tablet, or cellular phone (Android, iOS) and is supported by multiple browsers (Chrome, Internet Explorer, Firefox and Safari). The survey is free, but data usage charges may apply. For your participation, you will receive a $5 gift card from a wide range of merchants.

The privacy of all survey participants is protected, and maintaining confidentiality is our highest priority. Your personal information is never shared, sold or made public. However, there may be circumstances where this information must be released (for instance, if required by state law). Also, your records may be reviewed by the following groups (as applicable to the research): Office for Human Research Protections or other federal, state, or international regulatory agencies; The Ohio State University Institutional Review Board or Office of Responsible Research Practices.

All data provided by you will be protected in transit by encryption (NIST 800-53 Moderate compliant information system). However, when using the Internet, there is always a chance that someone could access your responses without permission. In some cases, this information could be used to identify you.

For questions about the study or if you feel you have been harmed by study participation, you may either email your questions to panel@chrr.osu.edu or call 866-448-6075 and leave a message. You may also contact the study's Principal Investigator, Dr. Elizabeth Cooksey, at Cooksey.1@osu.edu.

For questions about your rights as a participant in this study or to discuss other study-related concerns or complaints with someone who is not part of the research team, you may contact Ms. Sandra Meadows at the Office of Responsible Research Practices at 1-800-678-6251.

Do you consent to participate in this survey?

Yes [clicking on Yes will open to the first part of the survey]

No [clicking on No will open to a screen saying "Thank you for your time. We hope you will consider joining us for another survey in the future].

The first few questions ask how you think of yourself in terms of political affiliation and potential voting behavior.

1. Generally speaking, do you usually think of yourself as a:
   a. Republican
   b. Democrat
   c. Independent
   d. Other
   e. No preference

2. (IF REPUBLICAN OR DEMOCRAT) "Would you call yourself a strong (REPUBLICAN/DEMOCRAT)?"
   a. Yes
   b. No

3. (IF INDEPENDENT, OTHER, OR NO PREFERENCE) "Do you think of yourself as closer to the Republican or Democratic party?"
   a. Closer to the Republican party
   b. Closer to the Democratic party
   c. Neither

4. When it comes to politics do you usually think of yourself as:
   a. extremely liberal
   b. liberal
   c. slightly liberal

d. moderate or middle of the road

e. slightly conservative

f. extremely conservative

g. None of the above

5. Did you vote in the 2016 presidential election?

___ YES   ___ NO

6. Are you likely to vote in the 2020 presidential election?

a. I definitely will vote

b. I probably will vote

c. There is a 50/50 chance I will vote

d. I probably will not vote

e. I definitely will not vote

The next few questions ask you to think about how public universities in (text fill for STATE here—California, Florida, New York State, Ohio, Texas or West Virginia) might spend taxpayer money, build connections to communities, provide financial aid to students, and emphasize local/global issues.

7. **In an ideal world**, how should every $100 of taxpayer money provided to public universities in (STATE TEXT FILL) be spent in terms of teaching, research, and community outreach programs and services?

Assume that all basic operating costs (electricity, heating/cooling, etc.) and other expenses (student housing, dining services, recreation, etc.) already are covered.

Your answers must add up to $100.

How much taxpayer money should be spent on teaching? ___
How much taxpayer money should be spent on research? ___
How much taxpayer money should be spent on community outreach programs and services? ___

8. **In an ideal world**, who should be prioritized by public universities in (STATE TEXT FILL), rural or urban communities?

___ Rural communities should be prioritized

___ Urban communities should be prioritized

___ There should be no difference between how rural and urban communities are prioritized

9. **In an ideal world**, what should be prioritized for funding by public universities in (STATE TEXT FILL), needs-based aid (based on family income) or merit-based aid (based on student academic performance)?

___ Needs-based aid should be prioritized for funding over merit-based aid

___ Merit-based aid should be prioritized for funding over needs-based aid

___ There should be no difference in funding provided for needs-based aid and merit-based aid

___ None of the above. I do not believe public universities should provide either needs-based or merit-based aid

10. **In an ideal world**, should our public universities place more of their emphasis on global/international issues, or on issues closer to home that affect the community you live in?

___ Global/international concerns should be emphasized more than issues impacting my community

___ Issues impacting my community should be emphasized more than global/international concerns

___ There should be no difference in emphasis between global/international concerns and issues impacting my community

The next few questions ask your opinion on how much you care about university rankings, and provide a place for you to make a suggestion about what universities could do to make you more comfortable about how they spend taxpayer money.

11. How much do you agree or disagree with the following statement: When it comes to university rankings like US News and World Report, it matters a lot to me where the public universities of (my state) are ranked?

___ Strongly Agree

___ Agree

___ Neither agree or disagree

___ Disagree

___ Strongly Disagree

12. If there was one thing that the public universities in (STATE TEXT FILL) could do that would make you feel more comfortable about how taxpayer money was being used to support higher education, what would it be?
(open text box)

Finally, we have a few demographic background questions which help to keep our records updated:

13. According to your American Population Panel profile, you were born in [{APP_YOB}]. Is this correct?
    1 Yes (skip Q14)
    0 No   (ask next question)

14. What is your year of birth?

15. What is your gender?
    1 Male
    2 Female
    3 Other (please specify)

16. What is your zip code?

17. What is the highest level of education you have completed?
    0 No formal schooling
    1 Elementary School
    2 Middle School or Junior High
    3 Some High School
    4 High School diploma, GED or equivalent
    5 Some College
    6 Associate's degree
    7 Bachelor's degree
    8 Master's degree
    9 Doctoral degree (PhD)
    10 Professional degree (MD, LLD, DDS)
    97 Other (please specify)

18. Are you of Hispanic or Latino origin?
    1 Yes
    0 No

19. What is your race? (*Please select all that apply*)
    1 White
    2 Black or African American
    3 Asian
    4 Native Hawaiian or other Pacific Islander
    5 American Indian or Alaska Native
    6 Hispanic only
    97 Other (please specify)

APPENDIX 2 *Multivariate Tests*

Effect		Value	F	Hypothesis df	Error df	Sig.
Intercept	Pillai's Trace	.767	960.238	2.000	585.000	.000
	Wilks' Lambda	.233	960.238	2.000	585.000	.000
Gender	Pillai's Trace	.039	5.870	4.000	1172.000	.000
	Wilks' Lambda	.961	5.912	4.000	1170.000	.000
EdAttain	Pillai's Trace	.040	6.024	4.000	1172.000	.000
	Wilks' Lambda	.960	6.076	4.000	1170.000	.000
race	Pillai's Trace	.002	.505	2.000	585.000	.604
	Wilks' Lambda	.998	.505	2.000	585.000	.604
libcon	Pillai's Trace	.005	.776	4.000	1172.000	.541
	Wilks' Lambda	.995	.775	4.000	1170.000	.542
party	Pillai's Trace	.014	2.022	4.000	1172.000	.089
	Wilks' Lambda	.986	2.025	4.000	1170.000	.089
vote2016	Pillai's Trace	.004	1.032	2.000	585.000	.357
	Wilks' Lambda	.996	1.032	2.000	585.000	.357
defvote2020	Pillai's Trace	.004	1.203	2.000	585.000	.301
	Wilks' Lambda	.996	1.203	2.000	585.000	.301
age	Pillai's Trace	.043	13.116	2.000	585.000	.000
	Wilks' Lambda	.957	13.116	2.000	585.000	.000
geolocate	Pillai's Trace	.001	.182	2.000	585.000	.833
	Wilks' Lambda	.999	.182	2.000	585.000	.833

Note: Design: Intercept + Gender + EdAttain + race + libcon + party + vote2016 + defvote2020 + age + geolocate

APPENDIX 3 *Tests of Between-Subjects Effects*

Source	Dependent Variable	Type III Sum of Squares	df	Mean Square	F	Sig.
Corrected Model	PUB_UNIV_SPEND_7_1	21701.819[a]	14	1550.130	6.134	.000
	PUB_UNIV_SPEND_7_2	3083.888[b]	14	220.278	1.576	.080
	PUB_UNIV_SPEND_7_3	18757.699[c]	14	1339.836	7.693	.000
Intercept	PUB_UNIV_SPEND_7_1	463239.699	1	463239.699	1833.137	.000
	PUB_UNIV_SPEND_7_2	195517.130	1	195517.130	1398.925	.000
	PUB_UNIV_SPEND_7_3	196357.393	1	196357.393	1127.488	.000
PARTY	PUB_UNIV_SPEND_7_1	740.651	3	246.884	.977	.403
	PUB_UNIV_SPEND_7_2	163.924	3	54.641	.391	.760
	PUB_UNIV_SPEND_7_3	876.598	3	292.199	1.678	.170
liberal-conservative	PUB_UNIV_SPEND_7_1	965.774	3	321.925	1.274	.282
	PUB_UNIV_SPEND_7_2	778.710	3	259.570	1.857	.135
	PUB_UNIV_SPEND_7_3	407.478	3	135.826	.780	.505
VOTE2016	PUB_UNIV_SPEND_7_1	620.857	1	620.857	2.457	.117
	PUB_UNIV_SPEND_7_2	7.736	1	7.736	.055	.814
	PUB_UNIV_SPEND_7_3	767.195	1	767.195	4.405	.036
VOTE2020	PUB_UNIV_SPEND_7_1	1061.583	1	1061.583	4.201	.041
	PUB_UNIV_SPEND_7_2	316.823	1	316.823	2.267	.133
	PUB_UNIV_SPEND_7_3	218.520	1	218.520	1.255	.263
GENDER	PUB_UNIV_SPEND_7_1	856.345	1	856.345	3.389	.066
	PUB_UNIV_SPEND_7_2	885.938	1	885.938	6.339	.012
	PUB_UNIV_SPEND_7_3	3484.315	1	3484.315	20.007	.000

(continued)

Source	Dependent Variable	Type III Sum of Squares	df	Mean Square	F	Sig.
AGE	PUB_UNIV_SPEND_7_1	4985.619	1	4985.619	19.729	.000
	PUB_UNIV_SPEND_7_2	376.072	1	376.072	2.691	.101
	PUB_UNIV_SPEND_7_3	2623.114	1	2623.114	15.062	.000
raceethnicity	PUB_UNIV_SPEND_7_1	764.551	1	764.551	3.025	.082
	PUB_UNIV_SPEND_7_2	3.696	1	3.696	.026	.871
	PUB_UNIV_SPEND_7_3	874.568	1	874.568	5.022	.025
URBANRURAL	PUB_UNIV_SPEND_7_1	15.844	1	15.844	.063	.802
	PUB_UNIV_SPEND_7_2	5.895	1	5.895	.042	.837
	PUB_UNIV_SPEND_7_3	2.410	1	2.410	.014	.906
EDATTAIN	PUB_UNIV_SPEND_7_1	5213.715	2	2606.857	10.316	.000
	PUB_UNIV_SPEND_7_2	271.058	2	135.529	.970	.380
	PUB_UNIV_SPEND_7_3	3537.221	2	1768.611	10.155	.000
Error	PUB_UNIV_SPEND_7_1	209491.019	829	252.703		
	PUB_UNIV_SPEND_7_2	115863.060	829	139.762		
	PUB_UNIV_SPEND_7_3	144374.257	829	174.155		
Total	PUB_UNIV_SPEND_7_1	2024741.000	844			
	PUB_UNIV_SPEND_7_2	790310.000	844			
	PUB_UNIV_SPEND_7_3	720493.000	844			
Corrected Total	PUB_UNIV_SPEND_7_1	231192.838	843			
	PUB_UNIV_SPEND_7_2	118946.948	843			
	PUB_UNIV_SPEND_7_3	163131.956	843			

a. R Squared=.094 (Adjusted R Squared=.079)

b. R Squared=.026 (Adjusted R Squared=.009)

c. R Squared=.115 (Adjusted R Squared=.100)

APPENDIX 4 *Multiple Comparisons*

LSD Dependent Variable	(I) EDATTAIN	(J) EDATTAIN	Mean Difference (I-J)	Std. Error	Sig
PUB_UNIV_SPEND_7_1	high school or less	some college	−2.75	1.455	0.059
		4 year degree or higher	−7.14*	1.334	0.000
	some college	high school or less	2.75	1.455	0.059
		4 year degree or higher	−4.39*	1.311	0.001
	4 year degree or higher	high school or less	7.14*	1.334	0.000
		some college	4.39*	1.311	0.001
PUB_UNIV_SPEND_7_2	high school or less	some college	1.30	1.082	0.232
		4 year degree or higher	.57	.992	0.567
	some college	high school or less	−1.30	1.082	0.232
		4 year degree or higher	−.73	.975	0.456
	4 year degree or higher	high school or less	−.57	.992	0.567
		some college	.73	.975	0.456
PUB_UNIV_SPEND_7_3	high school or less	some college	1.45	1.208	0.229
		4 year degree or higher	6.57*	1.107	0.000
	some college	high school or less	−1.45	1.208	0.229
		4 year degree or higher	5.11*	1.088	0.000
	4 year degree or higher	high school or less	−6.57*	1.107	0.000
		some college	−5.11*	1.088	0.000

NOTES

Introduction

1. Andrew Ferguson, Can Marriage Counseling Save America? *The Atlantic,* December 2019, https://www.theatlantic.com/magazine/archive/2019/12/better -angels-can-this-union-be-saved/600775/.

2. David French, We're Not in a Civil War, but We Are Drifting toward Divorce, *National Review,* June 8, 2017, http://www.nationalreview.com/article/448385 /americans-left-right-liberal-conservative-democrats-republicans-blue-red-states -cultural-segregate.

3. John Halpin and Marta Cook, Social Movements and Progressivism: Part Three of the Progressive Tradition Series, Center for American Progress, April 14, 2010, https://www.americanprogress.org/issues/democracy/reports/2010/04/14/7593/social -movements-and-progressivism/.

4. *National Review,* Our Mission Statement, November 19, 1955, https://www .nationalreview.com/1955/11/our-mission-statement-william-f-buckley-jr/.

5. Conor Friedersdorf, Truth vs. Social Justice: Academic Recognition Shouldn't Hinge on a Scholar's Moral Character, *The Atlantic,* November 1, 2018, https://www .theatlantic.com/ideas/archive/2018/11/academics-truth-justice/574165/.

6. Scott Jaschik, Is College Worth It? Yes, *Inside Higher Ed,* June 10, 2019, https://www.insidehighered.com/news/2019/06/10/new-data-show-economic-value -earning-bachelors-degree-remains-high.

7. *Pew Research Center,* Sharp Partisan Divisions in Views of National Institutions, July 10, 2017, https://www.people-press.org/2017/07/10/sharp-partisan-divisions-in -views-of-national-institutions/.

8. Frank Newport and Brandon Busteed, Why Are Republicans Down on Higher Ed? *Gallup Education,* August 16, 2017, https://news.gallup.com/poll/216278/why -republicans-down-higher.aspx.

9. Abraham Lincoln Online, First Political Announcement, New Salem, Illinois, March 9, 1832, http://www.abrahamlincolnonline.org/lincoln/speeches/1832.htm.

10. Stephen M. Gavazzi, Teaching Excellence: The Core of the Land-Grant Mission. *Journal on Empowering Teaching Excellence* 4, no. 1 (Spring 2020), https://doi .org/10.15142/3f6f-xc61.

11. Roy P. Basler, ed., The Collected Works of Abraham Lincoln (New Brunswick, New Jersey: Rutgers University Press, 1953).

12. Nathan M. Sorber, *Land-Grant Colleges and Popular Revolt: The Origins of the Morrill Act and the Reform of Higher Education* (Ithaca, NY: Cornell University Press, 2018).

13. Holden Thorp and Buck Goldstein, *Our Higher Calling: Rebuilding the Partnership between America and its Colleges and Universities* (Chapel Hill, NC: University of North Carolina Press, 2018).

14. Michael T. Nietzel, *Coming to Grips with Higher Education* (Lanham, MD: Rowman & Littlefield, 2018).

15. Philip G. Altbach, ed., *Global Perspectives on Higher Education* (Baltimore: Johns Hopkins University Press, 2016).

16. David J. Staley, *Alternative Universities: Speculative Design for Innovation in Higher Education* (Baltimore: Johns Hopkins University Press, 2019).

17. Stephen M. Gavazzi and David J. Staley, *Fulfilling the 21st Century Land-Grant Mission: Essays in Honor of The Ohio State University's Sesquicentennial Celebration* (Columbus: The Ohio State University Press, 2020).

18. Stephen M. Gavazzi, Prima Inter Pares: Ohio State's Position as the First Among Equals Within the US Public and Land-Grant System, in *Fulfilling the 21st Century Land-Grant Mission: Essays in Honor of The Ohio State University's Sesquicentennial Celebration*, ed. Stephen M. Gavazzi and David J. Staley (Columbus: The Ohio State University Press, 2020).

19. E. Gordon Gee, Adventures of Being a University President, In *Fulfilling the 21st Century Land-Grant Mission: Essays in Honor of The Ohio State University's Sesquicentennial Celebration*, ed. Stephen M. Gavazzi and David J. Staley (Columbus: The Ohio State University Press, 2020), 346.

Chapter 1. Opportunities and Threats to Higher Education

1. Abraham Lincoln Online, Annual Message to Congress, Concluding Remarks, accessed November 15, 2020, http://www.abrahamlincolnonline.org/lincoln/speeches/congress.htm.

2. Kellogg Commission on the Future of State and Land-Grant Universities, *Returning to Our Roots: Executive Summaries of the Reports of the Kellogg Commission on the Future of State and Land-Grant Universities* (Washington, DC: National Association of State Universities and Land-Grant Colleges, 2001).

3. Carnegie Community Engagement Classification, New England Resource Center for Higher Education, accessed November 13, 2019, http://nerche.org/index.php?option=com_content&view=article&id=341&Itemid=618.

4. Innovation and Economic Prosperity Universities, Association of Public and Land-Grant Universities, accessed April 29, 2017, www.aplu.org/projects-and-initiatives/economic-development-and-community-engagement/innovation-and-economic-prosperity-universities-designation-and-awards-program/index.html.

5. Kellogg Commission on the Future of State and Land-Grant Universities, *Returning to Our Roots: The Engaged Institution* (Washington, DC: National Association of State Universities and Land-Grant Colleges, 1999).

6. Stephen M. Gavazzi, What Public Universities Must Do to Regain Public Support, *The Conversation*, December 4, 2018, https://theconversation.com/what-public-universities-must-do-to-regain-public-support-107772.

7. Stephen M. Gavazzi, Engaged Institutions, Responsiveness, and Town-Gown Relationships: Why Deep Culture Change Must Emphasize the Gathering of Community Feedback, *Planning for Higher Education* 43 (2015): 1–9.

8. Stephen M. Gavazzi and E. Gordon Gee, *Land-Grant Universities for the Future: Higher Education for the Public Good* (Baltimore: Johns Hopkins University Press, 2018).

9. IEP Submission Process and Guidelines, Association of Public and Land-Grant Universities, accessed November 18, 2019, www.aplu.org/projects-and-initiatives /economic-development-and-community-engagement/innovation-and-economic -prosperity-universities-designation-and-awards-program/submission-process.html.

10. John McCormick, *George Santayana: A Biography* (New Brunswick, NJ: Transaction Publishers, 2003).

11. Nathan M. Sorber, *Land-Grant Colleges and Popular Revolt: The Origins of the Morrill Act and the Reform of Higher Education* (Ithaca, NY: Cornell University Press, 2018).

12. Holden Thorp and Buck Goldstein, *Our Higher Calling: Rebuilding the Partnership between America and its Colleges and Universities* (Chapel Hill: University of North Carolina Press, 2018).

13. Jonathan Cole, *Toward a More Perfect University* (New York: Public Affairs, 2016).

14. Stuart M. Butler, Business Is Likely to Reshape Higher Ed, Brookings Institution, December 20, 2016, https://www.brookings.edu/opinions/business-is-likely-to -reshape-higher-ed/.

15. Lumina Foundation, What America Needs to Know About Higher Education Redesign: The 2013 Lumina Study of the American Public's Opinion on Higher Education and U.S. Business Leaders Poll on Higher Education, February 25, 2014, https://www.luminafoundation.org/resources/what-america-needs-to-know-about -higher-education-redesign.

16. Scott Jaschik and Doug Lederman, 2017 Survey of College and University Presidents, *Inside Higher Ed* (Washington, DC: Inside Higher Ed, 2017).

17. Michael Porter, What Is Strategy? *Harvard Business Review* 74, no. 6 (1996): 61–78.

18. Martin J. Finkelstein, Valerie Martin Conley, and Jack H. Schuster, *The Faculty Factor: Reassessing the American Academy in a Turbulent Era* (Baltimore: Johns Hopkins University Press, 2016).

19. Robert J. Sternberg, *What Universities Can Be: A New Model for Preparing Students for Active Concerned Citizenship and Ethical Leadership* (Ithaca, NY: Cornell University Press).

20. Katherine Mangan, Have Campuses Become Ideological Echo Chambers? Not Necessarily, *Chronicle of Higher Education*, September 22, 2019, https://www.chronicle .com/article/Have-Campuses-Become-/247165.

21. Robert K. Greenleaf, *The Servant as Leader* (Westfield, IN: Greenleaf Center for Servant Leadership, 1970).

22. Michelle Popowitz and Cristin Dorgelo, Report on University-Led Grand Challenges, February 13, 2018, https://escholarship.org/uc/item/46f121cr.

23. Nicholas Lemann, Can a University Save the World? *Chronicle of Higher Education*, November 21, 2019, https://www.chronicle.com/interactives/20191121 -Lemann.

24. Brian Pascus, Every Charge and Accusation Facing the 33 Parents in the College Admission Scandal, *CBS News*, June 3, 2019, https://www.cbsnews.com/news /college-admissions-scandal-list-operation-varsity-blues-every-charge-plea -accusation-facing-parents-2019-05-16/.

25. Aaron Katersky and Justin Doom, New Charges in College Admissions Scandal Affect 11 Parents, Including Lori Laughlin, *ABC News*, October 22, 2019, https://abcnews.go.com/US/charges-filed-college-admissions-scandal/story?id =66447670.

26. E. Gordon Gee, College Admissions Scandal: Lincoln's Land-Grant Universities Are Still Helping Students to Grow, *USA Today*, March 25, 2019, https://www .usatoday.com/story/opinion/2019/03/25/college-president-admissions-scandal -shows-land-grant-college-success-column/3238575002/.

Chapter 2. What Citizens Think about Their State's Public Universities

1. National Park Service, First Debate: Ottawa, Illinois, August 21, 1858, https:// www.nps.gov/liho/learn/historyculture/debate1.htm.

2. David Zarefsky, "Public Sentiment Is Everything": Lincoln's View of Political Persuasion, *Journal of the Abraham Lincoln Association* 15, no. 2 (1994): 23–40.

3. Scott Jaschik, Professors and Politics: What the Research Says, *Inside Higher Ed*, February 27, 2017, https://www.insidehighered.com/news/2017/02/27/research-confirms -professors-lean-left-questions-assumptions-about-what-means.

4. Andrew Small, The Ultimate 2016 Presidential Map? *CityLab*, April 3, 2017, www .citylab.com/politics/2017/04/is-this-the-ultimate-2016-presidential-election-map /521622/?utm_source=SFTwitter.

5. Michael A. Neblo, *Politics with the People: Building a Directly Representative Democracy* (Cambridge University Press, 2018).

6. Michael A. Neblo, *Deliberative Democracy between Theory and Practice* (Cambridge University Press, 2015).

7. American Population Panel, The Ohio State University, https://american populationpanel.org.

8. William J. Wolf, *The Almost Chosen People: A Study of the Religion of Abraham Lincoln* (Garden City, NJ: Doubleday and Company, 1959).

Chapter 3. Public Funding for Teaching, Research, and Community Engagement

1. P. D. Warner, J. A. Christenson, D. A. Dillman, and P. Salant, Public Perception of Extension, *Journal of Extension* [online serial] 34, no. 4 (1996), https://www.joe.org /joe/1996august/a1.php.

2. D. A. Dillman, J. A. Christenson, P. Salant, and P. D. Warner, What the Public Wants from Higher Education: Workforce Implication's from a 1995 National Survey, Technical Report no. 95-52 (Pullman: Washington State University Social and Economic Sciences Research Center, 1995).

3. U. S. Department of Education, Digest of Education Statistics, National Center for Education Statistics, accessed January 30, 2020, https://nces.ed.gov/programs /digest/d18/tables/dt18_334.10.asp.

4. U. S. Department of Education, Fast Facts, National Center for Education Statistics, accessed January 30, 2020, https://nces.ed.gov/fastfacts/display.asp?id=75.

5. Andrea E. Abele and Bogdan Wojciczke, *Agency and Communion in Social Psychology* (New York: Routledge, 2019).

6. M. Diehl, S. K. Owen, and L. M. Youngblade, Agency and Communion Attributes in Adults' Spontaneous Self-Representations, *International Journal of Behavioral Development* 28, no. 1 (2004): 1–15.

7. MaryBeth Walpole, Socioeconomic Status and College: How SES Affects College Experiences and Outcomes, *The Review of Higher Education* 27, no. 1 (2003): 45–73.

8. Kim Parker, Rich Morin, and Juliana Menasce Horowitz, Looking to the Future, Public Sees an America in Decline on Many Fronts, Pew Research Center, March 21, 2019, https://www.pewsocialtrends.org/2019/03/21/public-sees-an-america-in-decline -on-many-fronts/.

9. Bill Bishop, *The Big Sort: Why the Clustering of Like-Minded America Is Tearing Us Apart* (New York: Houghton Mifflin Harcourt, 2008).

10. 1940 Statement of Principles on Academic Freedom and Tenure, American Association of University Professors, accessed October 9, 2017, www.aaup.org/report /1940-statement-principles-academic-freedom-and-tenure.

11. Jack H. Schuster and Martin J. Finkelstein, *The American Faculty: The Restructuring of Academic Work and Careers* (Baltimore: Johns Hopkins University Press, 2006).

12. Adrianna Kezar and Cecile Sam, "Understanding the New Majority of Non-Tenure-Track Faculty in Higher Education: Demographics, Experiences, and Plans of Action," *ASHE Higher Education Report* 36, no. 4 (2010): 1–133.

13. Helen Stubbs, Restoring University Faculty's Role of Teaching and Student Service, September 16, 2016, *Gallup News*, https://news.gallup.com/opinion/gallup /195569/restoring-university-faculty-role-teaching-student-service.aspx.

14. John T. McGreevym, The Great Disappearing Teaching Load, *Chronicle of Higher Education*, February 8, 2019, https://www.chronicle.com/article/The-Great -Disappearing/245582.

15. Richard Vedder, Is It Wise to Increase Teaching Loads? *Chronicle of Higher Education*, March 24, 2011, https://www.chronicle.com/blogs/innovations/is-increasing -teaching-loads-a-wise-idea/28897.

16. Colleen Flaherty, Should Professors Teach More to Avoid Program Cuts? *Inside Higher Education*, November 1, 2018, https://www.insidehighered.com/news /2018/11/01/when-institutions-look-teaching-loads-instead-academic-program-cuts -face-budget.

17. Naomi Schaefer Riley, Academia's Crisis of Irrelevance, *Wall Street Journal*, July 20, 2011, https://www.wsj.com/articles/SB10001424052702303661904576453803765138870.

18. Vannevar Bush, *Science—The Endless Frontier: A Report to the President for Postwar Scientific Research*, A Report to the President by the Director of the Office of Scientific Research and Development (United States Government Printing Office, July 1945), https://www.nsf.gov/od/lpa/nsf50/vbush1945.htm.

19. Michael M. Crow and William B. Debars, University-Based R&D and Economic Development: The Morrill Act and the Emergence of the American Research University, in *Precipice or Crossroads: Where America's Great Public Universities Stand Are and Where They Are Going Midway through Their Second Century*, ed. Daniel M. Fogel and Elizabeth Malson-Huddle (Albany: SUNY Press, 2012).

20. Christopher Newfield, *The Great Mistake: How We Wrecked Public Universities and How We Can Fix Them* (Baltimore: Johns Hopkins University Press, 2016).

21. Kellogg Commission on the Future of State and Land-Grant Universities, *Returning to Our Roots: Executive Summaries of the Reports of the Kellogg Commission on the Future of State and Land-Grant Universities* (Washington, DC: National Association of State Universities and Land-Grant Colleges, 2001).

22. Carnegie Community Engagement Classification, New England Resource Center for Higher Education, accessed April 29, 2017, http://nerche.org/index.php?option=com_content&view=article&id=341&Itemid=618.

23. Innovation and Economic Prosperity Universities, Association of Land-Grant and Public Universities, accessed April 29, 2017, http://www.aplu.org/projects-and-initiatives/economic-development-and-community-engagement/innovation-and-economic-prosperity-universities-designation-and-awards-program/index.html.

24. Kellogg Commission on the Future of State and Land-Grant Universities, *Returning to Our Roots: The Student Experience*, 1997, http://www.aplu.org/library/returning-to-our-roots-the-student-experience/file.

25. Kellogg Commission on the Future of State and Land-Grant Universities, *Returning to our Roots: Student Access*, 1998, http://www.aplu.org/library/returning-to-our-roots-student-access-1998/file.

26. Kellogg Commission on the Future of State and Land-Grant Universities, *Returning to our Roots: A Learning Society*, 1999, http://www.aplu.org/library/returning-to-our-roots-a-learning-society/file.

27. Kellogg Commission on the Future of State and Land-Grant Universities, *Returning to Our Roots: Toward a Coherent Campus Culture*, 2000, http://www.aplu.org/library/returning-to-our-roots-toward-a-coherent-campus-culture/file.

28. Kellogg Commission on the Future of State and Land-Grant Universities, *Returning to our Roots: The Engaged Institution*, 1999, http://www.aplu.org/library/returning-to-our-roots-the-engaged-institution/file.

29. Lorilee R. Sandmann, Courtney H. Thornton, and Audrey J. Jaeger, The First Wave of Community-Engaged Institutions, *New Directions for Higher Education* (2009): 99–104.

30. Seyyedmilad Talebzadehhosseini, Ivan Garibay, Heather Keathley-Herring, Zahra Rashid Said Al-Rawahi, Ozlem Ozmen Garibay, and James K. Woodell, Strategies to Enhance University Economic Engagement: Evidence from US Universities, *Studies in Higher Education* (2019). https://doi.org/10.1080/03075079.2019.1672645.

31. Jorge H. Atiles, Chris Jenkins, Patricia Ryas-Duarte, Randal K. Taylor, and Hailin Zhang, Service, Cooperative Extension, and Community Engagement, in *The Modern Land-Grant University*, ed. Robert J. Sternberg (West Lafayette, IN: Purdue University Press, 2014).

32. George R. McDowell, *Land Grant Universities and Extension into the 21st Century: Renegotiating or Abandoning a Social Contract* (Ames: Iowa State University Press, 2001).

33. Extension Committee on Organization and Policy, *The Extension System: A Vision for the 21st Century* (Washington, DC, National Association of State Universities and Land-Grant Colleges, 2002).

34. N. H. Bull, L. S. Cote, P. D. Warner, and M. R. McKinnie, Is Extension Relevant for the 21st Century? *Journal of Extension* 42 no. 6 (2004): Article 6COM2, https://www.joe.org/joe/2004december/comm2.php.

35. D. A. King and M. D. Boehlje, Extension: On the Brink of Extinction or Distinction? *Journal of Extension* 38, no. 5 (2000): Article 5COM1, https://www.joe.org/joe/2000october/comm1.php.

36. D. King, Hey, Siri, What Is the Future of Extension? *Journal of Extension* 56, no. 5 (2018): Article 5COM1, https://joe.org/joe/2018september/comm1.php.

37. Jean M. Bartunek and Michael K. Moch, First-Order, Second-Order, and Third-Order Change and Organization Development Interventions: A Cognitive Approach, *Journal of Applied Behavioral Science* 23, no. 4 (1987): 483–500.

38. E. Gordon Gee, Stephen M. Gavazzi, Roger Rennekamp, and Steve Bonanno, Cooperative Extension Services and the 21st Century Land-Grant Mission, *The EvoLLLution*, February 19, 2019, https://evolllution.com/revenue-streams/extending_lifelong_learning/cooperative-extension-services-and-the-21st-century-land-grant-mission/.

39. E. Gordon Gee, Stephen M. Gavazzi, Jennifer Sirangelo, and Karen Pittman. Placing 4-H Within the 21st Century Land-Grant Mission. *The EvoLLLution*, May 13, 2019, https://evolllution.com/revenue-streams/extending_lifelong_learning/placing-4-h-within-the-21st-century-land-grant-mission/.

40. David Campbell and Gail Feenstra, Community Food Systems and the Work of Public Scholarship, in *Engaging Campus and Community: The Practice of Public Scholarship in the State and Land-Grant University System*, ed. Scott J. Peters, Nicholas R. Jordan, Margaret Adamek, and Theodore R. Alter (Dayton, OH: Kettering Foundation Press, 2005).

41. Steven J. Diner, *Universities and Their Cities: Urban Higher Education in America* (Baltimore: Johns Hopkins University Press, 2017).

42. George R. McDowell, *Land Grant Universities and Extension into the 21st Century: Renegotiating or Abandoning a Social Contract* (Ames: Iowa State University Press, 2001).

Chapter 4. Focusing Attention on Rural and Urban Communities

1. Rural Education at a Glance, 2017 Edition, United States Department of Agriculture, Economic Research Service, April 2017, https://www.ers.usda.gov /webdocs/publications/.

2. High School Benchmarks 2016, National Student Clearinghouse Research Center, October 27, 2016, https://nscresearchcenter.org/hsbenchmarks2016/.

3. C. B. Flora and J. L. Flora, *Rural Communities: Legacy +Change*, 4th ed. (Boulder, CO: Westview Press, 2013).

4. The Status of Rural Education, National Center for Education Statistics, May 2013, https://nces.ed.gov/programs/coe/indicator_tla.asp.

5. John Marcus and Mark Krupnick, Who's Missing from America's Colleges? Rural High School Graduates, *National Public Radio*, February 15, 2018, https://www .npr.org/sections/ed/2018/02/15/581895659/whos-missing-from-america-s-colleges -rural-high-school-graduates.

6. Rich Morin, Behind Trump's Win in Rural White America: Women Joined Men in Backing Him, Pew Research Center, November 17, 2016, https://www.pewresearch .org/fact-tank/2016/11/17/behind-trumps-win-in-rural-white-america-women-joined -men-in-backing-him/.

7. Nicholas W. Hillman, Geography of College Opportunity: The Case of Educa- tion Deserts, *American Educational Research Journal* 53, no. 4 (August 2016): 987–1021.

8. A. L. Griffith and D. S. Rothstein, Can't Get There from Here: The Decision to Apply to a Selective College, *Economics of Education Review* 28, no. 5 (2009): 620–28.

9. Richard Florida, Where Do College Grads Live? The Top and Bottom U.S. Cities. City Lab, August 23, 2019, https://www.citylab.com/life/2019/08/education -talent-city-ranking-college-degree-us/596509/.

10. United States Census, New Census Data Show Differences Between Urban and Rural Populations, December 8, 2016, https://www.census.gov/newsroom/press -releases/2016/cb16-210.html.

11. Aaron M. Renn, Where College Grads Are Moving, *New Geography*, May 21, 2018, https://www.newgeography.com/content/005980-where-college-grads-are-moving.

12. Michael Barone, The New/Old Politics of the Capital Versus the Countryside, *Washington Examiner*, April 27, 2017, http://www.washingtonexaminer.com/the -newold-politics-of-the-capital-versus-the-countryside/article/2621529.

13. Dante J. Scala and Kenneth M. Johnson, Political Polarization along the Rural-Urban Continuum? The Geography of the Presidential Vote, 2000–2016, *Annals of the American Academy of Political and Social Science* 672, no. 1 (2017): 162–84.

14. Dan Kopf, The Rural-Urban Divide Is Still the Big Story of American Politics, *Quartz*, November 6, 2020, https://qz.com/1927392/the-rural-urban-divide-continues -to-be-the-story-of-us-politics/.

15. Gabe Bullard, The Surprising Origin of the Phrase "Flyover Country," *National Geographic*, March 14, 2016, https://www.nationalgeographic.com/news/2016/03 /160314-flyover-country-origin-language-midwest/.

16. Musa Al-Gharbi, Why Should We Care About Ideological Diversity in the Academy? Heterodox Academy, May 23, 2018, https://heterodoxacademy.org/why -should-we-care-about-ideological-diversity-in-the-academy-the-definitive-response/.

17. A. Koricich, X. Chen, and R. Hughes, Understanding the Effects of Rurality and Socioeconomic Status on College Attendance and Institutional Choice in the United States, *Review of Higher Education* 41, no. 2 (2017): 281–305, https://doi.org10.1353/rhe .2018.0004.

18. P. McDonough, R. E. Gildersleeve, and K. M. Jarsky, The Golden Cage of Rural College Access: How Higher Education Can Respond to the Rural Life, in *Rural Education for the Twenty-First Century: Identity, Place, and Community in a Globalizing World*, ed. K. A. Schafft and A. Y. Jackson, 191–209 (University Park: The Pennsylvania University Press, 2010).

19. Stephen M. Gavazzi, To Promote Diversity, Land-Grant Universities Must Return to their Roots, *Heterodox Academy*, January 21, 2019, https://heterodoxacademy .org/viewpoint-diversity-land-grant-universities/.

20. Simon Baker, Land-Grant Universities: Losing their Way in Rural America? *Times Higher Education*, April 17, 2019, https://www.timeshighereducation.com/news /land-grant-universities-losing-their-way-rural-america.

21. A. R. Thomas, B. M. Lowe, G. M. Fulkerson, and P. J. Smith, *Critical Rural Theory: Structure, Space, Culture* (Lanham, MD: Lexington Books, 2011).

22. R. Delgado and J. Stefancic, *Critical Race Theory: An Introduction* (New York: New York University Press, 2001).

23. R. Tong, *Feminist Thought: A More Comprehensive Introduction*, 3rd ed. (Boulder, CO: Westview Press, 2009).

24. K. Donehower, C. Hogg, and E. E. Schell, *Rural Literacies* (Carbondale: Southern Illinois University Press, 2007).

25. Naoki Masuda and Feng Fu, Evolutionary Models of In-Group Favoritism, *Prime Reports*, March 3, 2015, https://www.ncbi.nlm.nih.gov/pmc/articles/PMC 4371377/.

26. Gregory M. Fulkerson and Alexander R. Thomas, eds., *Urbanormativity: Rural Community in Urban Society* (Lanham, MD: Lexington Books, 2014).

27. Kathleen Gillon, The Middle of Somewhere: An Exploration of Rural Women, Communities of Place, and College-Going, *Graduate Theses and Dissertations*, 2015, https://lib.dr.iastate.edu/etd/14577.

28. Sonja Ardoin, *College Aspirations and Access in Working-Class Rural Communities: The Mixed Signals, Challenges, and New Language First-Generation Students Encounter* (Lanham, MD: Lexington Books, 2017).

29. Thomas, Lowe, Fulkerson, and Smith, *Critical Rural Theory*.

30. Ann R. Tickamyer and Cynthia M. Duncan. Poverty and Opportunity Structure in Rural America, *Annual Review of Sociology* 16 (1990):67–86.

31. William B. Meyer and Jessica K. Graybill, The Suburban Bias of American Society? *Urban Geography* 37, no. 6 (2016): 863–82.

32. Laura Pappano, Colleges Discover the Rural Student, *New York Times,* January 31, 2017, https://www.nytimes.com/2017/01/31/education/edlife/colleges -discover-rural-student.html.

33. Benjamin Wermund, In Trump Country, A University Confronts Its Skeptics, *Politico,* November 9, 2017, https://www.politico.com/story/2017/11/09/university-of -michigan-admissions-low-income-244420.

Chapter 5. Global Footprint versus Closer to Home

1. Gary Ecelbarger, Before Cooper Union: Abraham Lincoln's 1859 Cincinnati Speech and Its Impact on His Nomination, *Journal of the Abraham Lincoln Association* 30, no. 1 (2009): 1–17.

2. Robert J. Sternberg, ed., *The Modern Land-Grant University* (West Lafayette, IN: Purdue University Press, 2014).

3. P. G. Altbach and J. Knight, The Internationalization of Higher Education: Motivations and Realities, *Journal of Studies in International Education* 11, no. 3-4 (2007): 290–305.

4. R. King, S. Marginson, and R. Naidoo, *A Handbook of Globalization and Higher Education* (Cheltenham, UK: Edward Elgar, 2011).

5. G. Edward Schuh, Revitalizing Land-Grant Universities, *Choices* 1, no. 2 (1986): 6.

6. Lou Anna K. Simon, World Grant Universities: Meeting the Challenges of the Twenty-First Century, *Change: The Magazine of Higher Learning* 42, no. 5 (2010): 42–46.

7. John Hudzik and Lou Anna K. Simon, From a Land-Grant to a World-Grant Ideal: Extending Public Higher Education Core Values to a Global Frame, in *Precipice or Crossroads: Where America's Great Public Universities Stand Are and Where They Are Going Midway through Their Second Century,* ed. Daniel M. Fogel and Elizabeth Malson-Huddle (Albany: SUNY Press, 2012).

8. David Eastwood, Being Global, Sounding Local: Why Place Still Matters in Higher Education, *Chronicle of Higher Education* 61, no. 15 (December 12, 2014): 7.

9. Colin Dueck, Understanding Conservative Populism, *American Enterprise Institute,* November 19, 2019, https://www.aei.org/op-eds/understanding-conservative -populism/.

10. Party Platform: The Democratic Party, *On the Issues: Every Political Leader on Every Issue,* accessed October 23, 2020, https://www.ontheissues.org/Democratic _Party.htm.

11. Philip G. Altbach, Liz Reisberg, and Laura Rumbley, Tracking a Global Academic Revolution, in *Global Perspectives on Higher Education,* ed. Philip G. Altbach (Baltimore: Johns Hopkins University Press, 2016).

12. Philip G. Altbach, The Emergence and Reality of Contemporary International- ization, in *Global Perspectives on Higher Education,* ed. Philip G. Altbach (Baltimore: Johns Hopkins University Press, 2016).

13. Leelian Kong, Charted: How International Student Fees at US Universities Are Going Up, Up, Up, *Study International News,* December 20, 2018, https://www.studyinter

national.com/news/charted-how-international-student-fees-at-us-universities-are
-going-up-up-up/.

14. Elizabeth Redden, Study Abroad Numbers Continue Steady Increase, *Inside Higher Ed*, November 18, 2019, https://www.insidehighered.com/news/2019/11/18
/open-doors-data-show-continued-increase-numbers-americans-studying-abroad.

15. Karin Fischer, College 'Embassies' Advance their Interests Abroad, *Chronicle of Higher Education*, April 25, 2010, https://www.chronicle.com/article/Colleges-Set-Up
-Their-Own/65225.

16. Ian Wilhelm, Northern Arizona University Overhauls Curriculum to Focus on "Global Competence," *Chronicle of Higher Education*, May 25, 2012, https://www
.chronicle.com/article/Northern-Arizona-U-Overhauls/131925.

17. Karin Fischer, Northeastern, Once Local, Goes Global, *Chronicle of Higher Education*, January 16, 2011, https://www.chronicle.com/article/A-Once-Local
-University/125959.

18. Karin Fischer, Foreign Students Aren't Edging Out Locals, Numbers Show, *Chronicle of Higher Education*, February 2, 2015, https://www.chronicle.com/article
/Foreign-Students-Arent-Edging/151547.

19. McKay Jenkins, Why I'm Not Preparing My Students to Compete in the Global Marketplace, *Chronicle of Higher Education*, January 20, 2012, https://www
.chronicle.com/article/Forget-About-the-Global/130337.

20. Karin Fischer, How International Education's Golden Age Lost Its Sheen, *Chronicle of Higher Education*, March 28. 2019, https://www.chronicle.com/interactives
/2019-03-28-golden-age.

21. Philip G. Altbach, *Global Perspectives on Higher Education* (Baltimore: Johns Hopkins University Press, 2016).

Chapter 6. Merit-Based Aid and Needs-Based Aid for Students

1. Roy P. Basler, The Eulogy of Henry Clay, *The Collected Works of Abraham Lincoln*, The Abraham Lincoln Association, 2006, http://www.abrahamlincolnonline.org
/lincoln/speeches/clay.htm.

2. Edward P. St. John and Michael D. Parsons, *Public Funding of Higher Education: Changing Contexts and New Rationales* (Baltimore: Johns Hopkins University Press, 2015).

3. U. S. Department of Education, Trends in Undergraduate Nonfederal Grant and Scholarship Aid by Demographic and Enrollment Characteristics: Selected Years, 2003–04 to 2015–16, National Center for Education Statistics, accessed January 31, 2020, https://nces.ed.gov/pubs2019/2019486.pdf.

4. Ashley A. Smith, Poll: Voters Oppose Free College, Loan Forgiveness, *Inside Higher Education*, May 1, 2019, https://www.insidehighered.com/quicktakes/2019/05
/01/poll-voters-oppose-free-college-loan-forgiveness.

5. U. S. Department of Education, Digest of Education Statistics, National Center for Education Statistics, accessed January 30, 2020, https://nces.ed.gov/programs
/digest/d18/tables/dt18_334.10.asp.

6. U. S. Department of Education, Trends in Undergraduate Nonfederal Grant and Scholarship Aid by Demographic and Enrollment Characteristics: Selected Years, 2003–04 to 2015–16. National Center for Education Statistics, accessed January 31, 2020, https://nces.ed.gov/pubs2019/2019486.pdf.

7. U. S. Government, Financial Aid for Students, https://www.usa.gov/financial-aid.

8. U. S. Government, Federal Student Aid, https://studentaid.gov/about.

9. Suzanne Kahn, A Progressive Framework for Free College, Roosevelt Institute, December 2019, https://rooseveltinstitute.org/wp-content/uploads/2019/12/RI_AProg ressiveFrameworkForFreeCollege_Report_201912.pdf.

10. Victor Davis Hanson, Ivy-League Schools Wither, *National Review*, March 19, 2019, https://www.nationalreview.com/2019/03/elite-universities-ignore-merit-advance -progressive-agenda/.

11. Richard Kreitner, January 20, 1937: FDR is Inaugurated for the Second Time, *The Nation*, January 20, 2015, https://www.thenation.com/article/archive/january-20 -1937-fdr-inaugurated-second-time/.

12. Ronald Reagan, Remarks to Members of the National Governors' Association, February 22, 1988, National Archives, Ronald Reagan Presidential Library and Museum, https://www.reaganlibrary.gov/research/speeches/022288a.

13. John R. Thelin, Higher Education and the Public Trough, in *Public Funding of Higher Education: Changing Context and New Rationales*, ed. Edward P. St. John and Michael D. Parsons (Baltimore: Johns Hopkins University Press, 2004).

14. Andrew P. Kelly, Reforming Need-Based Aid, in *Policy Reforms to Strengthen Higher Education*, ed. Andrew P. Kelly, Jason D. Delisle, Kevin J. James, and Mark S. Schneider, *National Affairs*, Winter 2020, https://www.nationalaffairs.com/unleashing-opportunity.

15. Andrew P. Kelly and Sara Goldrick-Rab, *Reinventing Financial Aid: Charting a New Course to College Affordability* (Cambridge, MA: Harvard Education Press, 2014).

16. Sandy Baum, Hard Heads and Soft Hearts: Balancing Equity and Efficiency in Institutional Student Aid Policy, *New Directions for Higher Education* 140 (Winter 2007): 75–85.

17. T. G. Mortenson, Georgia's HOPE Scholarship Program: Good Intentions, Strong Funding, Bad Design, *Postsecondary Education Opportunity* 56 (1997): 1–3.

18. William R. Doyle, Does Merit-Based Aid "Crowd Out" Need-Based Aid? *Research in Higher Education* 51 (2010): 397–415.

19. Donald E. Heller and Patricia Marin, *Who Should We Help? The Negative Social Consequences of Merit Scholarships* (Cambridge, MA: The Civil Rights Project at Harvard University, 2002).

20. Stephen Burd, Crisis Point: How Enrollment Management and the Merit-Aid Arms Race Are Derailing Public Higher Education, *New America*, February 10, 2020, newamerica.org/education-policy/reports/crisis-point-how-enrollment-management -and-merit-aid-arms-raceare-destroying-public-higher-education/.

21. Ozan Jaquette and Bradley R. Curs, Creating the Out-of-State University: Do Public Universities Increase Nonresident Freshman Enrollment in Response to

Declining State Appropriations? *Research in Higher Education* 56, no. 6 (2015): 535–65.

22. Michael S. McPherson and Morton O. Schapiro, The Blurring Line Between Merit and Need in Financial Aid, *Change: The Magazine of Higher Learning* 34 no. 2 (2010): 38–46.

23. Tuan D. Nguyen, Jenna W. Kramer, and Brent J. Evans, The Effects of Grant Aid on Student Persistence and Degree Attainment: A Systematic Review and Meta-Analysis of the Causal Evidence, *Review of Educational Research* 89, no. 6 (2019): 831–74.

24. James C. Hearn and Janet M. Holdsworth, Federal Student Aid: The Shift from Grants to Loans. In *Public Funding of Higher Education: Changing Context and New Rationales*, ed. Edward P. St. John and Michael D. Parsons (Baltimore: Johns Hopkins University Press, 2004).

25. Sandy Baum and Michael McPherson, "Free College" Does Not Eliminate Student Debt, Urban Institute, August 22, 2019, https://www.urban.org/urban-wire /free-college-does-not-eliminate-student-debt.

26. Estelle James, Student Aid and College Attendance: Where Are We Now and Where Do We Go from Here? *Economics of Education Review* 7, no. 1 (1988): 1–13.

27. Lauren D. Appelbaum, The Influence of Perceived Deservingness on Policy Decisions Regarding Aid to the Poor, *Political Psychology* 22, no. 3 (2001): 419–42.

28. Jacob A. Hester, Social Construction and Policy Design in State Financial Aid Policy, PhD dissertation, University of Alabama, 2018, https://ir.ua.edu/handle /123456789/3634.

29. American Talent Initiative, https://americantalentinitiative.org/.

30. Emily Schwartz, Martin Kurzweil, Cindy Le, Tania LaViolet, Linda Perlstein, Elizabeth Davidson Pisacreta, and Josh Wyner, Expanding Opportunity for Lower-Income Students: Three Years of the American Talent Initiative, American Talent Initiative, February 19, 2020, https://3utufq1jg9va1hzfs93qmq34-wpengine.netdna-ssl .com/wp-content/uploads/2020/02/ATI-Impact-Report_Feb-2020_Expanding-Oppor tunity-for-Lower-Income-Students.pdf.

31. Michael T. Nietzel, The Momentum on Enrolling 50,000 More Lower-Income College Students Has Slowed—Four Steps for Getting It Back, *Forbes*, February 25, 2020, https://www.forbes.com/sites/michaeltnietzel/2020/02/25/the-momentum-on -enrolling-50000-more-lower-income-college-students-has-slowedfour-steps-for -getting-it-back/#17585da94497.

32. Michael T. Nietzel, *Coming to Grips with Higher Education* (Lanham, MD: Rowman & Littlefield, 2018).

Chapter 7. National Rankings

1. David B. Barker, "You Can Fool All the People": Did Lincoln Say It? History News Network, 2016, https://historynewsnetwork.org/article/161924.

2. G. Bogue and K. B. Hall, *Quality and Accountability in Higher Education: Improving Policy, Enhancing Performance* (Westport: Praeger Publishers, 2003).

3. Giljae Lee, Thomas Sanford, and Jungmi Lee, Variables that Explain Changes in Institutional Rank in U.S. News & World Report Rankings, *KEDI Journal of Educational Policy* 11, no. 1 (2014): 27–48.

4. Robert Morse, About the U.S. News Education Rankings Methodologies, *US News and World Report Education*, 2019, https://www.usnews.com/education/articles /rankings-methodologies.

5. Zachary A. Goldfarb, These Four Charts Show How the SAT Favors Rich, Educated Families, *The Washington Post*, March 5, 2014, https://www.washingtonpost .com/news/wonk/wp/2014/03/05/these-four-charts-show-how-the-sat-favors-the-rich -educated-families/.

6. A. F. J. van Raan, Challenges in Ranking Universities, in *The World-Class University and Ranking: Aiming Beyond Status*, ed. J. Sadlak and L. Nian Cai, 87–121 (Bucharest: UNESCO-CEPES, 2007).

7. Jung Cheol Shin and Robert K. Toutkoushian, The Past, Present, and Future of University Rankings, in *University Rankings: Theoretical Basis, Methodology and Impacts on Global Higher Education*, ed. Jung Cheol Shin, Robert K. Toutkoushian, and Ulrich Teichler (New York: Springer Press, 2011).

8. J. Shin and G. Harman, New Challenges for Higher Education: Global and Asia-Pacific Perspectives, *Asia Pacific Education Review* 10, no. 1 (2009): 1–13.

9. A. H. Eagly, M. C. Johannesen-Schmidt, and M. L. van Engen, Transformational, Transactional, and Laissez-Faire Leadership Styles: A Meta-Analysis Comparing Women and Men, *Psychological Bulletin* 129, no. 4 (2003): 569–91.

10. D. Dill and M. Soo, Academic Quality, League Tables, and Public Policy: A Cross-National Analysis of University Rankings, *Higher Education* 49 (2005): 495–533.

11. M. L. Stevens, *Choosing a Class: College Admissions and the Education of Elites* (Cambridge, MA: Harvard University Press, 2007).

12. G. R. Pike, Measuring Quality: A Comparison of US News Rankings and NSSE Benchmarks, *Research in Higher Education* 45 (2004): 193–208.

13. Pew Research Center, Sharp Partisan Divisions in Views of National Institutions, July 10, 2017, http://www.people-press.org/2017/07/10/sharp-partisan-divisions -in-views-of-national-institutions.

14. Bernard Longden, Ranking Indicators and Weights, in *University Rankings: Theoretical Basis, Methodology and Impacts on Global Higher Education*, ed. Jung Cheol Shin, Robert K. Toutkoushian, and Ulrich Teichler (New York: Springer Press, 2011).

15. Jung Cheol Shin, Organizational Effectiveness and University Rankings, in *University Rankings: Theoretical Basis, Methodology and Impacts on Global Higher Education*, ed. Jung Cheol Shin, Robert K. Toutkoushian, and Ulrich Teichler (New York: Springer Press, 2011).

16. R. Parloff, Who's Number One? And Who's Number 52, 91, and 137, *American Lawyer*, 1998, p. 5.

17. Ulrich Teichler, Social Context and Systemic Consequence of University Rankings: A Meta-Analysis of the Ranking Literature, in *University Rankings:*

Theoretical Basis, Methodology and Impacts on Global Higher Education, ed. Jung Cheol Shin, Robert K. Toutkoushian, and Ulrich Teichler (New York: Springer Press, 2011).

18. Grant Harmon, Competitors of Rankings: New Directions in Quality Assurance and Accountability, in *University Rankings: Theoretical Basis, Methodology and Impacts on Global Higher Education*, ed. Jung Cheol Shin, Robert K. Toutkoushian, and Ulrich Teichler (New York: Springer Press, 2011).

19. N. Bowman and M. Bastedo, Getting on the Front Page: Organizational Reputation, Status Signals, and the Impact of *U.S. News and World Report* on Student Decisions, *Research in Higher Education* 50, no. 5 (2009): 415–36.

20. M. Clarke, Weighing Things Up: A Closer Look at US News & World Report Ranking Formulas, *College and University Journal* 79, no. 3 (2004): 3–9.

21. Jonathan S. Gagliardi, Amelia Parnell, and Julia Carpenter-Hubin, *The Analytics Revolution in Higher Education: Big Data, Organizational Learning, and Student Success* (Sterling, VA: Stylus Publishing, 2018).

22. Julie Carpenter-Hubin, Why We Count: Using Data to be Our Best Selves, in *Fulfilling the 21st Century Land-Grant Mission: Essays in Honor of The Ohio State University's Sesquicentennial Celebration*, ed. Stephen M. Gavazzi and David J. Staley (Columbus: The Ohio State University Press, 2020).

Chapter 8. Jobs and Politics and Sports, Oh My!

1. David Zarefsky, "Public Sentiment Is Everything": Lincoln's View of Political Persuasion, *Journal of the Abraham Lincoln Association* 15, no. 2 (1994): 23–40.

2. A. L. Strauss, *Qualitative Analysis for Social Scientists* (Cambridge: Cambridge University Press, 1987).

3. H. F. Wolcott, *Transforming Qualitative Data: Description Analysis and Interpretation* (Newbury Park, CA: Sage, 1994).

4. NVivo Qualitative Data Analysis Software (version 12), QSR International Pty Ltd., Windows, 2018.

5. J. F. Gilgun, Qualitative Research and Family Psychology, *Journal of Family Psychology* 19, no. 1 (2005): 40–50.

6. Samantha Cooney, Should You Share Your Salary with Co-Workers? Here's What the Experts Say, *Time Magazine*, August 14, 2018, https://time.com/5353848/salary-pay-transparency-work/.

7. Dennis Prager, Coming Home from College, *National Review*, March 12, 2019, https://www.nationalreview.com/2019/03/college-indoctrination-leftism-rampant/.

8. David Gooblar, What Is Indoctrination? And How Do We Avoid It in Class? *Chronicle of Higher Education*, February 19, 2019, https://www.chronicle.com/article/What-Is-Indoctrination-/245729.

9. American Civil Liberties Union, Speech on Campus, accessed June 17, 2020, https://www.aclu.org/other/speech-campus.

10. Foundation for Individual Rights in Education, Campus Rights: What We Defend, accessed June 17, 2020, https://www.thefire.org/about-us/campus-rights/.

11. Chris Murphy, Madness, Inc: How Everyone is Getting Rich off College Sports, Except the Players, accessed June 17, 2020, https://www.murphy.senate.gov/download /madness-inc.

12. Michael McCann, Chris Spielman's Lawsuit Against Ohio State Could Set Monumental Precedent, *Sports Illustrated*, July 16, 2017, https://www.si.com/college /2017/07/16/chris-spielman-ncaa-ohio-state-football-img-college-ed-obannon-honda -nike.

13. Matt Bonesteel, In Unanimous Vote, NLRB Rejects Northwestern Football Team's Attempt to Unionize, *The Washington Post*, August 17, 2015, https://www .washingtonpost.com/news/early-lead/wp/2015/08/17/in-unanimous-vote-nlrb-rejects -northwestern-football-teams-attempt-to-unionize/.

14. Stephen M. Gavazzi, Sports Scandals Soil the Land-Grant Legacy, *Chronicle of Higher Education*, August 23, 2018, https://www.chronicle.com/article/Sports-Scandals -Soil-the/244343.

15. Matt Brown and Jason Kirk, Be Skeptical When Big College Athletics Pro- grams Act Broke. *Banner Society*, August 12, 2019, https://www.bannersociety.com /2019/8/12/20704195/college-football-athletic-budgets.

16. Will Hobson and Steven Rich, Why Students Foot the Bill for College Sports, And How Some Are Fighting Back, *The Washington Post*, November 30, 2015, https:// www.washingtonpost.com/sports/why-students-foot-the-bill-for-college-sports-and -how-some-are-fighting-back/2015/11/30/7ca47476-8d3e-11e5-ae1f-af46b7df8483_story .html.

Chapter 9. Disdain the Beaten Path

1. David Lowenthal, The Mind and Art of Abraham Lincoln, Philosopher States- man: Texts and Interpretations of Twenty Great Speeches (Lanham, Maryland: Lexington Books, 2012).

2. Anthony L Fisher, It Wasn't a Disaster, But This Election Shows the Fragility of American Democracy, *Business Insider*, November 4, 2020, https://www.business insider.com/2020-election-american-democracy-fragile-as-ever-trump-biden -2020-11.

3. Andrew Edgecliffe-Johnson, US Business Leaders Call for Peaceful Transfer of Power, *Financial Times*, November 7, 2020, https://www.ft.com/content/0df2cc72 -69e8-41a1-925a-b0bd4a9aec15.

4. Derek Newton, 5 Things That Covid-19 Will Make the New Normal in Higher Ed, *Forbes*, June 26, 2020, https://www.forbes.com/sites/dereknewton/2020/06/26/5 -things-that-covid-19-will-make-the-new-normal-in-higher-ed/.

5. Stephen M. Gavazzi, Have Public Universities Failed Their Communities on Covid-19 and Racism? *Forbes*, September 28, 2020, https://www.forbes.com/sites /stephengavazzi/2020/09/28/have-public-universities-failed-their-communities-on -covid-19-and-racism/.

6. Kim Parker, Rich Morin, and Juliana Menasce Horowitz, Looking to the Future, Public Sees an America in Decline on Many Fronts, Pew Research Center, March 21,

2019, https://www.pewsocialtrends.org/2019/03/21/public-sees-an-america-in-decline -on-many-fronts/.

7. Madeline St. Amour, Political Influence on Fall Plans, *Inside Higher Education*, September 3, 2020, https://www.insidehighered.com/news/2020/09/03/state-politics -influenced-college-reopening-plans-data-show.

8. Matt Barnum, Despite Setbacks, Trump Administration Doubles Down on Push to Reopen School Buildings, *Chalkbeat*, August 12, 2020, https://www.chalkbeat.org /2020/8/12/21365758/trump-devos-school-reopening-safety.

9. Tom Brew, Debate Fact-Checker: Donald Trump DID NOT Bring Back Big Ten Football, *Sports Illustrated*, October 2, 2020, https://www.si.com/college/indiana /football/debate-fact-check-trump-did-not-save-big-ten-football.

10. Stephanie Marken, Half in U.S. Now Consider College Education Very Important. *Gallup*, December 30, 2019, https://www.gallup.com/education/272228 /half-consider-college-education-important.aspx.

11. Steve Crabtree, Six College Experiences Linked to Student Confidence on Jobs, *Gallup*, January 22, 2019, https://news.gallup.com/poll/246170/six-college -experiences-linked-student-confidence-jobs.aspx.

12. Philip Altbach and Hans de Wit, COVID-19: The Internationalisation Revolu- tion That Isn't, *University World News*, March 14, 2020, https://www.universityworld news.com/post.php?story=20200312143728370.

13. Elizabeth Redden, U.S. Visa Data Show 21% Decline in International Students, *Inside Higher Education*, November 18, 2020, https://www.insidehighered.com/quick takes/2020/11/18/us-visa-data-show-21-decline-international-students.

14. Elizabeth Struck, New International Student Enrollment Falls 43% in the US, *Voice of America News*, November 16, 2020, https://www.voanews.com/student-union /new-international-student-enrollment-falls-43-us.

15. NAFSA: Association of International Educators, New NAFSA Data Show First Ever Drop in International Student Economic Value to the U.S., *PR Newswire*, November 16, 2020, https://www.prnewswire.com/news-releases/new-nafsa-data-show -first-ever-drop-in-international-student-economic-value-to-the-us-301173172.html.

16. Hans de Wit and Philip G. Altbach, Addressing Research Inequalities Exacer- bated by COVID-19, *International World News*, September 26, 2020, https://www .universityworldnews.com/post.php?story=20200923130840933.

17. H. Holden Thorp, Suspend Tests and Rankings, *Science*, May 22, 2020, https://science.sciencemag.org/content/368/6493/797.

18. Robert Morse, About the U.S. News Education Rankings Methodologies, *U.S. News and World Report*, April 20, 2020, https://www.usnews.com/education/articles /rankings-methodologies.

19. Frances Diep, Why One Former Campus Leader Thinks College Rankings Should Stop During the Pandemic, *Chronicle of Higher Education*, May 21, 2020, https://www.chronicle.com/article/Why-One-Former-Campus-Leader/248831.

20. Stephen M. Gavazzi, Need Proof That College Rankings Don't Matter? Ask the Editor of Science, *Forbes*, May 22, 2020, https://www.forbes.com/sites/stephengavazzi

/2020/05/22/need-proof-that-college-rankings-dont-matter-ask-the-editor-of
-science/.

21. Derek R.B Douglas, Jonathan Grant, and Julie Wells, Advancing University
Engagement, *Nous Group*, accessed November 24, 2020, https://www.kcl.ac.uk/policy
-institute/assets/advancing-university-engagement.pdf.

22. Impact Rankings 2020, Times Higher Education World University Rankings,
accessed November 24, 2020, https://www.timeshighereducation.com/impact
rankings#!/page/0/length/25/sort_by/rank/sort_order/asc/cols/undefined.

23. Ellie Bothwell, Leaders Create System to Rank Universities' Societal Engagement, *Times Higher Education*, July 22, 2020, https://www.timeshighereducation.com
/news/leaders-create-system-rank-universities-societal-engagement.

24. Stephen M. Gavazzi, Amid Covid-19 Pandemic, New University Ranking
System Emerges Based on Social Impact, *Forbes*, July 23, 2020, https://www.forbes
.com/sites/stephengavazzi/2020/07/23/amid-covid-19-pandemic-new-university
-ranking-system-emerges-based-on-social-impact/.

25. E. Gordon Gee, College Admissions Scandal: Lincoln's Land-Grant Colleges
Are Still Helping Students Grow, *USA Today*, March 25, 2019, https://www.usatoday
.com/story/opinion/2019/03/25/college-president-admissions-scandal-shows-land
-grant-college-success-column/3238575002/.

26. Will Patch, 2020 Niche Senior Survey: College Search to Enrollment, *Niche
.com*, September 22, 2020, https://www.niche.com/about/enrollment-insights/2020
-niche-senior-survey-college-search-to-enrollment/.

27. Heather Long and Danielle Douglas-Gabriel, The Latest Crisis: Low-Income
Students Are Dropping Out of College This Fall in Alarming Numbers, *Washington
Post*, September 16, 2020, https://www.washingtonpost.com/business/2020/09/16
/college-enrollment-down/.

28. Will Patch, Impact of Coronavirus on Students' Academic Progress and
College Plans, *Niche.com*, March 25, 2020, https://www.niche.com/about/enrollment
-insights/impact-of-coronavirus-on-students-academic-progress-and-college-plans.

29. Aaron Cantu, To Help First-Generation Students Succeed, Colleges Enlist
Their Parents, *Hechinger Report*, August 15, 2019, https://hechingerreport.org/to-help
-first-generation-students-succeed-colleges-enlist-their-parents/.

30. Association of Public and Land-Grant Universities, Innovation and Economic
Prosperity Universities, accessed December 1, 2020, https://www.aplu.org/projects-and
-initiatives/economic-development-and-community-engagement/innovation-and
-economic-prosperity-universities-designation-and-awards-program/index.html.

31. Association of Public and Land-Grant Universities, Economic Engagement
Framework, accessed December 1, 2020, https://www.aplu.org/projects-and
-initiatives/economic-development-and-community-engagement/economic
-engagement-framework/index.html.

32. Stephen M. Gavazzi, Innovation and Prosperity Amidst the Covid-19 Pandemic: Universities and Our Economic Future, *Forbes*, May 20, 2020, https://www

.forbes.com/sites/stephengavazzi/2020/05/20/innovation-and-prosperity-amidst-the
-covid-19-pandemic-universities-and-our-economic-future/.

33. Brian Finch, Future Pandemic Battles Depend on Manhattan (Kansas), *The Hill*, March 26, 2020, https://thehill.com/opinion/national-security/489617-future
-pandemic-battles-depend-on-manhattan-kansas.

34. K-State News, Kansas State University Is the 'Silicon Valley for Biodefense,' According to Blue Ribbon Study Panel, January 30, 2017, https://www.k-state.edu
/media/newsreleases/2017-01/blueribbon13017.html.

35. K-State News, K-State Expands Licensing Agreement for Covid-19 Antiviral Treatment, April 25, 2020, https://www.k-state.edu/media/newsreleases/2020-04
/cocrystal_extend42520.html.

36. Innovate Carolina, Protecting Those Who Protect Us, accessed December 2, 2020, https://innovate.unc.edu/unc-face-shield-maker-initiative/.

37. Robert H. Donaldson, Presidential Success and Intercollegiate Athletics, in *Leading Colleges and Universities*, ed. Stephen Joel Trachtenberg, Gerald B. Kauvar, and E. Gordon Gee (Baltimore: Johns Hopkins University Press, 2018).

38. Gerald B. Kauvar, Stephen Joel Trachtenberg, and E. Gordon Gee, That's My Budget Running Up and Down the Field, in *Leading Colleges and Universities*, ed. Stephen Joel Trachtenberg, Gerald B. Kauvar, and E. Gordon Gee (Baltimore: Johns Hopkins University Press, 2018).

39. Chris Murphy, Madness, Inc: How Everyone Is Getting Rich Off College Sports, Except the Players, accessed December 2, 2020, https://www.murphy.senate
.gov/imo/media/doc/NCAA%20Report_FINAL.pdf.

40. Steve Berkowitz, NCAA Slashes Payouts to Schools by $375 Million in Wake of Coronavirus Cancellations, *USA Today*, March 26, 2020, https://www.usatoday.com
/story/sports/ncaab/2020/03/26/coronavirus-issues-cause-ncaa-slash-payouts
-member-schools/2916805001/.

41. Stephen M. Gavazzi, The College Student-Athlete: Endangered Species in the COVID-19 Crisis? *Forbes*, April 22, 2020, https://www.forbes.com/sites/stephen
gavazzi/2020/04/22/the-college-student-athlete-endangered-species-in-the-covid-19
-crisis/.

42. Mark Schlabach and Paula Lavigne, Financial Toll of Coronavirus Could Cost College Football at least $4 Billion, *ESPN*, May 21, 2020, https://www.espn.com/college
-sports/story/_/id/29198526/college-football-return-key-athletic-departments-deal
-financial-wreckage-due-coronavirus-pandemic.

43. Ross Delenger, Bipartisan Name, Image, Likeness Bill Focused on Endorse-ments Introduced to Congress, *Sports Illustrated*, September 24, 2020, https://www.si
.com/college/2020/09/24/name-image-likeness-bill-congress-endorsements.

44. Emanual Cleaver, Press Release: Reps. Cleaver, Gonzalez Unveil Bipartisan Bill to Grant Name, Image and Likeness Rights to College Athletes, September 24, 2020, https://cleaver.house.gov/media-center/press-releases/reps-cleaver-gonzalez
-unveil-bipartisan-bill-to-grant-name-image-and.

45. Anthony Gonzalez, Press Release: Reps. Gonzalez, Cleaver Unveil Bipartisan Bill to Grant Name, Image, and Likeness to College Athletes, September 24, 2020, https://anthonygonzalez.house.gov/news/documentsingle.aspx?DocumentID=288.

46. Anthony Gonzalez and Emanual Cleaver, The Student Athlete Level Playing Field Act, accessed December 2, 2020, https://cleaver.house.gov/sites/cleaver.house .gov/files/The%20Student%20Athlete%20Level%20Playing%20Field%20Act%20 -%20One%20Pager.pdf

47. Greta Anderson, Federal Lawmakers Propose New Player-Pay Bill, *Inside Higher Ed*, September 25, 2020, https://www.insidehighered.com/quicktakes/2020/09 /25/federal-lawmakers-propose-new-player-pay-bill.

48. NCAA, NCAA Statement on Gonzalez-Cleaver Bill, September 24, 2020, https://www.ncaa.org/about/resources/media-center/news/ncaa-statement-gonzalez -cleaver-bill.

49. Stephen M. Gavazzi, The College Student-Athlete: Endangered Species in the COVID-19 Crisis? *Forbes*, April 22, 2020, https://www.forbes.com/sites/stephengavazzi /2020/04/22/the-college-student-athlete-endangered-species-in-the-covid-19 -crisis/.

50. Robert M. Hutchins, Football Is an Infernal Nuisance, *Sports Illustrated*, October 18, 1954, https://vault.si.com/vault/1954/10/18/college-football-is-an-infernal -nuisance.

51. Knight Commission on Intercollegiate Athletics, Knight Commission Recommends a New Governing Structure for the Sport of FBS Football, December 3, 2020, https://www.knightcommission.org/2020/12/knight-commission-recommends -a-new-governing-structure-for-the-sport-of-fbs-football/.

52. Andrew Howard Nichols, Segregation Forever? *The Educational Trust*, July 23, 2020, https://edtrust.org/resource/segregation-forever/.

53. Danette Gerald and Kati Haycock, Engines of Inequality: Diminishing Equity in the Nation's Premier Public Universities, *The Education Trust*, December 4, 2020, https://edtrust.org/wp-content/uploads/2013/10/EnginesofInequality.pdf.

54. Alex Usher, Flagship Universities Versus World-Class Universities, *Inside Higher Ed*, September 20, 2017, https://www.insidehighered.com/blogs/world-view /flagship-universities-vs-world-class-universities.

55. Vimal Patel, Black Students Have Less Access to Selective Public Colleges Now Than 20 Years Ago, Report Finds, *Chronicle of Higher Education*, July 21, 2020, https://www.chronicle.com/article/black-students-have-less-access-to-selective -public-colleges-now-than-20-years-ago-report-finds.

56. Jeremy F. Huckins, Alex W. da Silva, Weichen Wang, Elin Hedlund, Courtney Rogers, Subigya K. Nepal, Jialing Wu, Mikio Obuchi, Eilis I. Murphy, Meghan L. Meyer, Dylan D. Wagner, Paul E. Holtzheimer, and Andrew T. Campbell. Mental Health and Behavior of College Students During the Early Phases of the COVID-19 Pandemic: Longitudinal Smartphone and Ecological Momentary Assessment Study, *Journal of Medical Internet Research* 22, no. 6 (2020): https://www.jmir.org/2020/6 /e20185/.

57. Timon Elmer, Kieran Mepham, and Christoph Stadtfeld, Students Under Lockdown: Comparisons of Students' Social Networks and Mental Health Before and During the COVID-19 Crisis in Switzerland, *Plos One*, July 23, 2020, https://journals.plos.org/plosone/article?id=10.1371/journal.pone.0236337.

58. Stephen M. Gavazzi, College Students Want to Party: How They Keep Their Social Life This Fall, *Forbes*, May 26, 2020, https://www.forbes.com/sites/stephengavazzi/2020/05/26/college-students-want-to-party-how-they-keep-their-social-life-this-fall/.

59. Lawrence Steinberg, Expecting Students to Play It Safe if Colleges Reopen Is a Fantasy, *New York Times*, June 15, 2020, https://www.nytimes.com/2020/06/15/opinion/coronavirus-college-safe.html.

60. Peg O'Connor, College Drinking and Students' Mental Health, *Psychology Today*, July 31, 2018, https://www.psychologytoday.com/us/blog/philosophy-stirred-not-shaken/201807/college-drinking-and-students-mental-health.

61. Terry Gross, College Students (and Their Parents) Face a Campus Mental Health 'Epidemic,' *National Public Radio*, May 28, 2019, https://www.npr.org/sections/health-shots/2019/05/28/727509438/college-students-and-their-parents-face-a-campus-mental-health-epidemic.

62. Phebe Tucker and Christopher S. Czapla, Post-COVID Stress Disorder: Another Emerging Consequence of the Global Pandemic, *Psychiatric Times*, October 5, 2020, https://www.psychiatrictimes.com/view/post-covid-stress-disorder-emerging-consequence-global-pandemic.

63. Alisha Matthewson-Grant, Life Under Lockdown, Cambridge University, accessed December 8, 2020, https://www.cam.ac.uk/alumni/life-in-lockdown.

64. Stephen M. Gavazzi, David Rosowsky, and Chuck Pezeshki, The Path to Failure in the University: A Tragedy in Multiple Acts, *Inside Higher Education*, January 29, 2021, https://www.insidehighered.com/views/2021/01/29/satiric-look-how-faculty-and-administrators-can-realize-failure-grand-scale-opinion.

65. Scott Galloway, NYU Professor Scott Galloway Predicts Hundreds of Universities Will Shutter, Possibly for Good, if They Reopen in the Fall, *Business Insider*, July 17, 2020, https://www.businessinsider.com/scott-galloway-colleges-must-cut-costs-to-survive-covid-2020-7.

Cooksey, Elizabeth, 7, 12, 38, 184
Cooperative Extension Services: 4-H program initiative, 64; challenges of, 62–63, 65; community engagement efforts, 8, 54, 62, 63, 142; development of, 21–22, 62; public perceptions of, 48, 51, 62; rural-based programs, 64, 65; status of, 63; urban communities and, 64–65
COVID-19 pandemic: college sports and, 172–73; community impact, 169; economic consequences of, 171; higher education and, 5–6, 9, 11, 163, 166–67; international education and, 96, 160–61; mental health and, 178–79; public opinion poll about, 153–54, 155; public universities response to, 149, 153, 154; schools reopening plans, 158–59; university-community partnerships and, 170; vaccine race, 161–62
critical rural theory, 79, 82
cultural wars, 2–3

Daschle, Tom, 170
Davis, Rodney, 173
deliberative democracy, 36
Democratic party: attitude to public universities, 36–37, 42, 71, 88, 102, 120–21, 124
deservingness: concept of, 110, 114
diversity, 149, 175–76, 177
"division of labor," 65
Dorhout, Peter K., 170
Douglas, Derek, 165
Douglas, Stephen, 30, 131, 155
Duke University, 171
Duncan, Jeff, 173

"education deserts," 74
Education Trust, 175, 176, 177
Emancipation Proclamation, 15
engaged institutions, 17–18, 61–62
equal rights issues, 138, 144, 146

faculty: community engagement, 151–52; practical and vocational coursework, 136; public sentiment about, 10, 133, 134, 136, 141–42, 146; time spent on instruction, 136. *See also* nontenure-track faculty; tenure-track faculty

fair access to higher education, 135, 140, 141, 166
financial stewardship, 10, 133, 134, 135–36, 141
"flagship universities," 176
Floyd, George, 6
Foundation for Individual Rights in Education (FIRE), 143
4-H program initiative, 64
Free Application for Federal Student Aid (FAFSA), 105
free speech rights, 138, 143–44, 146
Freud, Sigmund, 76
Fudge, Marcia, 173
Fulfilling the 21st Century Land-Grant Mission (Gavazzi and Stanley), 13
Fulkerson, Gregory, 79, 81
funding allocation: on community programs, 48, 50–51, 60, 66; demo-graphic variables related to, 49–50, 52–53; educational level and perception of, 50; needs-based *vs.* merit-based, 33, 34; on noninstructional activities, 51; political variables related to, 53–54; on research, 48, 50–51, 56, 60; survey of public opinion, 8, 31–32, 47–48, 66; on teaching, 48, 50–51, 52, 54–56, 60, 156–57

Gallup, 23, 159
Gavazzi, Stephen M., 13, 180
Gee, Gordon E., 4, 13–14, 28–29, 78, 117, 155–56, 165
GI Bill, 108
Gillen, Andrew, 12
Gillon, Kathleen, 79
global/local concerns: demographic variables, 85–87, 93–94, 98; educational attainment and, 87–88, 98; initial reactions to findings about, 90–91; methodological approach, 85; political affiliation and, 86, 88–90, 94–95, 98; survey findings, 96, 97–98, 160; voting behavior and, 86, 90, 95
Goldstein, Buck, 7, 20, 22–23, 25–26, 29; *Our Higher Calling*, 12
Gonzalez, Anthony, 173, 174
Gottheimer, Josh, 173
Grant, Jonathan, 165
Great Plague, 180
Greenleaf, Robert, 27

Harmon, Grant, 127
Hess, Rick, 12
Hester, Jacob, 110
higher education: bifocal nature of, 6;
  business connections, 19; COVID-19
  pandemic and, 5–7, 9; economic damage
  of, 161; evolution of, 19–20; future of, 11;
  Great Reset of, 180–81; international
  programs, 91–93; opportunities and
  threats, 7, 15–16, 180, 182; politics and,
  34–36; as public good, 21; public
  perception of, 3, 4, 7, 10–11, 18, 30–31, 46,
  168, 182; social unrest and, 6; survey of,
  31–34, 183–87; urbanormativity and,
  79–80
Hillman, Nicholas, 13, 74
Hutchins, Robert, 175

Innovation and Economic Prosperity (IEP)
  designation, 17, 18, 61, 169–70, 171
Inside Higher Ed, 23
Integrated Postsecondary Education Data
  System (IPEDS), 158
international higher education: COVID-19
  pandemic and, 96–97, 160; decline of,
  161; economic benefits, 92–93, 95, 98;
  public perception of, 96; research
  collaboration, 161–62; statistics, 161, 162;
  student recruitment and retention,
  95–96, 97, 98; Trump administration
  policy, 97, 162; tuition and fees, 93, 95

Jones, Diane, 13
Jung Cheol Shin, 126
Jyotishi, Shalin, 169

K–12 schools, 158
Kansas State University, 170
Kellogg Commission on the Future of
  State and Land-Grant Universities, 17–18,
  61, 62
Kelly, Andrew, 13
Kelly, Walt, 4
Kittlison, Miki, 13
Knight Commission on Intercollegiate
  Athletics, 175
knowledge creation, 60
Koch Foundation, 5
Kogan, Vladimir, 12

Land-Grant Colleges and Popular Revolt
  (Sorber), 12, 15, 19, 20
land-grant colleges and universities:
  curriculum of, 21; mission of, 16, 21, 84;
  rural communities and, 65, 78–79
Land-Grant Universities for the Future
  (Gavazzi and Gee), 5, 12, 29, 31, 34, 48,
  68, 85, 100, 116, 125, 132, 137, 168
Lavertu, Stephane, 12
Lincoln, Abraham: on agriculture, 67; on
  American public, 46; Congressional
  address, 15; debate with Stephen
  Douglas, 30, 131; on duty of government,
  84; on fragility of public institutions, 147;
  gratitude of, 11; inauguration address,
  1–2; promise of public education, 3; on
  public opinion, 30, 115, 130, 131, 134, 155,
  182; on value of education, 47, 99
Lowe, Brian, 79
Lumina Foundation, 23
Luntz, Frank, 158

Marsicano, Chris, 156
Mayhew, Matthew, 12
McCluskey, Neal, 12
Meadows, Sandra, 184
mediocrity, 26–27
mental health issue, 149, 178–79
merit-based student aid, 9, 10, 100–101,
  105, 106, 109, 110, 112, 113–14, 140
"Mickey Mouse" evaluation system, 126
Morrill Land-Grant Act, 3, 20, 47, 91

Name, Image, and Likeness (NIL) issue,
  174–75
National Agricultural Biosecurity Center,
  170
National Center for Education Statistics
  (NCES), 51, 104, 105
National Collegiate Athletic Association
  (NCAA), 172, 173, 174
National Institutes of Health (NIH), 57
National Science Foundation (NSF), 57
Neblo, Michael, 7, 12, 36
needs-based student aid, 9, 10, 100–101,
  105–6, 109, 112, 140
Newfield, Christopher: The Great Mistake,
  57; on knowledge creation, 60; on
  research funding, 57, 58–59, 60–61

Newton, Isaac, 180
Niche.com, 166, 167
Nichols, Andrew Nichols, 177
Nietzel, Michael, 113; *Coming to Grips with Higher Education*, 12, 111–12
Nixon, Jay, 112
nontenure-track faculty: responsibilities of, 54–55, 56
North Carolina State University at Chapel Hill, 170–71
NVivo, 132

Obama, Barack, 107
Ohio State University, 183–87
open-ended responses: categories, 131–32, 133, 134; data analysis, 132–33; emergent themes, 134
Our Higher Calling (Thorp and Goldstein), 12, 20, 22

participants of public universities study: "buckets" of, 39; demographic variables, 8–9, 39, 41–44, 49–50; education, 39, 41; gender, 40, 49; geographic variability, 39, 41–42, 44; political affiliations, 8–9, 36–37, **42**, 42–43; recruitment of, 7–8, 39, 40–41; voting behavior, 37, 43–44
Pasque, Penny, 12
Pell Grants, 106, 108
Penn State University, 176
Pittman, Karen, 64
political views and indoctrination, 138, 143, 146
polling: limitations of, 155
"post-COVID stress disorder," 179
proof of positive impact theme, 138–39, 144, 146
provision of student support theme, 138, 142, 146
public health issues, 148, 154, 164, 166–67, 178, 179
public institutions: fragility of, 147–48
public sentiment on higher education: importance of, 7, 19, 29, 30–31, 39, 55, 130, 149–50, 155, 182; study of, 36, 51, 73, 91, 104, 122–23
public universities: admission tests, 116–17; affordability, 24; assessment of, 18–19; communities and, 4–5, 24–26,

61–62, 64–65, 81, 152–53, 165; cultural wars and, 2; current trends, 4; data collection about, 38–39, 40; dialogue with the public, 22–23, 155; donors, 151; finances, 24, 51; future of, 11, 22; global reach of, 9, 85, 90–91; idealized vision of, 45–46; IEP designation, 169–71; instructional activities, 55; international activities, 95; local impact, 85; low- and middle-income student enrollment, 110–11; as "people's universities," 16–17; politicization of, 27, 34–35, 158–59; post-pandemic reopening plans, 158, 160, 180–82; public perception of, 4, 19–20, 159; resistance to change, 25; rural/urban divide and, 8–9, 32, 77, 78–79, 81; state funding, 92; stewardship responsibilities, 27–28

racial (in)justice, 149, 153, 154, 155
ranking. *See* university ranking
Reagan, Ronald, 108
Rennekamp, Roger, 63
Republican party: attitude to public universities, 42, 124, 153, 154; electoral support, 120, 159
research: business and industry partners, 57; cost of, 54, 56, 57–58, 59–60; cross-subsidization of, 58; external stakeholders, 58, 60; federal funding of, 57, 60; grants, 57; internal stakeholders, 58; public funding allocation for, 48, 50–51, 57, 58–59, 60, 66; public opinion about, 133, 139, 143, 145; tuition dollars and, 57, 58–59
"Returning to Our Roots" reports, 17
Roosevelt, Franklin Delano, 107
routine reports theme, 139, 144, 146
rural communities: challenges of, 20–21; Cooperative Extension Services and, 64, 65; interest to higher education, 21, 79, 80; land-grant colleges and, 21; statistics, 67; stereotypes of, 79, 81
rural/urban communities prioritization: binary narrative of, 79; demographic variables related to, 68–71, 75–76; educational attainment and, 70–71, 73–74, 75; geographic variables related to, 70, 75; political variables related to,

71–72, 76, 82; survey findings, 68–69,
82–83; voting behavior and, 72–73, 78, 82
rural/urban divide, 76–77

safety from violence issue, 138, 144, 146
St. Louis Race riot, 147
Santayana, George, 20, 24
*Science—The Endless Frontier: A Report to
the President for Postwar Scientific
Research* (policy guideline), 57
"Segregation Forever?" report, 175
servant university, 27–28
Sirangelo, Sirangelo, 64
Smith-Lever Act, 21, 62
social unrest, 6, 148
Sorber, Nathan, 7, 20–21, 22, 29; *Land-
Grant Colleges and Popular Revolt*, 12, 15,
19, 20
Staley, David J., 13
standardized test scores, 116–17, 126,
163–64
State Student Incentive Grant, 108
Sternberg, Robert, 26
Stivers, Steve, 173
student aid: access to, 100; expansion of,
108; inequality and, 114; merit-based *vs.*
needs-based, 100–101, 105, 106, 109, 110,
140; public sentiments about, 125, 140;
shift in "generational responsibilities,"
109–10; sources of, 104–6; statistics of,
99–100, 105, 112, 140; university rankings
and, 116–17, 121–22, 125, 126
Student Athlete Level Playing Field Act,
173–74
student-centered experiences theme, 10,
133, 137, 142–43
student debt reduction, 107, 110, 135, 140,
146, 166
student-directed funding prioritization:
demographic differences as related to,
101–2, 106; merit-based *vs.* needs-based,
100–101; political variables as related to,
102–3, 106–7; voting behavior and, 103–4,
107
student loans, 105–6, 109, 114
students: college choice, 74, 167–68; of
color, enrollment statistics of, 176, 177;
concern for equal rights of, 138; family
support, 168; financial problems, 167;

post-pandemic educational plans,
166–67; preparedness for college,
167–68; preparedness for labor market,
159–60; provision of support for, 138,
142, 146; research skills, 159–60; social
gatherings, 178, 179
study abroad programs, 95, 160
SUNY public university system, 79, 80
Supplemental Educational Opportunity
Grant, 108

teaching: funding of, 48, 50–51, 56, 66,
156–57; public sentiment about, 10, 133,
134, 136, 141–42, 146
tenure process, 54–55
tenure-track faculty, 55–56
Thomas, Alexander, 79, 80
Thorp, Holden, 7, 20, 22–23, 24–25, 29, 163,
164; *Our Higher Calling*, 12
Times Higher Education College Rankings, 165
Trump, Donald, 148, 158, 162
tuition and fees: of international students,
93, 95; public opinion about, 135;
research funding and, 57–59

university-community partnership, 17–18,
169, 170
university expenditures: "central idea"
themes, 133, 134, 135–38, 139–43, 146;
demand for transparency, 136, 141;
emergent themes, 133, 134, 138–39, 143–45,
146; need to increase/reduce, 136, 140, 141,
146; proof of positive impact, 138, 144;
qualitative data, 145–46; survey of, 131–32
university leaders: community stakeholders and, 7, 17, 29, 150; fiscal influence on,
151; government relations, 150, 151;
narratives of, 25–26; political biases, 35;
promotion of diversity, 177; public
opinion perception, 11, 151–52, 155; public
outreach, 155–56; ranking system and,
115, 126; survey of, 16, 91; view of higher
education, 23–24, 96–97
University of California, Berkeley, 176
University of Georgia, 176
University of Nebraska-Lincoln, 176
university ranking: analysis of, 118–19, 122,
128–29; contextualization of, 129;
criticism of, 126–27, 128, 162–63; data